Events and Their Names

Events and Their Names

Jonathan Bennett

Hackett Publishing Company
Indianapolis/Cambridge

Printed in the United States of America

The paper in this book meets the guidelines for permanence and durability established by the Committee on Production Guidelines for Book Longevity of the Council on Library Resources.

Cover design by Ken Farnhill

Interior design by Dan Kirklin

For further information, please address

Hackett Publishing Company
Box 44937
Indianapolis, Indiana 46024

Library of Congress Cataloging-in-Publication Data

Bennett, Jonathan Francis.
Events and their names.

Bibliography: p.
Includes indexes.
1. Events (Philosophy) I. Title.
B105.E7B46 1988 111 88-5261
ISBN 0-87220-046-9 (alk. paper)
ISBN 0-87220-045-0 (pbk. : alk. paper)

CONTENTS

PREFACE ix

I. INTRODUCTION 1

1. Identifying the subject matter 1
2. Two kinds of sentence nominal 4
3. Fact language and event language 6
4. The fineness of facts 9
5. Events are supervenient 12
6. Challenges to supervenience 15
7. A sceptical conclusion 18

II. FACTS 21

8. Event causation and fact causation 21
9. How they differ 23
10. The noun-infinitive form 24
11. Some theses of Vendler's 26
12. Vendler's four challenges 28
13. Fact causation and explanation 31
14. Highlighting 32
15. What are facts? 35
16. V-facts 37

III. FACT CAUSATION 42

17. Approaches to singular causation statements 42
18. Fact causation: NS conditions 42
19. Transitivity 46
20. Fact causation: the counterfactual analysis 49

IV. EVENT CAUSATION 51

21. Event causation: the relational approach 51
22. Counterfactuals and essences 54
23. The search for data about event essences 56
24. Three approaches to the essences of events 58
25. Counterparts and modal continuants 62
26. The essences of events 64
27. Ordinary names for Lewis's events 65
28. Essences and times 69

V. KIM'S SEMANTICS 73
29. Kim's semantics for event names 73
30. Kim's causal example 75
31. Facts and events in Kim 76
32. The intuitive data about event identity 78
33. Constitution and character 79
34. Cardinality 82
35. What sorts of facts are Kim's "events"? 83

VI. THE TRUE METAPHYSICS OF EVENTS 88
36. What are events? 88
37. The supposed link with semantics 93
38. "Identity criteria" and circularity 95
39. What is a criterion of identity? 99
40. Two possible answers 100

VII. CONCRETE EVENTS 103
41. Quine's metaphysic of events 103
42. Some nonproblems about event location 105
43. A Quinean semantics of event names 106
44. Defending the Quinean semantics 108
45. The Quinean treatment of event causation 111
46. Events and physical objects 113
47. The immanence thesis 116

VIII. THE TRUE SEMANTICS OF EVENT NAMES 119
48. The search for middle ground 119
49. Surveying the relevant data 122
50. The true semantics of event names 126
51. Events and their companion facts 128

IX. EVENT CAUSATION AGAIN 135
52. Getting it right 135
53. Why do we have event causation? 137
54. Why event causation is inferior 139

X. THE FISSION AND FUSION OF EVENTS 143
55. Nonzonal fusion 143
56. Nonzonal fission 147
57. Parts and wholes 151
58. Zonal fusion 153
59. Zonal fission 156
60. Are all events changes? 157
61. Judith Thomson's theory of events 159
62. Parts and causes in Thomson's work 161

XI. ADVERBS AND EVENTS 165
63. Explaining entailments 165
64. Adverbs and first-order logic 168
65. Predicate modifiers 173
66. Stretching Davidson's ontology 176
67. Two other quantifying theories 178
68. Nonstandard adverbs 182
69. Dependency 183

XII. THE ANSCOMBE THESIS 188
70. The Anscombe thesis 188
71. What are the reasons for it? 191
72. The times of actions 194
73. Still looking for reasons 199
74. Logical form and the Anscombe thesis 200

XIII. GOLDMAN ON THE "BY"-LOCUTION 203
75. Goldman's program 203
76. Conventions 205
77. Augmentation 207
78. Goldman's first three conditions 208
79. The fourth condition 210

XIV. AN ANALYSIS OF THE "BY"-LOCUTION 213
80. Contrasting two patterns of analysis 213
81. An analysis of the "by"-locution 214
82. Positive and negative 218
83. Instrumental verbs 221
84. "Pictured as the sole input" 224
85. No wholly intervening agency 226
86. Idiosyncrasies in instrumental verbs 229

BIBLIOGRAPHY 232

INDEXES 240

PREFACE

This book arises from inquiries that I have pursued intermittently for about a decade, starting with a graduate class at the University of British Columbia and continuing in classes at Syracuse University, Princeton University and the University of Pittsburgh, and in an N.E.H. Summer Seminar for College Teachers in 1984. It was my especial good fortune that these groups included Nuel Belnap, Sara Bennett, William Blattner, Douglas Butler, Jan Cover, John Hawthorne, Frances Howard, Paul Hurley, Michael Kremer, Mark Lance, David Lewis, Steven Luper-Foy, Alison McIntyre, Brian McLaughlin, Leroy Meyer, Alastair Norcross, Shekhar Pradhan, John Quilter and Alexander Rosenberg. To them and to other members of the groups as well I am grateful for stimulus, criticism, insights, and other kinds of help.

A long paper from which some of the book grew was commented on by Robert Stalnaker, and parts or all of a late draft of the work were read and commented on by W.V. Quine, Jaegwon Kim, Judith Thomson, Lawrence Lombard, and Philip Peterson. All have enabled me to make significant improvements, which is not to say that any would be entirely satisfied with the result.

I am grateful to the National Endowment for the Humanities and to Syracuse University, which provided me with a year's leave in 1984–1985, giving me the leisure I needed to discover how inadequate was all my work on events up to then.

I am continually aware of my debt to the pioneers of the events literature. I here express my respectful gratitude to those who are still with us: Donald Davidson, Alvin Goldman, Jaegwon Kim, W.V. Quine, and Zeno Vendler, and I salute the memory of the one who is not: G.W. Leibniz.

I

INTRODUCTION

1. *Identifying the subject matter*

According to good dictionaries, an "event" is "anything that happens; an incident or occurrence." So weddings and explosions are events, as are attacks of nostalgia, quarrels, avalanches, fights, fires, traffic jams, reconciliations, slumps, elections, strolls, births, deaths. Various as these are, they have enough in common for them all to count as events, and in recent years philosophers have turned their attention to this presumed common nature. They have wanted to know: What marks events off from other categories of existent—how do we tell the dancer from the dance? How do events relate to space and time? What is needed for two events to be parts of a single larger or fuller event? What is needed for a single event to have smaller or more abstract parts? Could we tell the whole truth about the universe without using the concept of an event? How does that concept figure in causal statements? What determines whether a pair of event descriptions could fit a single event?

Those are conceptual questions: no empirical work such as geographers or physicists or psychologists do is relevant to any of them. If you want to understand what distinguishes events from substances or to know whether two events can fill the same region of space-time or the like, you must get your answers by thinking; there is no other way. Since your thinking will include reflection on your own patterns of thought and speech, it will be necessary to include empirical inquiry of a kind, but not a kind that need get you out of your armchair.

If we are to study the concept, we must know how to tell when we are in its presence. It won't do just to look for the word "event": few occurrences of the concept involve that word, just as few occurrences of the concept of a physical thing include the phrase "physical thing". Furthermore, some uses of "event" do not involve the item that I call our "event concept", or "our concept of a particular event". For example, in the sentence "I'll after him, and see the event of this", as in all Shakespeare's other uses of "event", the word means "outcome" and has no special tie to the event concept that I want to explore. We still sometimes use the word like that, as in "In the event, he turned out to be no braver than anyone else."

What we must steer by, mainly, is whether we are talking about particular things that happen or occur either at moments or through periods of time, that can be seen or heard etc., that can cause and be caused. (And I shall confine myself to ones that occur in places; if there are mental events that do not occur in space, I ignore them as a complication that I can't afford.) If you are wondering whether a given noun N is an event sortal—i.e. a general term that stands for some kind of event—test it to see whether its syntax is appropriate for a word that stands for a kind of particular: does it admit of "the [N]"? of "an [N]"? of the plural "[N]s"? of qualification in the form "[adjective] [N]"?[1] Also, see whether it creates good sense when used in such forms as "The [N] occurred at noon (or: throughout the day)", "An [N] has taken place on this island", "We watched the [N] as it occurred", "The most interesting [N] on record was . . . ", "There have been two [N]s during . . . ". If it passes all these tests, N probably is an event sortal; otherwise, it probably isn't. Everything on my opening list of samples passes the tests.

Hundreds of event sortals, including some on that list, are derived from verbs. For example:

explosion	explode
marriage	marry
reconciliation	reconcile
payment	pay
intervention	intervene
performance	perform
discovery	discover
refusal	refuse
departure	depart

1. Whenever I use a variable such as "N" or "ES" to refer indifferently to any member of a class of expressions and also use that variable between square brackets, replace the unbracketed occurrences by *the name of* some expression of the kind in question, and replace the bracketed occurrences (and the brackets) by that same expression, not by its name. For example, if I write, "If you are wondering whether a given noun N is an event sortal, see whether it can be used in the form 'the [N]' ", take me to have asserted indefinitely many things like this: "If you are wondering whether 'horse' is an event sortal, see whether it can be used in the form 'the horse' ". A second example: When I write "If a sentence S expresses a Russellian proposition, then the fact that [S] is a Russellian fact", take me to have asserted indefinitely many things like "If the sentence 'Quine lives in Cambridge' expresses a Russellian proposition, then the fact that Quine lives in Cambridge is a Russellian fact".

death	die
birth	bear
quarrel	quarrel

You can easily verify that each of the above nouns passes the rough tests I have offered, from which I infer that each is an event sortal. The change in sound and spelling between noun and verb varies greatly, as the list shows.

Just as nouns that are derived from verbs can function as event sortals ("explosion", "marriage", "payment"), so can noun phrases that are derived from verb phrases, as "explosion in the attic" comes from "explode in the attic", "marriage to Helen" from "marry Helen", and "payment of five dollars" from "pay five dollars". Going a step further, event kinds can be picked out by noun phrases that are grammatically derived from whole sentences, as "a boiler's explosion in the attic" is from "A boiler explodes in the attic", "John's marriage to Helen" from "John marries Helen", and "Henry's payment of a dollar" from "Henry pays a dollar".

To see that those last three are event sortals, reword them slightly to get "explosion of a boiler in the attic", "marriage of John to Helen", and "payment by Henry of a dollar". Then they pass my grammatical and other tests. I watched the explosion of a boiler in the attic; there have been two marriages of John to Helen; the belated payment by Henry of a dollar occurred at noon; and so on.

If a sortal is strong enough to pick out a one-membered kind, it can be used in a definite description, like "U.S. Senator who was once an astronaut" and "philosopher who was excommunicated by his synagogue". So it is with event sortals, as for instance "award by Syracuse University of an honorary degree to W.V. Quine" and "civil war in the U.S.A.". When I refer to any particular event, it will nearly always be through a definite description, that is, by an expression of the form "the [ES]", where ES is an event sortal or something synonymous with such an expression. My examples will be truncated, for brevity's sake. When I offer "Wagner's stay in Venice" as an event name, let us pretend that I have specified which stay is meant, and for that matter which Wagner and which Venice.

Some events get proper names. A hurricane frightened a householder into building walls that spoiled his neighbor's view, and the neighbor sued, making it true that Gloria caused *Arkwright v. Jenkins*. But such proper naming of events is ordinarily parasitic on reference to them by definite descriptions: there is no practicable way of giving a hurricane the name "Gloria" unless you say something like "Gloria is the *hurricane* that . . . ". You might stand in the middle of the hurricane, wave your arms, and shout "*This* is Gloria", but the rest of us don't know how far your "this" is meant to reach, and so we don't know what you are calling "Gloria". Nor will it do just to say, "Gloria is what caused *Arkwright* v. *Jenkins*", for that lawsuit—like every event—had many causes, the hurricane being only one of them.

For that and other reasons, I shall dispense with proper names of events. That frees me to use the word "name" in its broadest sense of "individual referring expression", knowing that in practice the only "names" that will concern me are definite descriptions.

When a noun phrase is derived from a whole sentence in the way I have illustrated, it is said to result from "nominalizing" the sentence—that is, turning it into a nounlike expression, something that could in its turn be the subject of further sentences. The resultant phrase is called a "sentence nominal" or "nominal" for short. I shall follow this usage.

2. *Two kinds of sentence nominal*

A *gerund* is a noun formed by adding "ing" to the end of a verb. This is of course a way of deriving a noun from a verb, but I choose to employ the label "derived nominal" in a technical sense that excludes gerunds. In this usage, then, "baptism" is a derived nominal, but "baptising" isn't; "slump" is a derived nominal, but "slumping" isn't.

To get a grip on the philosophical literature about events, one must understand a certain contrast between some uses of gerunds and all uses of derived nominals. Most of what I know about this I have learned from Zeno Vendler, whose principal linguistic data and explanations thereof I shall now present.[2] I shall confine myself to nominalizations of indicative sentences.

The sentence "Quisling betrays Norway" is the source of the following two nominals, one derived and the other gerundial:

D: Quisling's betrayal of Norway.
G: Quisling's betraying Norway.

There are four big grammatical differences between these. (1) In D but not in G, the first word can be replaced by a definite or indefinite article, and D but not G can be pluralized. (2) D takes adjectives in the attributive position, G takes adverbs: Quisling's treacherous betrayal of Norway, Quisling's treacherously betraying Norway. (3) In G the gerund can be negated, tensed, and modalized through auxiliaries:

2. An important source of our understanding of this matter is Robert B. Lees, *The Grammar of English Nominalizations*. But the pioneering work in connecting the grammatical matter with our present philosophical topic was by Zeno Vendler, "Facts and Events". See also Noam Chomsky, "Some Remarks about Nominalization", and Richmond Thomason, "Some Issues Concerning the Interpretation of Derived and Gerundive Nominals".

Quisling's not betraying—having betrayed—being going to betray—having to betray—being (un)able to betray—Norway. None of these operations can be peformed on D. (4) In D the relation to Norway is expressed through "of" whereas in G it is direct.

These differences are summed up in the statement that "betrayal" is perfectly a noun, whereas "betraying", as it occurs in the phrase "Quisling's betraying Norway", is a sort of noun that still has, as Vendler puts it, a verb alive and kicking inside it. (*The Shorter Oxford Dictionary* says, perfectly: "Gerund: A form of the . . . verb capable of being construed as a substantive, but retaining the regimen of the verb.") It is therefore labeled as an imperfect nominal, whereas "betrayal" is a perfect nominal—its status as a noun is pure and untainted by any grammatical reminders of the verb that is its source. In a nutshell: "Quisling's betrayal of Norway" is grammatically like "the fjords of Norway", whereas "Quisling"s betraying Norway" is much more like "Quisling betrays Norway".

The two sorts of nominals, as thus syntactically distinguished, also differ semantically in two ways that matter to philosophy.

Firstly, D is at home in many contexts where G will not go comfortably, if at all. Try each in the contexts

. . . occurred over a period of months;
. . . was consummated in this room;
I powerlessly watched . . . ;
. . . was more reprehensible than Eklund's.

Secondly, some contexts will take either phrase but mean different things according to which is used. For example, "Quisling's betrayal of Norway surprised us" might be true just because we were surprised that he betrayed Norway or because something surprised us about how he did it. On the other hand, "Quisling's betraying Norway surprised us" is true only if we were surprised that he betrayed Norway. There are analogous differences when the two phrases are put into the contexts

. . . was without precedent in Norwegian history,
. . . was disgraceful,
. . . was pleasing to Hitler,
. . . was a stroke of genius,

and so on. In each case, the meaning of the sentence you get when G is inserted is most clearly exhibited in the "that [S]" form, where S is a sentence: to say that his betraying Norway was disgraceful is to say that it was disgraceful that he betrayed Norway.

In my two contrasted examples, the perfect nominal is derived, and the imperfect nominal is gerundial. But gerunds can also be used in perfect nominals. To satisfy yourself of this, compare "Quisling's betraying of Norway" with the two examples. It sounds stilted, especially in the plural, but there can be no doubt that it is English and is perfect rather than imperfect.

The characteristic features of perfect nominals come as a package, and nothing in this package is privileged. If you start with a genitive object, as in "Quisling's betraying of Norway", you are committed to the rest, but so you are if you start with some other item from the package, e.g. with "Quisling's wicked betraying" or with "the betraying". What about "Quisling's betraying"? Or, to take a less conspicuously transitive verb, "Hotter's singing"? Is that perfect or imperfect? The answer is that out of context it is neither, but it could be built into either: "Hotter's wonderful singing of *Die Winterreise*", "Hotter's wonderfully singing *Die Winterreise*".

Some perfect gerundial nominals are familiar, comfortable bits of English, as secure in their event-sortal roles as are derived nominals: "I have been to three weddings", "it was a sad parting", "they watched the landing", "there was a drowning in this lake yesterday". Countless others, though they are lawful English and do qualify as event sortals by any reasonable standard, sound awkward and are not likely to be used. Sometimes this is because of pressure from a corresponding derived nominal: it sounds odd to speak of "the wayward flying of KAL 007" because we prefer to use "flight"; and the perfect "betraying" is under competitive pressure from "betrayal". In other cases, there must be some other explanation: if she dried herself, then there was a drying of her by her, but this gerund falls strangely on our ears, and I don't know why.

Perfect gerundial nominals are apt to be confused with their imperfect cousins. I shall play safe by not using perfect gerundial nominals at all. When I want a nominal that is perfectly a noun phrase, I shall choose a derived one, using gerunds only to form imperfect nominals. Some writers about events slide into a kind of philosophers' pidgin in naming events, producing such horrors as "an event of someone's doing things" and "the event of the Empire State Building ceasing to be the tallest building in New York",[3] as though they could form an event name by shoving the words "the event of" in front of a fact name. I shall not follow them in this.

3. *Fact language and event language*

My exemplary perfect nominal passes all the tests, syntactic and semantic, for counting as an event sortal. *In most of our event names, the descriptive part is a perfect nominal.* The converse, however, seems

3. No names, no pack-drill. But I have not made these up.

not to hold. One reason is that many perfect nominals pertain to states rather than events: "his hatred towards her", "their possession of the house", "your ignorance of physics", "my amusement at your antics". Later on I shall suggest that any philosophical theory of events should be extended to cover states as well, because the differences between them are of the superficial kind that would seem significant only to someone doing the kind of "conceptual analysis" that shades off into mere lexicography. Until that is argued for, however, we should respect the appearances and allow that perfect nominals are not always event names or sortals. Another reason for that is that sometimes a perfect nominal seems to be the name of a fact. It is difficult to hear "I am aware of his continuation of the loan" as meaning anything but "I am aware that he has continued the loan". Still, perfect nominals are our main device for talking about events, and that is the only function that most of them have.

In contrast, no imperfect nominals pertain to events. Imperfect nominals fail all the tests for event sortals. They don't behave syntactically as though they were applicable to located particulars: they don't take articles or attributive adjectives, they don't have plural forms, and so on. Their semantic behavior is wrong, too: they don't go comfortably into contexts about being observed, occurring at stated times or lasting for stated periods, and so on.

That is the negative part of Vendler's doctrine about imperfect nominals. The positive part says that *imperfect nominals name facts*. More generally, they name states of affairs: A fact is a state of affairs that obtains, and it is named by a nominal whose parent sentence is true; when the parent sentence is false, as with "Quisling's rescuing France", what it names is a state of affairs that is not a fact. From now on I shall take this complication as understood. What about propositions? My purposes in this work give me no need to distinguish them from states of affairs or, therefore, to distinguish facts from true propositions. Where it doesn't itch, don't scratch.

I now state Vendler's case for the thesis which I express in the short form "Imperfect nominals name facts."

First, let us notice another kind of imperfect nominal, namely the kind that contains a complete sentence within it, as do "the fact that there are warm superconductors" and "that there are warm superconductors". These are sentence nominals—they function as noun phrases and they come from sentences—and they pass all the tests for imperfectness, which is not surprising since they *visibly* have verbs alive and kicking inside them. I take it for granted that these "that [S]" constructions name facts.

I contend that any sentence using an imperfect gerundial nominal is synonymous with one in which that gerundial nominal's work is done instead by a "that [S]" nominal. Test this, and if you find no counterexamples you will agree that imperfect gerundial nominals are basically interchangeable with "that [S]" nominals and are therefore names of facts. If you do find counterexamples, Vendler and I must back off, saying merely that many gerundial imperfect nominals name facts and that none name events, and it will be a further problem to know what marks off the fact names from the rest. But I shall stay with the stronger claim until it is refuted.[4]

The grammatical behavior of "that [S]" nominals is not exactly the same as that of imperfect gerundial ones. For example, we can say

I was aware of Quisling's betraying Norway,

but not

I was aware of that Quisling betrayed Norway.

Still, the latter can be made honest by deleting "of" or inserting "the fact" or rearranging a little:

I was aware that Quisling betrayed Norway,
I was aware of the fact that Quisling betrayed Norway,
That Quisling betrayed Norway is something I was aware of.[5]

We also refer to facts by means of pronouns tied to whole sentences. In this: "She turned him down. That is why he was so depressed", the word "that" refers to the fact that she turned him down, which hasn't been named but has been expressed.

I said that many perfect nominals are event *sortals*, and I explained how sortals can be used to form names. On the other side of the fence, however, I have said only that imperfect nominals are fact *names*, suggesting that they cannot be employed as fact sortals. Nor indeed can they. The very syntax of imperfect nominals forbids them to function as sortals, because they can't be pluralized or prefixed with articles in such expressions as "a stealing the bicycle", "three (betraying Norway)s", "the singing *Die Winterreise* tomorrow", and so on. But syntax reflects something deeper. Given an event name, we can turn it into a sortal under which many events fall, by omitting some of its detail. Suppose that "performance of 'Stormy Weather' that Lena Horne gave on November 4th, 1983" is a sortal that fits only one event, so that we can put "the" in front of it and get an event name. Now, we can turn this sortal into one that covers two or more events by omitting detail from it. Here are some of the ways of doing this:

4. There is a mass of doctrine about how our language handles facts and events, but since I know little of it at first hand (not needing to for my limited purposes) I shall not presume to offer references.

5. I am guided here by Vendler, *op. cit.*, p. 129n.

performance of "Stormy Weather" that Lena Horne gave in 1983,
performance of "Stormy Weather" that Lena Horne gave,
performance that Lena Horne gave,
performance.

Each of these sortals applies to, among other events, the performance of "Stormy Weather" that Lena Horne gave on November 4th, 1983. Now, contrast that with what happens when we take a *fact* named and omit detail from it. I could exhibit this through gerundial nominals, but, to make it as clear and persuasive as I can, I shall use "that [S]" nominals instead. So we start with the fact *that Lena Horne performed "Stormy Weather" on November 4th, 1983*. If we omit detail from that fact name, we get such items as

that Lena Horne performed "Stormy Weather" in 1983,
that Lena Horne performed "Stormy Weather",
that Lena Horne performed something,
that someone performed something.

This list mirrors the list of increasingly capacious event sortals, but this time each item on the list names a single fact, namely the fact expressed by the nested sentence. We cannot pluralize "that Lena Horne performed 'Stormy Weather' ", because it is the *name* of a single fact, namely the fact that Lena Horne performed "Stormy Weather" (at least once), and an expression that cannot be pluralized cannot take articles and, in sum, is not a sortal.

There are sortals that cover facts, but they are never nominalizations of sentences and are always of the form "fact which is F". Each of the following: "fact which has been discovered by John over the past month", "fact which it would be better for Susan not to know", "fact the discovery of which would ruin Hart's career" is a sortal that might fit many facts, which is why they take indefinite articles and can be pluralized. They are not sentence nominals, however, and have no place in my discussion.

4. *The fineness of facts*

When it comes to naming facts by means of imperfect nominals, *what you see is what you get*. That is, any difference in content between two such fact names—corresponding to any failure of logical equivalence between the parent sentences—makes them names of different facts. If S_1 is not interdeducible with S_2, then the fact that [S_1], if there is such a thing, is not the fact that [S_2]. Actually, I shall soon be discussing a view about facts according to which that is not true, but it is near enough to right for present purposes. Nothing like it is true of the perfect nominals that name events: nominalizations of two nonequivalent sentences may well name a single event. I shall illustrate this.

Bernard travelled to Calais just once in his lifetime. So there is

e_1 his journey to Calais,

and, corresponding to that, there is

f_1 the fact that he journeyed to Calais, or
his journeying to Calais,

with the latter understood as an imperfect nominal. I add the information that Bernard got to Calais, this one time, by swimming the Channel. So there is

e_2 his cross-Channel swim

and, corresponding to that, there is

f_2 the fact that he swam the Channel, or
his swimming the Channel.

I contend that e_1 is e_2, whereas f_1 is not f_2. This is not an upshot of any special features of the example; rather, it illustrates the general truth that with fact names but not with event names differences in logical power create differences of referent.

How am I to justify saying that e_1 is e_2? That raises a general question that I want to discuss before coming to the case in point.

Many writers on events have debated about which pairs of nominals name the same event, or what the truth conditions are for statements of the form "the [ES_1] is the [ES_2]", where each ES is an event sortal. How can we decide this? What are our data for claims about this aspect of the common concept of an event? One might hope they would be provided by the facts about what intelligent and thoughtful people will say and what they will deny, of the form "the [ES_1] is the [ES_2]", but such naked assertions of event identity seldom occur in ordinary speech and writing. Fortunately, there is another source of evidence, because the concept of identity is being silently employed whenever we predicate two things of a single subject. It is not at work in this:

(a) There is an x and a y such that: Gx and Hy,

but it is in this:

(b) There is an x such that: Gx and Hx.

The difference is easily seen: If to (a) we add the identity clause " . . . and x is y", the result is equivalent to (b). So when philosophers discuss event identity, they are not working in a vacuum: what they say is relevant to double predications on events. For example, Davidson holds that every mental event is also physical, and some of his wordings have encouraged others to express this in the form "Every mental event is identical with some physical event"—an eccentric wording, like saying that all schizophrenics are ungrateful in the words "Every schizophrenic is identical with some ingrate." Even when it is expressed less eccentrically, however, Davidson's thesis still involves the concept of event identity, because in saying that some mental event is also physical we are implying that there is a mental event x and a physical event y such that x is y.

That, however, is not the same as saying that the [ES_1] is the [ES_2]—asserting an identity statement in which two names are used. To do that we must be able to form event names, which requires us to be able to count events: we cannot be competent with statements of the form "The [ES_1] is the [ES_2]" if we are never sure whether ES_1 applies to one event or to more than one. Fortunately, the counting of events under sortals is something we do all the time: there is plenty of evidence about how that is done, given the event concept we actually have.

Let us apply all this to my statement that Bernard's journey to Calais was his cross-Channel swim. If the statement is false, then it follows that either (i) his cross-Channel swim was not *a* journey to Calais or (ii) it was not his only journey to Calais (and in particular is not the one I mentioned first and called e_2). But (i) seems clearly wrong: the swim took him to Calais and has all the marks of a journey. And (ii) seems wrong, because it seems absurd to suggest that Bernard went to Calais only once yet made two journeys there. Furthermore, analogous arguments could raise the number of his journeys to Calais still higher.

I *argue* for the obvious conclusion that the swim was the journey, because some philosophers may have denied it. We shall see in due course that they have not understood the difference between perfect and imperfect nominals or between events and facts, so one must hesitate to attribute to them any doctrines about events. Still, they have *thought* they were saying that Bernard's journey to Calais was one event and his cross-Channel swim another; so I could not take the point for granted.

As for the claim that the two imperfect nominals name different facts and that in general two fact names have the same referent only if they have the same logical powers: I justify this by pointing to what can happen to the truth-value of a statement when an imperfect nominal that it contains is replaced by another. I am surprised that Bernard journeyed to Calais, but not that he swam the Channel; his having swum the Channel, but not his having journeyed to Calais, explains his fatigue; his interest in Calais hotels resulted from the fact that he was going to journey to Calais, not from the fact that he was going to swim the Channel.

Summing all this up: An event can be picked out by a definite description that (i) involves only its intrinsic nature (not its relational properties) and (ii) does not exhaust that nature. For example, "Watteau's arrival in Paris" names an event without telling anywhere near the whole monadic truth about it. In contrast with that, no fact name can satisfy both (i) and (ii). We can refer to a fact by a description that satisfies (i) but not (ii), as we do in every expression of the form "the fact that [S]"; or by a description that satisfies (ii) but not (i), as in "the fact which I called into question in our discussion yesterday" and "the fact which made all the difference to how she felt about his behavior". On the other hand, when facts are named through their intrinsic natures, by imperfect nominals, what you see is what you get.

5. *Events are supervenient*

Events are not basic items in the universe; they should not be included in any fundamental ontology. I do not say and do not believe that we can in practice tell all the truths about events without using the event concept, which is why I avoid the language of reduction or elimination, in favor of the language of supervenience. In shorthand, I shall say that events are supervenient entities, meaning that all the truths about them are logically entailed by and *explained* or *made true* by truths that do not involve the event concept. Similarly, all the truths about universities come from truths about people and buildings and equipment; all the truths about ecological niches come from truths about plants and animals and weather and terrain.

In discussing the supervenience of events, I shall use the word "zone" to mean "spatiotemporal zone" or "region of space-time". The "location" of an event is its spatiotemporal location, i.e. where and when it occurs. Thus, if we say of a certain mugging that it occurred in Hyde Park yesterday, we locate it in a certain stretch of space-time whose limits in three dimensions are those of Hyde Park and whose limits in the fourth dimension are set by the boundaries of yesterday. Locations of events can be more or less precise in any of the four dimensions. A zone may be sizeless along one or more of its dimensions: whereas examinations, journeys, and races take time, starts, arrivals, and victories are instantaneous and are therefore contained in zones that have no temporal extent; some fill spatial volumes, and presumably others occupy only planes, lines, even points. I shall make nothing of these differences. For example, I shall pick out the temporal aspect of an event's zone using the form ". . . at time T" with a meaning that is indifferent between "at instant T" and "throughout period T". Now back to the main thread.

My view about supervenience implies that what makes it the case that there is a run is the fact that something runs, so I can't also say that what makes it the case that something runs is the fact that there is a run. I don't mean that something's running *causes* it to be the case that there is a run; my point concerns the direction of conceptual explanation, not of causal flow. Our grasp of the idea that a run occurred yesterday comes from our grasp of the idea that something ran yesterday; our grasp of the idea there is a picnic in the park comes from our grasp of the idea that people are sitting around eating and conversing in the park. Someone could have a linguistic/conceptual upbringing that made him competent in talking about how things behave and where they are when, but stopped short of equipping him to use the event concept; nobody could have an upbringing that started at the other end and stopped in the same place. Or so I confidently believe, though I don't know how to defend my opinion.

The derivativeness of some truths about events can be displayed in simple algorithms, which would allow for a reductive treatment of some propositions about events, if we wanted one. This seems to be feasible for every truth of the form "There is an [ES]", where ES is an event sortal that is derived from a verb. There is a riot (in Vienna, today) because people riot (in Vienna, today); there will be a flight (over this forest, next week) because something will fly (over this forest, next week). In these cases, the fact that there is an [ES] at zone z comes from the fact that [S] at z, where S is a sentence whose principal verb is the parent of the principal noun in ES. In each case, the S in question does not itself contain any event sortals.

The scope of the algorithm can be enlarged a little, so that it covers statements to the effect that there is an [ES] *by* x or *of* y, where x and y are (as we might say) participants. When an event has just one participant, it can be called the subject of the event; where there are two, it may be plausible to call one the subject and the other the object; but sometimes when there are only two and always when there are more, it is best just to speak of the participants and identify them as occupying the first, second, etc. places in the event, according to some chosen ordering. These aspects of events can also be brought within the scope of an algorithm. Just as there will be a flight because something will fly, there will be a flight by a heron because a heron will fly; there was a quarrel between John and Marsha because John and Marsha quarreled.

All of that concerns event sortals that are derived from verbs: I have been pairing (i) sentences in which an event sortal ES occurs with (ii) sentences whose principal verb is the source of ES. Some event sortals, however, do not grammatically come from verbs at all—

e.g. "hurricane", "picnic", "traffic jam", "ball", "ceremony", and countless others. Events of these kinds are supervenient also, I submit, but now the supervenience cannot be displayed in a simple algorithm. Still, it can often be displayed somehow. It seems about right to say that if there is a picnic at z that is (noncausally) because a group of people sociably eat an informal outdoor meal at z, and that a traffic jam is a noncausal upshot of the fact that the traffic on a stretch of road is (nearly) stopped by a temporary blockage or by the road's containing more traffic than it can swiftly handle. It would be strange (to put it mildly) if one were to run either of these explanations in the reverse direction.

Sometimes, though, it is hard to display the supervenience at all. It would take a long time to work out exactly how to complete the sentence "If there is a hurricane at z, that is because . . .". But I don't doubt that it can be completed truthfully, and we do at least know what the subject of the completing clause will be, namely portions of air, water particles in the clouds, and so on.

With some kinds of events we do not even know that much—flashes and bangs, for example. As Strawson has pointed out: "That a flash or bang occurred does not entail that anything flashed or banged. 'Let there be light' does not mean 'Let something shine'."[6] So what do such statements mean? This question must be faced by any friend of the supervenience thesis. If flashes and bangs were mental occurrences, as Berkeley thought when he assumed that the so-called "sound of a coach" is really an "idea" in the mind, each fact about the occurrence of a flash or bang would owe its truth to some fact about how someone alters in a certain mental respect. But Berkeley was wrong: flashes and bangs are—and are conceived by us as being—extramental, with shapes, sizes and positions in space. I suggest, then, that when *there is a flash at zone* z this is (noncausally) because *something is the case about* z *that would have caused normal well-placed observers to alter* . . . with the gap filled in with a Berkeleian description of the subjective experience of a flash. (If you think there are no unseen flashes and no unheard bangs, add "and did cause one such observer to alter thus".) Analogously with "There was a bang".

That account of the supervenience of flashes and bangs does not go beyond what the ordinary person means and knows. For those who know more, the account can be improved and deepened: there is a flash because of a fact about how photons moved, and there is a bang because of how air undulated.

So much for event statements of the form "There is an [ES] at z" and elaborations of those to bring in participants. The supervenience thesis is harder to illustrate and defend in application to some other

6. P.F. Strawson, *Individuals*, p. 46.

uses of the event concept. Here are some of the principal ones.

(1) Statements attributing to events properties and relations other than existence, location, and participants. "The advance on Arnhem was slow and clumsy." "Your house-warming party was unlike mine in three main ways." "The funeral cost more than the wake." (2) Statements about numbers of events. "There were three forest fires in the state last month." "There are two conferences going on in the hotel right now." "She did seventeen laps." (3) Counterfactuals about events. "If there hadn't been so much logging over the past decade, the mudslide wouldn't have occurred."

We shall find in due course that none of them can be algorithmically equated with statements in which the event concept is not used. Even when ES is derived from a verb, there is no simple rule for constructing a sentence with the same informational content as "The [ES] is F" or "There are three [ES]s at z" and so on. However, we shall not find any reason to think that statements of the above three kinds make much trouble for the supervenience thesis.

6. *Challenges to supervenience*

The supervenience thesis can be challenged in any of three ways.

One depends on the fact that I am taking truths about events to be derivative from ones that do not involve *event* but do involve *substance* and *property* or, at any rate, that involve whatever concepts are needed for making predications on substances. A metaphysical view advanced by Donald C. Williams and some others implies that I have got this backwards.

It is a view about items that Leibniz called "individual accidents" and Williams called "tropes".[7] A trope is a case or instance of a property: My house is a concrete particular that has whiteness and other properties; whiteness is an abstract universal that is possessed by my house and other particulars; and *the whiteness of my house* is a trope, an abstract particular. It is unlike my house in that all there is to it is whiteness, and it is unlike whiteness in that it pertains only to my

7. Donald C. Williams, "The Elements of Being". An important precursor is G.F. Stout, "The Nature of Universals and Propositions", and a useful successor is Keith Campbell, "The Metaphysics of Abstract Particulars". For a helpful discussion, see Anthony Quinton, "Objects and Events". An attack on Stout's paper by G.E. Moore, "Are the Characteristics of Particular Things Universal or Particular?", was responded to in the same volume by Stout and was demolished by J.R. Jones, "Are the Characteristics of Things Particular or Universal?".

house. Now, Williams has maintained that at the deepest metaphysical level my house and the universal whiteness are both collections of tropes, with different principles of colligation. What makes it the case that my house is white is just the fact that the whiteness of my house belongs to both collections.

According to this metaphysical scheme, substances and properties are supervenient on tropes. To that can be added the plausible thesis that events are tropes and that indeed the concept of a trope differs from the concept of an event only in being slightly more general or abstract. The result is a position implying that substances and properties are supervenient on tropes (including events), rather than vice versa.

I shall later defend the second premise of that argument, namely that events are tropes. I have no opinion on the first premise and do not want to discuss it here. To stay clear of it, I assert my supervenience thesis in a conditional form: events are supervenient on substances and properties, unless the supervenience runs the other way because tropes are more fundamental than substances and properties. That is a substantive thesis, denied by some philosophers who put events on the same level as substances and properties.

One such philosopher is Julius Moravcsik. He has maintained, against a view of Strawson's, that, just as we cannot reidentify an event except by reference to substances that participate in it, so we cannot reidentify an enduring physical thing except by reference to events in which it is a participant. This goes against the supervenience thesis, which says that there is a one-way explanatory flow. Moravcsik puts it like this:

> Though part of the evidence [for reidentification of physical things] may be qualitative sameness (e.g. "The knife looks the same"), the statements of the evidence would have to connect this with events of observation (e.g. "The knife looks the same as the one someone saw an hour ago"). In short, reidentification involves correlating in certain ways objects, times, and places; and this is not possible without some reference—ultimately—to events. . . . Strawson argues that such events as strikes cannot be basic particulars, for we could not have the concept of a strike without having such concepts as those of tools and factories. To this, however, it should be replied that neither could we have the concepts of tools and factories without having such concepts as those of production, manufacturing, etc.[8]

This has been endorsed by Davidson, who cites Moravcsik as reaching "the same conclusion" as he, Davidson, does here:

8. J.M.E. Moravcsik, "Strawson and Ontological Priority", pp. 116, 117.

> Substances owe their special importance in the enterprise of identification to the fact that they survive through time. But the idea of survival is inseparable from the idea of surviving certain sorts of change—of position, size, shape, colour, and so forth. As we might expect, events often play an essential role in identifying a substance. Thus if we track down the author of *Waverley* or the father of Annette, it is by identifying an event, of writing, or of fathering. Neither the category of substance nor the category of change is conceivable apart from the other.[9]

Not so. We can track down the author of *Waverley* by locating the person who *wrote Waverley*; we don't have to think of him as the person who was the subject or agent or author or participant in *a writing of Waverley*. So we have no need to introduce the concept of a particular event. As for Moravcsik's statement that the knife looks the same as the one I saw an hour ago, that doesn't even seem to use the concept of an event. Of course, if the knife was seen twice then two events, specifically two observations, occurred, but that is irrelevant to the question at issue.

Of Davidson's various other reasons for esteeming the concept of an event, only one challenges the claim that events are supervenient. According to him, "Lincoln fell" should be understood as saying "There was a fall and Lincoln was its subject", and countless other predications on substances should also be understood on this same pattern as asserting the existence of events. This lets him equate "Lincoln fell heavily" with "There was a fall and Lincoln was its subject and it was heavy", and he argues that if we want to understand valid inferences in which adverbs are dropped—e.g. the inference from "He fell heavily" to "He fell"—we shall do best to explicate adverbs ("heavily") in terms of adjectives ("heavy").

Understood as a merely technical device—a way of organizing adverb-dropping inferences—this is no threat to the supervenience of events. But Davidson means more. He is doing psychology, claiming to lay bare the logical principles that do in fact guide us in our handling of adverbs. To take a concrete example: Someone tells me, "As Danton was being taken to the guillotine, he gestured derisively to Robespierre", and I believe this. Later, I hear someone else say that Danton, from the moment he was condemned to death, would not acknowledge that Robespierre existed, and I say, "But I was told that as Danton was being taken to the guillotine he gestured to Robespierre." I have inferred that he gestured from the premise that he gestured derisively, and Davidson holds that I have done this by understanding the premise as meaning "There was a derisive gesture . . ." and the conclusion

9. Donald Davidson, "The Individuation of Events", p. 175.

as meaning "There was a gesture . . .". The claim must be that whenever we say "He gestured . . ." we mean "There was a gesture . . ."; the equation couldn't hold only when there is an adverb in the vicinity! So Davidson seems to be denying that facts about events owe their truth to underlying truths in which the event concept is not involved. For, if his psychological thesis is right, the latter statements do use the event concept just below their surfaces.

Do we understand "He gestured" *through* the thought that he made a gesture? If Davidson's theory is correct, we do, and then one of the following must be true. (1) We could not educate a child into knowing a big fragment of English from which perfect nominals were absent—so that he came to understand "She reigns" but not "her reign", "They performed" but not "their performance", and so on. (2) We could do it, but the child would perform clumsily with adverb-dropping inferences, not having our smooth rules for handling them, and would process ordinary subject-predicate statements—even ones with no adverbs in them—by quite different processes from those the rest of us follow. (3) The child would not think differently from us, or perform worse than us, because he would employ the perfect-nominal apparatus in his thoughts: he would *think* "They performed well" in the form "Their performance was good", even though he could not *say* the latter.

Each of those is implausible enough to cast doubt on a thesis that implies that one of them is right.

7. *A sceptical conclusion*

One conclusion of this book will be that our event concept is adapted to the giving of rather small and indeterminate gobbets of information. That unfits it for bearing weight in disciplined theories such as those of semantics, ethics, "action theory", and philosophy of mind, in which philosophers have tried to put it to work; and the failures of those attempts (some of which will be examined later) can be traced to their putting onto our event concept a load it cannot carry.[10]

Objection: "Any imprecise concept—and what concept isn't?—

---

10. Although we cannot do much *with* our event concept, we can do philosophy *on* it. Even there, however, not too much should be expected. The persistent disagreements among philosophers about the nature of events—their role in causal statements, their "identity conditions", their relations to space-time, etc.—have arisen partly from the fact that some of the disputed questions have no answers. They ask for precision at the very points where our event concept does not have it.

can be polished into precision if there is need for it; and a concept that is used for giving small rations of information can be strengthened so as to give more." I don't agree. Our event concept is *essentially* imprecise and uninformative; change it in those respects, and it will no longer serve well in the hurly-burly of everyday thought and speech. I shall give evidence for this in due course.

If there are events, how can we theorize about them without using the event concept as a load-bearing part of the theory? We cannot, but I see no reason to want to have or to think we can have disciplined theories about events or at least about the kinds of events that loom large in our everyday thinking. Consider the example of "theories about *wars*", with which I have been challenged. I doubt that there could be much decent theory about the relation of *being-at-war* that sometimes obtains between nations; but even if there could, it would not follow that there could be decent theories that made real use of the notion of *wars*, individual complex events, things that happen. I am not arguing for this now; merely stating an attitude.

This does not follow from the supervenience thesis. The facts of thermodynamics, though they come from underlying facts about molecular motion, are sharp and orderly enough to be usable in theories. My contention is just that the particular way in which events are supervenient—the nature of *this* conceptual device for carrying news upstairs from the ground floor—unfits our event concept for serious theoretical use.

"Stop shilly-shallying! Are there such things as events, or aren't there?" Well, there was an earthquake in California last week and a birth in China this morning, so there are events. One might express the supervenience thesis in the form "*Basically* there are no events", but that is a needlessly provocative way of saying something rather humdrum. And I have no grounds for saying that [adverb] there are no events, with any of the other usual adverbs.

What about "*Strictly speaking* there are no events"? This might be said by someone who believes that if we press down hard on some of the things we are most sure of about events we can extract absurdities or contradictions—like those who are led by the puzzle about the ship of Theseus[11] to refuse to admit shoes and ships etc. into their strict inventory of the world's contents or like those who, assuming that the building bricks of the universe must be indivisible substances

11. The story is told that Theseus' ship was rebuilt over a period of years, one plank at a time, while it stayed in use. The planks removed from it were stored and later reassembled to form a perfect replica of the original ship. So now we have a ship that *is continuous with* the original and we also have one that *has the same matter as* the original. Which of them is the original ship of Theseus?

and that any occupant of a region of space can be split, have concluded that strictly speaking there are no physical things except the infinitely large one (Spinoza) or infinitely small ones (Leibniz). There is no reason to say such a thing about events.

So I am not embarking on a reductive or eliminative treatment of events. I want only to analyze our event concept: not to dismantle it into simpler constituents (that view of analysis has been a disaster, from Locke through to Moore) but just to describe how it works and how it relates to its neighbors. That should help us to get the concept of an event into perspective and to command a whole, clear view of what its strengths and weaknesses are.

II

FACTS

8. *Event causation and fact causation*

An event-causation statement picks out a pair of events and says of one of them that it caused the other: "The tidal wave caused the collapse of the oil rig", "Her fall caused the fracture", "The volcanic eruption caused the forest fire". We can also say such things using "effect", "result", "upshot", and other terms. I shall not attend to differences amongst these, except when discussing a thesis of Vendler's about them.

Event-causation statements are rich sources of data about the concept of an individual event. But they won't give us much of a handle on the concept until we understand how they work, and that involves grasping how they relate to fact-causation statements. I therefore start with the latter.

A fact-causation statement picks out two facts—two states of affairs that obtain—and says that one of them caused the other. Such statements are not most happily expressed in the form ". . . caused . . ." with a fact name in each gap. Indeed, it is only with imperfect gerundial nominals that such a form is English at all. The sentence "Her mocking him caused his hating her" may barely pass muster, but "That she mocked him caused that he hated her" is emphatically not English, and it becomes only slightly better if we replace "that" by "the fact that". Still, there are plenty of idiomatic ways of causally interrelating facts. Here are some examples:

His perpetually smoking cigarettes led to his getting cancer.
She sneered at him, which resulted in his sulking for a week.
One upshot of the wind's starting up when it did was that the fire was driven into the new timber.
That I dislike *Julius Caesar* is a consequence of my having to study it in high school.

Differences between "lead", "result", "upshot", "consequence", etc. seem not to matter for our present topic. All the above are fact-causation statements, and my concern is with what they have in common.

Those examples display some of our large repertoire of devices for referring to facts. They contain five imperfect gerundial nominals, two instances of the "that [S]" form, and (in the second example) one pronomial reference to a fact. This last device is always available. The first example could be replaced by either "He smoked etc., which led to his getting cancer", or "He smoked etc. That led to his getting cancer."

Indeed, a fact-causation statement need not *refer* to facts at all. For example, the statement "The fire went out because the rain came" expresses a pair of facts without in any way referring to them; and "In consequence of the rain's coming, the fire went out" names one fact and expresses the other. However, each gives the same information as do "The rain's coming led to the fire's going out" and "The rain came, and the fire went out, and the latter fact was a consequence of the former". The difference in logical form is philosophically unimportant. It is like the difference between "That grass is green entails that bananas are yellow", which relates two named propositions, and "If grass is green then it follows necessarily that bananas are yellow", in which the propositions are expressed, not named. I shall write as though fact-causation statements always relate named facts; everything I say can easily be adjusted to cover expressed-fact statements as well.

Some people have objected that facts are not the sorts of items that can cause anything. A fact is a true proposition (they say); it is not something *in* the world but is rather something *about* the world, which makes it categorially wrong for the role of a puller and shover and twister and bender. That rests on the mistaken assumption that causal statements must report relations between shovers and forcers. I grant that facts cannot behave like elbows in the ribs, but we know what items do play that role—namely elbows. In our world the pushing and shoving and forcing are done by *things*—elementary particles and aggregates of them—and not by any relata of the causal relation. Consider these:

> The vase broke because a heavy stone was dropped onto it.
> The vase's destruction was caused by the fall of a heavy stone.
> The vase broke when a heavy stone sent shock waves through it.

The first two of these report causes, a fact in one case and an event in the other. The third reports a pusher, an exerter of force, and this is neither a fact nor an event but a stone.

Objection: "But do you deny that when an explosion causes a

fire, the explosion emits force, pushes things around, acts as the elbow in the ribs?" Yes, I do. When an explosion causes a fire, what happens is that molecules bump into other molecules, increasing their velocity to the point where they react rapidly with the ambient gases, etc. The idea that the pushing is done not by the molecules but by the explosion is just the afterglow of ignorance about what an explosion is.

9. *How they differ*

Each kind of causation statement relates a pair of items in a certain way, the logical form being C(x,y). So each is transparent with respect to the x and the y. That means that if, in an event-causation statement, we replace the name of an event by another name for the very same event, the result will have the same truth-value as the original; and similarly for fact-causation statements.

The latter claim is sometimes disputed. It is sometimes said that "x caused y" is transparent with respect to x and y if they are events and opaque with respect to them if they are facts; but that is not so. Take the case of Bernard, who goes to Calais just once, by swimming the Channel. The truth of this:

> His getting pneumonia was due in large part to (1) the fact that he swam the Channel,

stands or falls with the truth of this:

> His getting pneumonia was due in large part to (2) the fact that he entered the water on one side of the Channel and propelled his body forward by movements of his hands and feet against the water until he reached the other side;

whereas each of them is consistent with the falsity of this:

> His getting pneumonia was due in large part to (3) the fact that he journeyed to Calais.

By any reasonable standard, this should count as evidence that (1) is (2) and that (1) is not (3). I don't see what stronger evidence one could have for such a conclusion. But the premises yield that conclusion only if the context in which the fact names appear is transparent rather than opaque (or, as some like to say, "intensional").

Here is the real difference between the two kinds of causation statement: If we substitute one imperfect nominal for another in a fact-causation statement, we risk moving from truth to falsity unless the two nominals in question are necessarily equivalent; in substituting one perfect nominal for another in an event-causation statement, we do not need so tight a constraint to be sure of preserving truth. That is because fact names corefer only if they are strictly equivalent, whereas coreference of event names is less demanding (see Section 4 above).

Let us test that. If Henry fell twenty feet from the rooftop and thereby broke his leg, the following pair need not have the same truth-value:

> Because of his coming down from the roof, he suffered a fracture.
> Because of his falling twenty feet, he suffered a fracture.

But these two must have the same truth-value:

> Henry's fracture was caused by his descent from the roof.
> Henry's fracture was caused by his twenty-foot fall.

The underlying idea is just that a single event was a descent of the free and fast kind known as a fall, from a roof to the ground twenty feet below, whereas the fact that Henry came down from the roof is not at all the same as the fact that he fell twenty feet.

Although I have spoken of event- and fact-causation statements, I should really classify not statements but positions within statements. We often make causal statements in which the cause is a fact and the effect an event, as in "The divorce resulted from their incessantly quarreling" and "The prime rate went up, which caused a fall in the price of gold". Conversely, we sometimes represent an event as a cause and a fact as an effect, as when we say "The discovery of penicillin has led to there being more resistant bacteria than there used to be". So let us stop pretending that proper Engish gives us only $C(e_1,e_2)$ or $C(f_1,f_2)$. There is nothing wrong with the mixtures C(f,e) and C(e,f).

10. *The noun-infinitive form*

The majority of causation statements in everyday English speech are of the form ". . . cause [noun phrase] to [verb phrase]" or the form ". . . make [noun phrase] [verb phrase]". For example: "The rain causes the fire to go out", "What the auditor did caused the managing director to resign", "The oration will make the crowd become restless", "Your amiability makes me wonder what you want". Facts, events, and perhaps other items can occur before the principal verb in these, but never mind that. What follows the verb in each case makes these statements about the causation of *facts*. In explaining why, I shall focus on " . . . cause [NP] to [VP]", which seems to differ only trivially from " . . . make [NP] [VP]".[1]

Suppose that Peter dislikes the music at a party and consequently decides to leave. As he moves towards the door, he gets a coughing fit, so he leaves noisily. Now consider these two statements about the causation of events:

1e. The music caused Peter's departure.
2e. The music caused Peter's noisy departure.

On any viable theory of events, a person who leaves only once is the subject of only one departure, and so "his departure" and "his noisy departure" refer to the same event, with the latter describing it more fully; and both statements are true, because that one event was caused by the music. Here now are two statements about the causation of facts:

1f. The music led to Peter's leaving the party.
2f. The music led to Peter's leaving the party noisily.

These name different facts, one richer than the other, so they could differ in truth-values. They not only could—they do. In the anecdote, 1f is true and 2f is false, though

3. The music led to his leaving the party, which he did noisily

is true.

Now consider these two:

1* The music caused him to leave.
2* The music caused him to leave noisily.

It seems clear that 1* is true and 2* is false, unlike

3* The music caused him to leave, which he did noisily,

which is true. So the noun-infinitive form behaves like an imperfect nominal, and that is why I take it to refer to facts rather than to events.

That gives us a rich store of examples of the mixed form C(e,f): "Their conversation caused him to rethink his position", "The removal of the tree caused the lawn to be torn up", "The acid rain made the lakes go sterile". And we now have no shortage of fact-causation statements with "cause" as their main verb. When two imperfect nominals are used, as in "Marian's mocking Robin caused his hating

---

1. Unless the latter should be classified with the form " . . . make [NP] [Adj]", as in "Your amiability makes me uneasy". I do not know what to say about this problem.

her", the sense of impropriety is all at the effect position, but now we can put a noun-infinitive in there, and the result—"Marian's mocking Robin caused him to hate her" is unstrained, acceptable English.

11. *Some theses of Vendler's*

Vendler doesn't just allow f/e mixtures; he insists on them. Let us examine his surprising views about the proper relata of various causal relations.[2]

(1) Where I am willing to use the verb "to cause" in linking pairs of facts, Vendler prefers the verb "to explain". I have no more to say about that. I am inclined to agree with him that ". . . explains . . ." cannot take anything but facts as relata. What about "His insulting her explains her anger"? Vendler replies that here we "feel the push towards saying that it is really something about [her anger]" that is explained, namely the fact that it occurs.

(2) According to Vendler, " . . . is the/an effect of . . . " relates events. It certainly can do so, as in "Among the effects of Lord Gordon's speech were a riot and many deaths". His view that *only* events can be effects seems wrong, though. It condemns such innocent exchanges as this: "The forest floor is covered with flowers." "Yes, that's an effect of the forest ire."

(3) Vendler says that " . . . is the/a result of . . . " relates only facts, not events. Here is a counterexample, drawn from his own writings: "As propositions are the results of an abstraction from the variety of [logically equivalent] forms, so facts are the results of a further abstraction from the variety of equivalent referring expressions." (p. 711) In this sentence, the phrase "are the results of an abstraction" is quite proper and cannot mean that the items in question are results of a fact! Actually, ". . . is the/a result of . . ." takes a wide variety of relata—facts, events, and items that are neither.

(4) By far the most striking of Vendler's doctrines in this area is that the relation ". . . is the/a cause of . . ." is properly used only to relate a fact to an event, as in "Oil's gradually becoming more expensive was the cause of the dollar's fall". I shall not discuss the view that the form " . . . causes (fact)" is improper, but I must examine the remarkable condemnation of the form "(event) causes . . . ". Where some philosophers hold that $C(e_1,e_2)$ is the only proper form of particular causation statement, Vendler condemns it as defective.

2. Zeno Vendler, "Causal Relations"; see also his *Linguistics in Philosophy*, pp. 163–69. In this section, unadorned page numbers will refer to these works.

Although I agree with Vendler that facts can be causes, his arguments for this are not strong. Here is some supposed evidence:

> Scientists can find, deduce, mention or state causes as much as they can find, deduce, mention, state facts. The causes themselves, like facts, may indicate, lead to or explain things. . . . Like facts, causes can be hidden or obvious, probable or unlikely, plausible or unbelievable. (p. 709)

Absolutely anything, in any metaphysical category, can be found, mentioned, hidden, or obvious—the fact that our planet is spherical, an underground nuclear explosion, a thimble, the virtues of Aaron Burr. We can "state the cause", but we can also state our name. To say that someone has "deduced the cause" may mean only that he has deduced what it is—like "deducing the culprit". As for "The cause was something unbelievable"—compare "What he bought her for Christmas was something unbelievable". Similarly with the rest of Vendler's list.

Two of Vendler's examples of fact causation are unpersuasive: "John's having arrived caused the commotion", "John's being able to be here caused our surprise" (p. 165). These are grammatically passable, but each is suspect on other grounds. The former implies that what caused the commotion at T_3 was its being the case at T_2 that *John had arrived*; but it would be better to say either that what caused the commotion was John's arrival at T_1 or that it was caused by people's memory at T_2 of his earlier arrival. I don't mind saying that the commotion was caused by *John's arriving at T_1*, which is a fact. I am not arguing that facts cannot be causes; merely complaining against Vendler's evidence that they can. As for "John's being able to be here caused our surprise": I submit that no modal facts—as distinct from their nonmodal bases—are causally efficacious. What caused our surprise was *our belief that* John could be here, which was caused not by John's ability to be here but rather by some nonmodal fact about John that was evidence that he could be here or that made it possible for him to be here.

It is significant that Vendler defends his thesis with unpersuasive arguments and suspect examples. Good examples can be given, and Vendler provides a couple, but ones that would satisfy him are not plentiful. This is because our most idiomatic and comfortable ways of causally interrelating facts do not use "cause" etc. but rather "because", "lead to", "upshot" etc., and Vendler ties the concept of cause pretty tightly to the word "cause". I do not.

Let us now look at Vendler's startling claim that *only* facts can be causes, implying that events cannot. One might expect him to defend this by adducing sentences of the form "[perfect nominal] caused . . ." that were so absurd as to suggest that everything of that form is defective. Vendler knows that he cannot do that, because such statements are idiomatically acceptable, so he must explain them away. He tries to disarm them by maintaining that (i) the context " . . . caused y" can take either perfect or imperfect nominals and that (ii) when a context can take either, it is the imperfect nominal that properly, strictly, literally gives the meaning. He argues for (ii) by looking at just a few examples; I am not convinced that he is right even about them, and, even if he is, that does not make him right about *all* contexts that could take nominals of either kind.

12. *Vendler's four challenges*

Still, Vendler has arguments of other sorts. I do not see how they could convince us that events cannot be causes, but each poses a challenge that ought to be met.

(i) He holds, as I have reported, that the proper way to use "effect" is in the form "(event) is an effect of (event)". He is now arguing against those who think that the proper way to use "cause" is in the form "(event) is a cause of (event)". According to them, "cause" and "effect" name converse relations, and Vendler challenges them: If "is an effect of" is the converse of "is a cause of", why do we have both words in our language?

This can be explained, as can other pairs of words that express converse relations—"parent" and "offspring", "creditor" and "debtor", "contain" and "occupy". In each case our having both words, rather than only one, makes for brevity and structural simplicity. Try dropping "parent" (along with "father" and "mother") and doing all its work with "offspring" (and with "son" and "daughter"). We can replace "x is a parent of y" by "y is an offspring of x", which is no worse, but sentences that do more than merely attribute parenthood are trickier. For example, the work of "One of my parents wrote a novel" has to be done by "One of those whose offspring I am wrote a novel", which is three words longer and one nested clause more complex. Similarly with "cause" and "effect". Vendler's first challenge is met.

His other three challenges are consecutive sentences. I shall discuss them separately.

(ii) "If the word 'cause' sometimes denotes an event, then why is it nonsense to say that a cause has occurred or taken place, that it began at a certain time, lasted for a while, and ended suddenly?" (p. 709) In answering this, let us get clear what we should be looking for. For obvious reasons, we ought to focus not on "the cause" but rather on "a cause" and "causes". It is seldom if ever literally true that e_1 is the cause of e_2. Now, to call an event "a cause", *tout court*, is to say little or nothing about it, for possibly all events are causes. For the same reason, we have no occasion to generalize about all causes. What we should be looking at, then, are uses of phrases of the form "cause(s) of e". For example:

The Versailles Treaty was a cause of World War II;
He is writing a book on the causes of the Reformation;
One of the causes of the landslide was also a cause of the flood.

That third example is a heroic attempt to find a plausible sentence in which the *subject* noun phrase includes "cause(s) of . . . ". It's an improbable subject term. When we want to refer to an item in order to say something about it, it seems very strained and unnatural to do so with help from the word "cause", as is done in that example. (We may well use "cause" in what we say *about* the event, i.e. in the predicate rather than the subject, as in the statement "Your speech was one of the causes of the riot.") Try it for yourself and you will see. The reason is clear. Most events can have a wide variety of causes, so that the phrase "a cause of e" gives almost no indication of the intrinsic nature of whatever item falls under it, and someone who did refer to an item in this way would almost certainly be able to refer to it more informatively than that. Why would anyone say "A cause of the riot occurred in this room yesterday" rather than, more informatively, "*A speech* that caused the riot occurred in this room yesterday"? Apart from the special case of hearsay, he could not know the former to be true without knowing that the latter, or something like it, is true.

Here is my answer to this challenge of Vendler's. It is perfectly all right to say that the speech was a cause of the riot and that the speech began at a certain time, lasted for a while, and so on. What we are not likely to say—though it is not "nonsense"—is anything of the form "A cause of the riot began at a certain time, lasted for a while", and so on. What makes this odd is merely the fact that the subject clause is so uninformative about the intrinsic nature of the item in question, together with the fact that the speaker—unless he was relying on hearsay—could not have been in a position to say that much unless he could have said more with equal brevity.

In trying to find more plausible uses of "cause(s) of e" in a subject NP, remember that, if you merely generalize about "the causes of e", you won't be able reasonably to say that they "began at a certain time, lasted for a while, and ended suddenly": for it goes without saying, at the actual world, that the causes of e began when the world began and reached the end of their career as causes of e when e occurred.

(iii) "[If the word "cause" sometimes denotes an event, then] why is it that no witness can ever watch or listen to causes, that no scientist can possibly observe them through a telescope or register them with a seismograph . . . ?" (p. 709) The oddity of "I was listening to a cause of the illegal strike" or "I was measuring some causes of the earthquake" can be explained in the same way as before. It is long-winded and uninformative to pick out the items you are talking about through phrases of the form "cause(s) of e", and you must be in a position to say more with fewer words.

In that case, why is it all right to say "The effects of the riot made themselves felt for weeks"? In general, "effect of" seems to be more at home in a subject noun phrase than does "cause of", and we cannot be at peace about Vendler's challenge until we know why. One explanation would be that, for most values of E, the variety of an E event's possible causes is much greater than the variety of its possible effects, so that "effect of the E" is more informative about the item's intrinsic nature than is "cause of the E". That cause/effect asymmetry, if it exists, has no tendency to imply that events can be effects but cannot be causes. Or perhaps there is no metaphysical cause/effect asymmetry but only a linguistic "cause"/"effect" asymmetry: perhaps the explanation is just that the kinds of events that we are accustomed to speaking about as "effects of the E" are more narrowly circumscribed than the kinds we are accustomed to speaking about as "causes of the E".

It is also relevant that any statement about someone's experiencing, perceiving, measuring, etc. "a cause of the E" strongly suggests that at the time in question he or she knew or believed that the item was indeed a cause of the E. Similarly with "an effect of the E". That allows "effect" to do more work than is happily assigned to "cause", because while an event is occurring we can know more about what it is an effect of than about what it is a cause of.

On some theories, indeed, a cause of e does not acquire that relational property until e occurs, or at least until it begins; that means that causes of the E attain that status only posthumously, after they are all over. If that is correct, then "He observed a cause of the E (at a time when it was a cause of the E)" will always be false except in the special case where the E takes over from its cause during the time it takes for the signal to get from it to the observer.

(iv) "[If the word 'cause' sometimes denotes an event, then why] are there no slow causes, no sudden, violent or prolonged ones, and so forth?" (p. 709) My first explanation in (ii) applies again here, strengthened by something else. The adjective "sudden" is noun-dependent: whether a given event counts as sudden depends in part on what event-kind it is thought of as belonging to. My first thought of devoting myself to philosophy rather than medicine was sudden *qua* change of life-plan but not *qua* thought. The same holds for "prolonged". And the description of an event as "violent" is so uninformative as to be pointless unless we are told something about the event's intrinsic nature—for example, whether it is the collision of two continents or the flaring of a struck match.

I conclude that Vendler has not made a good enough case for his doctrine that every statement of the form "e_1 caused e_2"—for example, "The earthquake caused the landslide"—is categorially defective. I shall continue to use all the forms C(e_1,e_2), C(f_1,f_2), C(e,f), and C(f,e). With a little adjustment, any mixture of our event concept and our fact concept can be used in a causal statement.

13. *Fact causation and explanation*

In my examples of fact-causation statements, I have excluded one of the commonest kinds, namely statements of the forms "[S_1], which is why [S_2]" and "[S_2] because [S_1]", and perhaps others that also involve the notion of one fact's *explaining* another.

Do "why" and "because" and the rest have specifically causal senses? If they do, then "because" is being used in its causal sense in (1) "I like the thought of Brian because we had good times together" and in a different, logical sense in (2) "Brian is my cousin because his father and mine were brothers". Really, there is no such ambiguity. Rather, "Q because P" means just one thing, namely that P's truth helps to explain Q's truth, and this may be the case either for logical or for causal reasons. Still, someone who asserted (1) would intend to communicate something about a causal connection and would succeed in doing so; it is obvious why. So it does no harm to say that (1) and its like are "causal explanatory statements", as though they used "because" in a special causal sense.

Afficionados of event causation sometimes categorize the likes of (1) as "explanations" and therefore not as meaning anything of the form C(x,y). That seems to be Strawson's thought here:

> If causality is a relation which holds in the natural world, explanation is a different matter. People explain things to themselves or others and their doing so is something that happens in nature. But we also speak of one thing explaining, or being the explanation of, another thing, as if explaining was a relation between the things. And so it is. But it is not a natural relation in the sense in which we perhaps think of causality as a natural relation. It is an intellectual or rational or intensional relation. It does not hold between things in the natural world, things to which we can assign places and times in nature. It holds between facts or truths.[3]

If it is nonlogically true that f_P explains f_Q, then this *is* a truth about how things are in the natural world and about nothing else. If Straw-

3. P.F. Strawson, "Causation and Explanation", p. 115.

son is denying this, he cannot be right.[4] If he is not denying it, then I do not see what his point is. It is perhaps worth mentioning also that, just as fact-causation statements can be explanatory, so can event-causation statements.[5]

There is a complication, however. Any statement of the form $C(f_1,f_2)$ can be evaluated for *truth* and for *fullness*: It is true if f_1 played some part in the causal ancestry of f_2, and it is full to the extent that that part was large. Each of these evaluations depends on what facts are named (or expressed) in the statement and not on how they are named. But the value of an explanation as a help for people, enabling them to understand one fact by seeing how it relates to another, may depend in part on how the relevant facts are named. One explanation could be better than another that involves the very same pair of facts, because the former makes it clearer what fact f_1 is or how it connects with f_2. That psychological matter, however, is irrelevant to present concerns. My topic is a certain relation between pairs of facts, a relation that gives one of them a certain role in the causal ancestry of the other: I am not concerned with whether the facts are so stated as to help people to grasp how one is linked to the other.

14. *Highlighting*

"Imperfect nominals name the same fact if and only if they are logically equivalent"—there are two challenges to that. One says that equivalence is too weak to be sufficient for coreference of fact names, and the other that it is too strong to be necessary. Let us look at these in turn.

Here are three sentences that give the same information or would be made true by the same states of affairs or, as we say nowadays, are true at the same worlds:

1. The bicycle is what Mary stole
2. It was Mary who stole the bicycle
3. What Mary did to the bicycle was steal it

They differ, however, in how they are *highlighted*. Each uses a "cleft" or "pseudocleft" construction, a syntactic device with the semantic effect of putting a split ("cleft") between two of the conceptual elements and the third, pushing the two into the background and high-

4. I am glad to be in agreement with Davidson at this point. See his "Reply to Strawson", pp. 226f.

5. See David K. Lewis, "Causal Explanation".

lighting the one. Highlighting can also be achieved by emphasis: "Mary stole *the bicycle*", "*Mary* stole the bicycle", "Mary *stole* the bicycle".

(The members of the latter trio lack the suggestions of uniqueness—(1) only the bicycle, (2) only Mary, (3) all she did to it was steal it. If you think that uniqueness is downright asserted in the former trio, you won't agree that its three members are true at exactly the same worlds: "At any world where Mary steals the bicycle and nothing else but isn't alone in the theft," you will say, "(1) is true and (2) false." If that is your view, substitute (1) "The bicycle is something that Mary stole", (2) "Mary is someone who stole the bicycle", and (3) "Stealing is something that Mary did to the bicycle".)

Each of those triples consists of three "propositional allomorphs"—that is what Fred Dretske called them in the first philosophical treatment of them.[6] Although they are logically equivalent, they cannot be substituted for one another *salva veritate* ("saving the truth") in all contexts; that is, replacing one by another in a sentence may make it go from true to false. If you know that Mary's gang planned to steal a bicycle and that Mary was trying to avoid doing the job herself, you might be greatly surprised that it was Mary who stole the bicycle, yet not in the least surprised that what Mary stole was the bicycle. Dretske notes that they also behave differently in counterfactuals. A completion that is right for "If it hadn't been Mary who stole the bicycle, . . . " might be wrong for "If it hadn't been the bicycle that Mary stole, . . . ". And—to move back to my proper topic—the fact that Mary desperately needed a bicycle may explain why it was the bicycle that she stole much better than it explains why what she did to the bicycle was steal it.[7]

Some writers have concluded that there are highlighted facts as well as plain ones and have made this central in their work in this area. Others have gone even further, trying to get distinctions between

---

6. Fred I. Dretske, "The Content of Knowledge". For other discussions of how allomorphs relate to causal explanation, see Fred I. Dretske, "Referring to Events", replied to by Jaegwon Kim, "Causation, Emphasis, and Events"; Peter Achinstein, "The Causal Relation", a revised version of which is Chapter 6 of his *The Nature of Explanation*; David H. Sanford, "Causal Relata".

7. Or, anyway, it does not explain why her way of taking the bicycle was illegal. Dretske mentions three allomorphs, but there are indefinitely many, including that one and the likes of: "What the bi-something that Mary stole had two of was wheels", and "The number of wheels on the cycle that Mary stole was two", and "The time when Mary steals (tenseless) the bicycle is in the past". See my Comments on Dretske's "The Content of Knowledge".

events out of differences of highlighting, so that Mary's *theft* of the bicycle is distinguished from her theft *of the bicycle*. The latter idea is a nonstarter, in my view—a result of not clearly distinguishing facts from events. The notion of a highlighted fact, though better, is still an inflated response to a quite minor linguistic affair.[8] The best way to cut highlighting down to size is to explain what happens in it. That is what I now try to do.

In highlighting we say something that could be expressed as a conjunction with the form "P and (P ⊃ Q)", and we treat the two conjuncts differently. For example, the proposition that Mary stole the bicycle is equivalent to the conjunction of (B_1) "Mary stole something" and (F_1) "Mary stole something ⊃ she stole the bicycle"; and someone who utters "What Mary stole was the bicycle" is—as I shall say—putting (B_1) in the background and (F_1) in the foreground. The original proposition is also equivalent to the conjunction of (B_2) "Someone stole the bicycle" and (F_2) "Someone stole the bicycle ⊃ Mary stole the bicycle"; and someone who utters "It was Mary who stole the bicycle" is putting (B_2) in the background and (F_2) in the foreground. Working out the story for (3) is left to the reader.

In each case, a highlighted version of P is a background treatment of some Q that is entailed by P and a foreground treatment of (Q ⊃ P).

What I have called a "background" treatment consists in the speaker's signalling that he believes (and takes his hearers to believe) the B component. The "foreground" treatment consists in applying some operation to the F component.

If the highlighted sentence stands alone as a complete statement, the treatment in question is just that of *assertion*—presenting the F component in a manner that is, normally, suitable only if one's hearers don't already believe it. For example, it is appropriate for me to say "It was Mary who stole the bicycle" if my hearers already think that someone did, but don't yet believe it was Mary. They have not ruled out the possibility that *someone stole the bicycle and Mary didn't*, which means that they don't yet believe the material conditional (F_2) "Someone stole the bicycle ⊃ Mary stole the bicycle", which is what I am asserting.

(It is because the B component is not outright asserted that one can plausibly hold that its falsity deprives the entire utterance of any truth-value rather than making it false. The falsity of the F component—someone stole the bicycle but it wasn't Mary—clearly does make the whole thing false. But don't think that the sentence "It

8. Steven E. Boer, in his "Meaning and Contrastive Stress", argues that Dretske has misunderstood the data and overestimated their significance. I go his way, but not so far.

wasn't Mary who stole the bicycle" (or "*Mary* didn't steal the bicycle") is the simple contradictory of (F_2) "Someone stole the bicycle ⊃ Mary stole the bicycle". Rather, it has (B_2) "Someone stole the bicycle" in the background and (F*) "Someone stole the bicycle ⊃ Mary didn't steal the bicycle" in the foreground.)

If the highlighted sentence is part of some larger complex, the "treatment" of the F component will be more complex. (i) For example, "I am surprised that it was Mary who stole the bicycle" gives the background treatment to (B_2) the proposition that someone stole the bicycle, and reports that the speaker was surprised that (F_2) someone stole the bicycle ⊃ Mary did. This is more informative than the report "I was surprised that Mary stole the bicycle", though the latter is more informative than "I was surprised that . . . " with the gap filled by a detailed account of what the whole gang did on the day in question. The stronger P is, the less informative it is to be told, "I was surprised that P". (ii) Another example: "Pressure from the gang leader explains why it was Mary who stole the bicycle" adds to the background treatment of "Someone stole the bicycle" the assertion that pressure from the gang leader brought it about that someone stole the bicycle ⊃ Mary did. This is a more precise, more informative statement than is "Pressure from the gang leader brought it about that Mary stole the bicycle". I conjecture that something along these lines will go for all the other contexts as well: "I have just discovered that . . . ", "If it were not the case that . . . ", and so on, though I haven't worked it out in detail for every kind of complex within which a highlighted sentence could occur. It seems safe to assume that highlighting can henceforth be neglected, as having little philosophical significance.

15. *What are facts?*

The aspects of explanation that depend upon helpfulness to human minds or upon highlighting take us beyond sheer fact identity. Or so I have assumed, believing that if two sentences are a priori interderivable then they express the same fact. There remains a question, however, about whether that condition is *necessary* for two sentences to express the same fact.

There are two views about (1) the meanings of individual referring expressions and thus of sentences containing them. This generates a pair of views about (2) what propositions there are, which in turn leads to two views about (3) what facts there are. At each level, I shall call one of the views Fregean and the other Russellian.[9] We get

9. For justification of these labels, see David Kaplan, "How to Russell a Frege-Church".

from (1) to (2) through the assumption that what a sentence means determines what proposition it expresses, and from there we get to (3) through the assumption that facts correspond to true propositions.

On the Fregean view, we can refer to a particular thing only through a description that fits it. Even proper names and demonstrative pronouns, on this view, stand for descriptions that the speaker has in mind. Thus, for example, when I say "Quine lives in Cambridge" I may express a different proposition from the one I expressed when I pointed to Quine and said "That man lives in Cambridge", because I use "Quine" to mean "the author of *Word and Object*" whereas I used "that man" to mean "the man I am now pointing out". According to this theory, pronouns and proper names are special, because their meanings may differ greatly from speaker to speaker, and from time to time: your uses of "she", Frege would have to say, have various meanings on different occasions of use. Still, they latch on to their referents in the same way that definite descriptions do, namely by somehow standing for a definite description and referring to the thing that fits it.

Since Fregean propositions are entirely built out of general concepts, what proposition a sentence expresses depends only on what concepts its words express—what they conventionally mean or (for proper names etc.) what description the speaker associates with them. Thus, if two sentences express the same Fregean proposition, they do so purely by virtue of the meanings of their constituent words, and perhaps the mind of the speaker, with no dependence on the rest of the world. So the principle *Two sentences express the same proposition if and only if they are a priori interderivable* is true of Fregean propositions.

The Russellian view is that one can refer to a thing without even implicitly describing it. Such a non-describing referring expression is a "logically proper name"—one that has no conceptual meaning but only a referent. Russell thought that demonstratives and some but not all grammatically proper names are logically proper names.[10]

A sentence with a Russellian name in it expresses a proposition with an object—the referent of the name—in it. We could call this a Russellian proposition. If "Quine" is a Russellian name and if demonstratives are too, then someone who says "Quine lives in Cambridge" expresses the same Russellian proposition as someone who says "He lives in Cambridge", referring to Quine, for they both apply the same predicate to the same thing. It clearly follows that the principle *Two sentences express the same proposition if and only if they are a priori*

10. Saul Kripke, in "Naming and Necessity", argues persuasively that no grammatically proper names are Fregean and theorizes that such a name gets a grip on its referent by being causally related to it.

interderivable is not true of Russellian propositions if there are any.[11] But the following principle, which I call "PC" (for "propositional coexpression") is true across the board:

> PC: Two sentences express the same proposition if and only if they are interderivable either (i) a priori or (ii) by the replacement of one Russellian name by another with the same referent.

If there are no Russellian names, option (ii) is vacuous and PC is still true because option (i) is right for Fregean propositions. (If there are any propositions at all, then certainly at least some of them are Fregean—e.g. ones expressed by sentences that don't refer to particulars or do so through descriptions.) On the basis of PC, we can easily tell the truth about when two sentences express the same fact:

> FC: Two true sentences express the same fact if and only if they are interderivable either (i) a priori or (ii) by the replacement of one Russellian name by another with the same referent.

For convenience, let us speak of (i) as the equivalence condition and of (ii) as the transparency condition.

16. *V-facts*

Now consider the items that I label "V-facts".[12] These are defined as obeying the following principle:

> VFC: Two true sentences express the same V-fact if and only if they are interderivable either (i) a priori or (ii) by the replacement of one name by another with the same referent.

This is FC with the adjective "Russellian" dropped from the transparency condition. Two true sentences express the same V-fact if one can be got from the other by replacing one name or pronoun or *definite description* by another that has the same referent. That difference between FC and VFC is fatal to V-facts, as is shown by a famous proof

---

11. Russellian names, if there are any, are presumably rigid designators, whereas Fregean names—definite descriptions—are nonrigid. So the principle *Two sentences express the same proposition if and only if they are true at the same worlds* is true for Fregean and for Russellian propositions. That is why I handle the former in terms of a priori interderivability, rather than of truth at the same worlds.

12. So named because Vendler commits himself to the view that all facts are V-facts, in his "Causal Relations", pp. 710f.

that *there is only one V-fact*. The proof, which was invented by Frege and adapted by Davidson to this present purpose, goes as follows.

Let S_1 and S_2 be any true sentences you like. Then

"the fact that [S_1]",

by the equivalence condition, names the same fact as does

"the fact that: the class of self-identical things is the class of things such that (they are self-identical and [S_1]";

and that, by the transparency condition, names the same fact as

"the fact that: the class of self-identical things is the class of things such that (they are self-identical and [S_2]",[13]

which, by the equivalence condition, names the same fact as

"the fact that [S_2]".

And so we get such results as that "the fact that Hillary climbed Everest" has the same referent as "the fact that Russia invaded Poland". There is only one V-fact.

Here are three responses to this argument. (1) Some philosophers have, though not in print, rejected this argument on the grounds that descriptions such as "the class of things such that (they are self-identical and grass is green)" are too artificial to be taken seriously. They object that "grass is green" is a complete sentence with no free variable, so that it doesn't really express an honest condition on the members of the class. (2) Others have claimed that the argument's first step is invalid, because S_1 might not entail that there are any classes, in which case it is not equivalent to the second line in the argument, since that does entail that there are classes.[14] (3) J. L. Mackie said that the argument would not hold if the notion of a V-fact were repaired a little. The trouble with V-facts is their prodigal transparency, Mackie said, and he proposed to reduce it thus: in a fact name we may single out one contained name as permitting substitution for identity, but

13. To see why this step is valid, consider the expressions "the class of things such that (they are self-identical and [S_1]" and "the class of things such that (they are self-identical and [S_2]". If S_1 and S_2 are both true, then each expression names the class of self-identical things, i.e. the universal class; if S_1 and S_2 are both false, each expression names the null class. (There is, for example, nothing such that (it is self-identical and grass is usually purple) or such that (it is self-identical and the speed of light is infinite).) Either way, they name the same class, and so the transparency condition lets us replace one by the other in any fact name.

14. Robert Cummins and Dale Gottlieb, "On an Argument for Truth-Functionality".

other names that are introduced through logical equivalence don't share the same privilege.[15]

None of these responses gets to the heart of the matter. They are all aimed narrowly at the Fregean argument and do not touch its teeming progeny—arguments that pose the same kind of threat, though less extensively. These arguments (1) do not use contrived definite descriptions, (2) imply nothing about classes, and (3) do not introduce any names through logical equivalence and then substitute for them. Here is one of these arguments.

My dinner host on a certain occasion was Saul Kripke, the man who invented a semantics for modal logic. So the V-fact that (i) my dinner host on that occasion showed me a trick mirror is, by the transparency condition, the V-fact that (ii) the man who invented a semantics for modal logic showed me a trick mirror, and that, by logical equivalence, is the V-fact that (iii) exactly one man invented a semantics for modal logic, and every such man showed me a trick mirror.[16] Thus, we have ended up with a fact that helps to explain why modal logic has blossomed in recent years, because it includes the fact that modal logic has a semantics. That alone proves that it is not the fact that my dinner host on that occasion showed me a trick mirror, since the latter has no power to explain how modal logic is faring.

This shows, without the contrived manoeuvres of the Fregean argument, that V-facts are not facts as ordinarily understood. It also makes evident what is wrong with them. The undamped transparency condition is what generates the heat that melts all the V-facts into one. Expressions of V-facts are transparent with respect not merely to uninformative Russellian names but also to definite descriptions, and *of course* that makes trouble. If we want facts that will stay decently separate from one another, their names must not be transparent with respect to any of the definite descriptions they contain, whether contrived or natural, whether introduced through logical equivalence or there from the start.[17] That is just to say that FC is correct.

Actually, we can allow more transparency than that. We sometimes use definite descriptions as though they were Russellian, re-

15. J.L. Mackie, *The Cement of the Universe*, pp. 250–254.

16. On some theories, (iii) could be false while (ii) is neither true nor false, making them non-equivalent. Even then, (ii) contains or entails (iii), which is enough for my purposes. This issue about failed definite descriptions—about "the F" where nothing is F—arises in connection with some versions of the Fregean argument and dominates the discussion of the latter by Barry Taylor, *Modes of Occurrence*, pp. 32–39.

17. Thus Terence Horgan, "The Case Against Events", pp. 33–35. The same view is hinted at by Mackie, *op. cit.*, p. 260.

garding them merely as pointers to their referents (and even substituting one for another when they corefer) and not using the information they contain for any other purpose. Mackie has pointed this out. A fact may be genuinely *about* some particular thing x, he said, so that a causal or explanatory statement involving it has the form "Concerning x: the fact that it is F explains [or is explained by] the fact that Q", or "Concerning x: its being F leads to [or is a consequence of] P's being the case", or the like; and a speaker might mean something like that while referring to x through a definite description.

For example, someone who says "The auditor turned in a terrible report; that explains the managing director's having to resign" has spoken falsely if Mrs. Exit (the one who resigned) was not managing director, so part of what has been said is that the person who resigned was the managing director. But we don't take this to mean that any part of *that* fact was a consequence of the auditor's giving an unfavorable report. Thus, the informative content of the definite description "the managing director" lies outside the scope of " . . . explains . . . ". On the other hand, the speaker probably doesn't mean "the auditor" in the same way: that Mr. Scan is an auditor may be part of what is said to explain the resignation. What makes the difference is sheer pragmatics: there is no grammatical clue that "the auditor" is being used in a purely Fregean way, while "the managing director" is being treated as (so to speak) Russellian in the complex. It's just that, if the speaker meant the latter phrase in any other way, what he was saying would be absurdly improbable.

As well as such *pragmatic* constraints, we have at least one *conventional* way of ensuring that a definite description occurs Russellianly within a complex. It is the noun-infinitive form discussed in Section 10 above. If we say "His harsh words caused the embarrassed child to cry", we cannot properly mean that his harsh words caused the child to be embarrassed. We hearers may suspect that what caused the crying also caused the embarrassment, but the utterance does not say so, any more than "His harsh words caused the little child to cry" means that his words caused the child's size. It is part of the conventional meaning of the NP-infinitive form, as used in causation statements, that the NP occurs Russellianly in the complex.

So we have resources for expressing fact-causation statements without falling into the clutches of the Frege-Davidson argument and its like. Names occurring in fact names may be treated as Russellian in the explanation or causal statement, in which case they can be replaced by any coreferring names, but their descriptive content has no role in the explanation, whether in the explanans or the explanandum. Or they may be treated as Fregean, in which case their descriptive content forms part of the explanation, but they cannot safely be replaced by coreferring names. To avoid the Frege-Davidson trap, we must only avoid using names in a manner that is Russellian so far as substitivity is concerned and Fregean with regard to the usability of descriptive content. Davidson writes:

> If the fact that there was a fire in Jones's house caused it to be the case that the pig was roasted, . . . then the fact that there was a fire in the oldest building on Elm Street caused it to be the case that the pig was roasted. We must accept the principle of extensional substitution, then.[18]

That example involves a pair of definite descriptions that are, quite reasonably, being treated as Russellian in the complex: that is, they can be intersubstituted without affecting the truth-value of the whole, *and their informative content does not enter into the complex*. Davidson ignores the second constraint, and concludes that all facts are V-facts, from which false premise he validly infers that there is only one of them.

Summing up, then: We have encountered three logically coherent fact concepts. If each has appplication, then there are Russellian facts, corresponding to each of which there are many Fregean facts, corresponding to each of which there are many highlighted facts. With these riches available, it is odd that Davidson should write as though there were only the degenerate concept of a V-fact.

In later chapters it will simplify things if I concentrate on Fregean facts and say that logical interdeducibility is the whole criterion for coreference of fact names. That is just short-hand, for the criterion is too strict for Russellian facts if there are any and too loose for highlighted ones if there are any, but readers can easily make the needed adjustments.

---

18. Donald Davidson, "Causal Relations", pp. 152f.

III

FACT CAUSATION

17. *Approaches to singular causation statements*

When we understand the forms $C(f_1,f_2)$ and $C(e_1,e_2)$, we shall have no trouble with the mixed e/f and f/e cases. So I shall confine my attention to the pure cases—f/f and e/e. These must be taken one at a time, for there is no way of analyzing both at once.

That division between analysanda splits the story into two, and a certain division between analysantia splits it into four. When we are analyzing something of the type C(x,y)—whether about facts or about events—we may be drawn to a *counterfactual* kind of analysis, according to which the causation statement means something to the effect that if there had not been x there would not have been y. Alternatively, we may hope to adopt a *relational* kind of analysis, according to which the causation statement means that a certain tetradic relation holds amongst x and y and their environment and the totality of causal laws.

Let us start with fact causation, by which I mean every way of wording fact-causation statements (with "that P" or whole sentences or imperfect nominals or noun-phrase plus infinitive, with "result" or "consequence" or "cause" and so on) in which the obtaining of one fact is said to contribute causally to the obtaining of another. With that kind of statement as our analysandum, let us take first the relational approach to analyzing it.

18. *Fact causation: NS conditions*

Three bits of shorthand: (1) "L" names the totality of actual causal laws. (2) It is "causally necessary" that P if P is true and L entails that P is highly probable. If no members of L are probabilistic, we always have the special case where L entails P. My uses of "required", "inevitable", and similar terms are also to be understood as allowing but not requiring that some basic causal laws are probabilistic. (3) Where P is any true proposition, f_P is the fact that P.

I shall be working with material conditionals (P ⊃ Q) that satisfy the following constraints: (i) Neither P nor Q entails the other. (ii) Each of P and Q is a truth to the effect that such-and-such is the case at time T (that is, at a given instant or throughout a given period). (iii) Neither P nor Q is entailed by L.

Why these three restrictions? Well, I am trying to creep up on $C(f_P,f_Q)$, and no statement of that form will be true unless the corresponding conditional (P ⊃ Q) satisfies (i) through (iii). You might think that even if L entails both P and Q, it could be the case that $C(f_P,f_Q)$; for example, that gravity's obeying an inverse square law brings it about that some other physical law holds. I don't agree, but I shall not defend my position here.[1] If it is wrong, then I am willing to stipulate my third condition, that is, to *restrict* myself to causal relations amongst particular matters of causally contingent fact.

Within that class of material conditionals, let us consider the causally necessary ones. They fall into three subclasses. *Forwards*: It is causally necessary that P's being the case leads to Q's being the case. *Backwards*: It is causally impossible for P to be the case except as a consequence of Q's being the case. *Mixed*, the simplest mixture being this: It is causally impossible for P to be the case except as a consequence of some R that necessarily leads to Q's being the case.

Given that a conditional is causally necessary, you cannot always tell which species it belongs to just by looking at it. For if Q is dated later than P, (P ⊃ Q) may be either forwards or mixed. Indeed, it may even be a backwards conditional if temporally backwards causation is somehow possible.

Then what does distinguish one species from the others? Three answers have been offered. (i) The nomological structure of the world distinguishes them: perfect knowledge of L would enable us first to pick out the causally necessary conditionals and then sort them into their forwards, backwards, and mixed species.[2] (ii) The notion of causal direction is well grounded, but not in L: our thinking about causation is based not on the notion of causal laws but rather on our everyday perceptions of things pushing one another around.[3] (iii) The

1. Something related to it is defended in my "Counterfactuals and Temporal Direction", pp. 82f.

2. See David H. Sanford, "The Direction of Causation and the Direction of Conditionship". For a helpful discussion of this whole matter, see Tom L. Beauchamp and Alexander Rosenberg, *Hume and the Problem of Causation*, Chapter 6.

3. For a development of that line of thought, see P.F. Strawson, "Causation and Explanation", pp. 134f.

line between consequences and prerequisites is not objectively grounded at all; it merely reflects our needs and interests, like the distinction between weeds and other plants or between dirt and other matter.[4] I don't mind whether (i) or (ii) is right; either way, we need the concept of causal direction if we are to make sense of the form $C(f_1,f_2)$; if the former is shallow and interest-relative, then so is the latter. On the other hand, if option (iii) is correct then my whole approach to causation is soft at its foundations. I hope it is not, but I have no arguments about this.

Before exploring the conceptual underlay of "a cause" and the verb "cause" and related expressions, a little should be said about "*the* cause".

If $(P \supset Q)$ is a causally necessary forwards conditional, then $C(f_P,f_Q)$ is true. But that is understating it, for in this case Q comes to obtain as a causally inevitable consequence of the fact that P—not of f_P aided by environmental circumstances, but of f_P all on its own. That makes it true not only that f_P caused f_Q to obtain, or was *a* cause of f_Q, but more strongly that f_P was—so far as the time to which it pertains is concerned—*the* cause of f_Q. We cannot easily formulate a precise, detailed truth about *the* cause at time T of a given fact's obtaining, because that would be too big a mouthful: it would involve antecedent conditions of such richness that nothing could possibly stop the consequent from arising from them. So we have no practical use for "*the* cause" in its strict and literal sense. In ordinary speech and writing, "the cause of x" always means "a salient cause of x" or "the most salient cause of x"; that use of the term does not need separate discussion.

One fact is a cause of another if the former is an operative part of some total cause of the latter. Borrowing from work by J.L. Mackie, we can say that $C(f_P,f_Q)$ is true if f_P is an NS condition of f_Q—a Necessary part of a Sufficient condition for f_Q, meaning that without it the condition would not be sufficient.[5] Here and throughout it is to be understood that the relevant sufficient condition always concerns the same instant or period as does f_P itself.

Mackie speaks of an INUS condition—not a mere NS condition. The vowels in his acronym come from his interest in the case where f_P is Insufficient on its own to produce f_Q and where the sufficient condition for f_Q of which f_P is a part is Unnecessary for f_Q in the sense that

4. For well-argued doubts about the objectivity of the notion of causal direction, see Robert J. Fogelin, "Kant and Hume on Simultaneity of Causes and Effects".

5. J.L. Mackie, "Causes and Conditions". The notion of sufficiency must be weakened if basic causation is probabilistic; I shall take that adjustment as read.

the latter might have come about through some other sufficient condition. Why should we confine ourselves to those cases? If we don't insist that f_P be insufficient on its own for f_Q, the harmless result is just that our account of "a cause" includes "the cause", strictly understood, as a special case. The other restriction seems to be equally pointless. In each of Mackie's examples, f_Q could indeed have come about through some different causal route, and perhaps there are no examples that are not like that; but why should we build that dubious thesis into our account of the form $C(f_P,f_Q)$? To be fair, Mackie (p. 247) allows for the possibility that the U in his acronym might not apply in some cases and says that then f_P is "at least an INUS condition" of f_Q; but that implies that something can be "at least an INUS condition of y" without being "an INUS condition of y". Mackie would have done better to dump his terminology and start again with the concept of an NS condition.

Here, as everywhere, pragmatic factors come into play. Speakers will be reluctant to say that f_P was a cause of f_Q if its causal role in the obtaining of f_Q is already well known or was extremely small in the sense that in its absence there would still have been an *almost* sufficient condition for f_Q. But those do not make the fact-causation statement false—merely a bad thing to say.

My account is not right as it stands, however, for it can happen that a causally sufficient condition for f_Q's obtaining was nevertheless not operative in its obtaining. My throwing a lighted match into the gasoline drum topped up a set of jointly sufficient conditions for the house to be in ruins an hour later; and the house was in ruins an hour later; but that is because a bomb was dropped onto it just as I threw the match, so that the fact that I threw the match was not a cause of the house's being destroyed.

How can we strengthen the sufficient conditions for $C(f_P,f_Q)$ so as to exclude this unwanted case? Not by saying that f_P is a necessary part of an *operative* sufficient condition for f_Q's obtaining, for that amounts to saying that f_P is a necessary part of something that brings it about that f_Q obtains, that is, of something x such that $C(x,f_Q)$—which is the very notion we are trying to analyze!

The best solution I can find to the problem is the following.[6] Granted that (f_1) my throwing the match onto the gasoline at T_1 is an NS condition of (f_2) the house's being in ruins at T_2, it is not the case that, for every time t_j between T_1 and T_2, there is a fact (f_j) of the form *P is the case at time* t_j such that f_1 is an NS condition of f_j, which in turn is an NS condition of f_2. On the other hand, this is true if we keep the

6. It is adapted from the treatment of the problem, as it confronts the counterfactual analysis of event causation, in David K. Lewis's "Causation", p. 567.

same f_2 but let f_1 be the fact about the dropping of the bomb: that the bomb is dropped is an NS condition not only of the ultimate ruin of the house but also of a continuous chain of facts linking the dropping to the subsequent ruin. The throwing of the match is NS related to the match's getting nearer and nearer to the gasoline, but when the bomb hits the house, including the not-yet-ignited gasoline, there is no fact f_j obtaining then such that the throwing of the match is an NS condition for f_j's obtaining *and* the obtaining of f_j is an NS condition for the house's being in ruins at T_2.

I shall express this by saying that the throwing of the match does not, as the dropping of the bomb does, satisfy *the continuity condition*.

This suggests that we can equate $C(f_1,f_2)$ with

> f_1 is an NS condition of f_2, and for every time t_j between the time to which f_1 pertains and the time to which f_2 pertains, there is a fact f_j pertaining to t_j such that f_j belongs to a temporally ordered sequence of facts, running from f_1 to f_2, each member of which is an NS condition of the next.

Although this is on the right road, we shall see in a moment that it is not correct as it stands.

19. *Transitivity*

I introduced the continuity condition by strengthening the analysans of $c(f_1,f_2)$: I retained the requirement that f_1 be an NS condition of f_2 and added the continuity condition. I proceeded in that way so as to take things one at a time. I now have to explain why the continuity condition is all that we need: for the truth of $C(f_1,f_2)$, it is not necessary that f_1 be an NS condition of f_2, which is to say that the original analysis was too strong in one way as well as being too weak in another. Here is an example that illustrates this point.

At noon Jorge lit a fuse (f_P), thereby topping up a sufficient condition for

> f_Q: At 12:05 there were two girders missing from the bridge;

and f_Q completed a sufficient condition for

> f_R: At 12:07 a truck fell through the bridge.

In this case, it is clearly true that $C(f_P,f_Q)$ and that $C(f_Q,f_R)$, and so by transitivity $C(f_P,f_R)$. Jorge's lighting the fuse caused the bridge to be weakened, which caused the truck to fall, and so his lighting the fuse caused the truck to fall.

This, however, does not automatically make it the case that f_P

completed any sufficient condition for f_R. That *would* be the case if at noon it was already causally determined that the truck would be on the bridge at 12:07. But suppose that the truck's presence there resulted from random or extremely improbable events, so that nobody, however well informed about causal laws and the state of the world up to noon, could have foreseen then where the truck would be at 12:07. In that case, the fuse's being lit and the truck's falling do not satisfy my sufficient condition for fact causation, although one did cause the other by causing something that caused it. The root of the trouble is that the relation " . . . is an NS condition for . . . " is not itself transitive.

Clearly, what we need is to build transitivity into the analysis, which we can do by adopting the continuity condition as our entire analysans. Here is how it works with the example (I owe a lot to Michael Kremer at this point):

> *The bridge's being interfered with at 12:05 is an NS condition for its being weak at 12:06* (and we can fill in the intervening minute in a way that satisfies the continuity condition). At 12:06 the driver freely decides to cross the bridge at 12:07, which makes it the case that *the bridge's being weak at 12:06 is an NS condition of the truck's crashing at 12:07* (and again we can fill in the intervening minute in a way that satisfies the continuity condition): it is a necessary part of a total sufficient condition, another part of which is the driver's decision.

Put the underlined clauses together and you get, through transitivity, the desired result that the bridge's being interfered with at 12:05 was a cause of the truck's crashing at 12:07, whereas, if the transitivity clause is not included, that result does not follow. The bridge's being weakened at 12:05 did not bring it about that the status "causally sufficient for the truck's crashing at 12:07" was possessed by any condition that obtained at 12:05.

By this account, fact causation is notably weak. Not only does one fact cause another if it plays *some* essential part in a sufficient condition for the other's obtaining, so that a given fact can have countless tiny facts as causes; but there is further weakness because of transitivity. Here is an example, adapted from one of David Lewis's: Having been the runner up to Topman in a competition for a job, Nearthing takes a post in another country, where he meets the future mother of his children; so everything that lies causally downstream from anything done by any of Nearthing's descendants is a consequence of Topman's applying for that job.

Objection: "You imply that, if one of Nearthing's great-grandsons commits a crime, one cause of this is Topman's applying for that job half a world away and a century earlier. That is an intolerable burden of responsibility." No, Topman is not morally accountable for the later crime, because no degree of prudence, caution, or foresight could have made it less likely to have such consequences. "Then why say that they *are* consequences of it or caused by it? Wouldn't it be better to restrict the notion of conduct that causes x to conduct making the agent morally accountable for x?"

This could be done, and it may be worth seeing how. It cannot be by developing a causation relation that is untouched by any kind of transitivity, i.e. that never allows a conclusion about f_1's causing f_3 to be inferred from premises about f_1's causing f_2 and the latter's causing f_3. Inferences of that general sort are at the heart of everyday uses of the concept of causation, and an analysis that made no provision for them would *ipso facto* be wrong. The problem is to find for plausible inferences of that kind some basis other than the unrestricted transitivity that makes causation so enormously weak. Here is a possible solution:

Continue using C to symbolize the relation that I have been calling "cause" up to here, but now let us call it "protocause". Then introduce the notion of e_1's being an n-degree protocause of e_2, where n lies on a scale from 0 to 1 and measures the salience and size of e_1's causal contribution to the occurrence of e_2; symbolize this by $C_n(e_1,e_2)$. Then adopt this principle:

$$C_n(e_1,e_2) \ \& \ C_m(e_2,e_3) \ .\supset. \ C_{n.m}(e_1,e_3),$$

using n.m to symbolize the product of n and m. If n and m are both $<$ 1, as they almost always will be, their product will be lower than either, and this expresses the intuitive idea that an unsalient protocause of an unsalient protocause of e_3 will itself be a *very* unsalient protocause of e_3. With this idea at our disposal, we can give an account of "cause" that builds salience into its meaning, rather than leaving it to pragmatics, by picking on some proper fraction F for which we can say:

$$e_1 \text{ causes } e_2 \ .\equiv. \ C_n(e_1,e_2) \quad \text{for some } n > F.$$

That relation obviously is not unrestrictedly transitive: it could hold from fact to fact along a chain, yet not hold between the first and last links in the chain because the product of all the fractions was $<$ F. There will, however, be some short, high-fraction causal chains where transitivity does hold, and that is just what we wanted.

That sketch of a possible theory is consistent and has the right shape. Unfortunately, though, I see no prospect of finding a quantifiable measure of degrees of salience, and without that the theory is nothing. Anyway, I don't believe it. Our actual concept of *cause* really is as weak as unrestricted transitivity makes it. Our best chance of getting clear about accountability, I believe, is to see it as having causation as one ingredient among others, such as foreseeability and importance. "Shouldn't we strengthen our concept of causation a little, rather than letting it sprawl so widely, leaving to other concepts most of the work of pinning down the upshots for which one is morally accountable?" No. The other concepts do the work quite well, and there is no useful way of tightening our concept of causation. If we are to keep it fairly clean and hard, we must keep it weak.

I sometimes feel oppressed by the thought that so much of the world's future history will have been caused by (among other things) my conduct; but this is a burden that one should bear honestly, rather than hiding it from oneself by misusing the language of causation.

20. *Fact causation: the counterfactual analysis*

Counterfactual conditionals say that if things had been different in one way from how they actually are, they would also have been different in some other way. It is sometimes thought that fact-causation statements can be analyzed with help from counterfactual conditionals. The idea is that instead of getting at $C(f_1,f_2)$ through the idea of a temporally continuous chain of facts $f_1, \ldots, f_2$, each member of which is an NS condition of each later member, we should get at it through the idea of a temporally continuous chain of facts each member of which has the CC relation to its immediate successor—by which I mean that if the former had not obtained the latter would not have obtained either. We still need to bring in the notion of a chain, guaranteeing transitivity, because the CC relation, like the NS one, is not transitive.[7]

You might think that the NS analysis itself involves counterfactual conditionals, on the grounds that "f_P is an NS condition of f_Q" means that a certain sufficient condition for f_P *would not be* sufficient if f_Q were removed from it. The NS analysis can be expressed in that way, but it need not. It suffices to say that "f_P is an NS condition of f_Q" means that

> There is a true R such that (P & R & L) entails Q, and (R & L) does not entail Q,

where L is the conjunction of all causal laws. That is expressed in hard logic, with none of the messy complications that counterfactual conditionals bring with them.

These two analyses have something important in common,

---

7. For help in seeing why, consult David K. Lewis, *Counterfactuals*, pp. 32–35.

namely a grounding in the concept of causal law. The NS relation is defined purely in terms of logical relations to L, the totality of causal laws; and the only plausible analyses of counterfactual conditionals also rely on the notion of causal law, either explicitly or as implied by the concept of a causally possible world, or of a miracle, or the like.[8]

It would be nice if the NS and CC analyses turned out to be equivalent, but I don't think that they can be, because counterfactual conditionals—on any plausible analysis of them—involve a concept of *closeness of worlds* that has no analogue in the NS analysis. If the two are not equivalent, I am pretty sure that the NS analysis is preferable. David Lewis thinks that the CC analysis can solve what he calls the problem of epiphenomena, i.e. the problem of sorting causally necessary conditionals into forwards, backwards, and mixed, and he offers this as an advantage over the NS approach. So it would be, if it were true, but I don't think it is. That, however, is a long story that I cannot go into here.

8. See, for example, Jonathan Bennett, "Counterfactuals and Temporal Direction"; David K. Lewis, "Counterfactual Dependence and Time's Arrow".

IV

EVENT CAUSATION

21. *Event causation: the relational approach*

Relational analyses of event-causation statements have dominated the philosophical literature on events. Davidson presents one when he suggests that "e_1 causes e_2" means:

> There are descriptions of e_1 and e_2 such that the sentence obtained by putting these descriptions for "e_1" and "e_2" in "e_1 causes e_2" follows from a true causal law.[1]

Davidson offers this as "rough", and so it is. It needs four large repairs if it is to have even a chance. Also, a small one. Because events could cause others even if there were no descriptions, no languages, we should rework Davidson's sketch into the material mode, moving from language to what language is about.[2] Then we shall say that e_1 causes e_2 only if there are features F and F′ such that e_1 has F and e_2 has F′ . . . etc. This commits us to the existence of features or properties, but that seems inevitable anyway.

(i) The first big repair must be preceded by some tidying up. Davidson speaks of replacing the event names in "e_1 causes e_2" by descriptions, but that is probably not quite what he means. No statement of the form "The F event causes the F′ event" could follow from a true causal law, since no law could imply that there is any F event. What Davidson probably means, and what best fits what he says about causal laws in his "Causal Relations" (p. 158), is this: e_1 causes e_2 if for some F and F′:

---

1. Donald Davidson, "Actions, Reasons, and Causes", p. 16n. Here and elsewhere I freely substitute my own symbols for those of authors from whom I quote. Here, for example, I have replaced Davidson's "A" and "B" by my "e_1" and "e_2".

2. Thus Jaegwon Kim, "Events and their Descriptions", n. 14 on pp. 214f.

> $F(e_1)$ and $F'(e_2)$ and the statement "Every F event causes an F′ event" or "For all x, if Fx then for some y: F′y and x causes y" is entailed by causal laws.[3]

I shall assume that that is what Davidson is saying.

My first substantive point is that Davidson's analysis is circular: the analysans could be understood only by someone who already grasped the form "x causes y", which is the analysandum. To break the circle, let us make the analysans say not that causal laws entail "Every F event *causes* an F′ event" but rather that they entail "Every F event *is followed by* an F′ event". In thus taking causal laws to be propositions about what (probably) follows what, not about what causes what, I am not implying that there is nothing to causality but de facto regularities. For all I have said to the contrary, a truth's being a causal law may depend on its being necessary in some strong sense that Hume, for instance, would have rejected; my point concerns the content of causal laws, not their status. In short, I propose an analysis of event causation in terms that involve the concept of causal law, but not the concept of event causation; Davidson's "rough" analysis involves both. I don't know whether Davidson would accept this revision; in his writings he wavers. In his "Causal Relations" paper he works with an example in which "Any stab . . . that is F *is followed by* the death of the stabbed" is described as a "law", as "unconditional", and as supporting counterfactuals, but on the next page he presents causal laws as speaking about what *causes* what.

(ii) The revised analysis, however, is still not right. It implies this:

> If $F(e_1)$, and it is causally necessary that any F event is followed by an F′ event, then e_1 causes some F′ event that follows it.

That is false because a potential cause may be preempted by another: it was causally necessary that such a rock falling from such a height onto a comatose man would be followed by a death, but while the rock was falling the man's heart stopped, and so the fall did not cause his death. Davidson's circular analysis can deal with this neatly, saying: "Causal laws imply that such rockfalls (in such circumstances) *are followed by* deaths, but not that they *cause* deaths." But that victory is won at too high a price.

We met a difficulty like this when dealing with fact causation; and the solution that worked there seems to work here too. Let us require, for the truth of $C(e_1,e_2)$, not merely that a certain relation R

---

3. Here and elsewhere I use the form "F(x)" as short for "x has feature F". Strictly speaking, "F(x)" requires that "F" be a predicate, whereas I mean it to be the name of a feature or property, but my usage makes for brevity and should do no harm.

hold between L (the totality of causal laws) and e_1 and e_2, but that there be a temporally continuous series of events $e_1, \ldots, e_2$ such that $R(L,e_i,e_j)$ for each successive pair in the series. That will take us from the heart failure to the death, but not from the rockfall to the death.

(iii) That uses continuity to strengthen the analysans, but in another way we want it weakened. The analysis as it stands does not imply that event causation is transitive—i.e. does not allow for the possibility that e_1 caused e_2 just because they were linked by a causal chain, a sequence of events $e_1, \ldots, e_2$ each member of which caused the next, even though $R(L,e_1,e_2)$ is not true. (An example can be constructed on an analogy with the bomb-on-the-bridge case in Section 19.) As with fact causation, so also here, the way to make the relation transitive is to *replace* $R(L,e_1,e_2)$ by the continuity condition rather than conjoining the two in the analysans. Then the analysis allows $C(e_1,e_2)$ to be true even when $R(L,e_1,e_2)$ is false, so long as a suitable causal chain links e_1 to e_2; and when $R(L,e_1,e_2)$ is true we still get $C(e_1,e_2)$ as a special case.

(iv) We have arrived at this: $C(e_1,e_2)$ just in case there is a continuous series of events $e_1, \ldots, e_2$ in which each successive pair e_i, e_j satisfies the following:

> There are properties F and F′ such that: $F(e_i)$ and $F'(e_j)$ and L entails that every F event is followed by an F′ event.

But if F and F′ are intrinsic features of events, involving no relations to anything else, it will seldom be a causal truth that F events are followed by F′ events: it hardly ever happens that one intrinsic kind of event leads to another except by virtue of the circumstances being right. Our analysans, on this understanding of it, is so strong that the analysis makes virtually all event-causation statements *false*.

The simplest repair is to unleash F and F′, allowing them to be as relational as you like. That won't do either, though, because it makes far too many event-causation statements *true*. Suppose that an explosion at t_1 caused a fire at t_2 and was accompanied by a quite irrelevant drumbeat. Now, the drumbeat has a feature, namely *occurring at a time when there also occurred an explosion which . . .* [etc., filling in details about the environment], such that causal laws entail that if an event with that feature occurs at t_1 then there is a fire at t_2. Our "repaired" analysis therefore has to conclude that the drumbeat caused the fire![4]

A superficially attractive idea that turns out not to work is to

---

4. The problem that arises from letting F and F′ be promiscuously relational is pointed out by Carnap, *Meaning and Necessity*, pp. 28f. For a fuller discussion, see Jaegwon Kim, "Causation, Nomic Subsumption, and the Concept of an Event"; Gerald Vision, "Causal Sufficiency".

confine F and F′ to intrinsic features of events and to mention the circumstances separately. (I surreptitiously did this a few paragraphs back, in connection with the rockfall.) This would be done by saying that "e_i caused e_j" means something like this:

> e_i had an intrinsic feature F, and e_j had an intrinsic feature F′, such that some set of jointly sufficient conditions for the occurrence of an F′ is not sufficient if the fact that an F event occurred is omitted from it.

This analyzes $C(e_1,e_2)$ as meaning that a certain fact about e_1 is an NS condition of the obtaining of a fact about e_2. (It is no coincidence that it reverts to NS condition *and* to fact causation, for the relevant notions of necessity and sufficiency make sense only as relating propositionally structured items such as facts. When Mackie first launched INUS conditions, his examples concerned events such as a short-circuit and a fire, but his discussion was, as it had to be, conducted in terms of facts. He evidently was not at that time sensitive to the difference.)

Although I like the idea of analyzing event causation through fact causation, this present proposal fails, because its analysans is too weak. It allows that $C(e_i,e_j)$ is true if some intrinsic feature of e_i was an NS condition of the occurrence of an event with *some* intrinsic feature of e_j. That could make it true that a puff of wind caused a fire because the fact that such a puff occurred was an NS condition of there being a fire with just precisely that average temperature rather than a slightly lower one. It could make it true that someone's reading of *Hamlet* caused his quarrel with his wife the next day because the fact that he read *Hamlet* was an NS condition of there being a quarrel between him and his wife in which he used the word "nunnery". The analysis is nowhere near to being right.

I shall present my own solution to these problems in Chapter VIII. A lot must be done first.

Let us now turn from relational to counterfactual analyses of event causation. That will complete the foursome announced in Section 17.

22. *Counterfactuals and essences*

The counterfactual analysis of event causation was one of Hume's two accounts of what causes are, and it has been revived more recently by David Lewis.[5] In its strongest form it says that "e_1 caused e_2"—where e_1 and e_2 are individual events—means that e_2 depended counterfactual-

5. David K. Lewis, "Causation".

ly on e_1, by which I mean that *if e_1 had not occurred, e_2 would not have occurred*. For reasons whose cousins we have already met, this simple counterfactual should be replaced by:

> There is a temporally continuous sequence of events $e_1, \ldots, e_2$ each successive pair in which satisfies this: If e_i had not occurred, e_j would not have occurred.

Other bits of tidying up may also be needed, but I shall not go into them here. There is a literature on them,[6] and I have other fish to fry.

If we are to counterfactualize about a particular item x, we must be able to distinguish worlds at which x is present-but-different from worlds that lack x altogether. So, as Lewis makes clear, any counterfactual about an event implies something about its essence. Suppose that at noon precisely I wave my right hand, and my companion later says (S) "If that handwave had not occurred, the auctioneer wouldn't have thought you were bidding." Now, if I had waved my right hand a fraction faster than I actually did or raised it an inch higher, the auctioneer would still have thought I was bidding; so if S is to come out true those possible waves must count as the wave I actually did. That implies that my actual wave could have been a bit faster or higher than it was, which means that its actual speed and trajectory are not of its essence.[7]

Now, suppose that at each of the nearest worlds where I don't wave my right hand I do wave my left, and the auctioneer thinks I am bidding. Is S true in this case? You might think not, because at those worlds my actual handwave doesn't occur, and yet the auctioneer still thinks I am bidding. Well, *doesn't* my handwave occur at those worlds? Perhaps the wave that I made with my right hand could have been made with my left, in which case worlds where I wave only with my left hand may still be ones where my actual wave occurs. Whether this is so depends on whether my wave was essentially or only accidentally right-handed.

Suppose now that if I hadn't waved I would have nodded, and the auctioneer would have thought I was bidding: Does *that* make S false? If you say Yes, that is because you think that my wave was essentially a wave. But maybe it wasn't. Perhaps it was an event that

---

6. See, for example, Jaegwon Kim, "Causes and Counterfactuals"; T. Yagisawa, "Counterfactual Analysis of Causation and Kim's Examples"; Marshall Swain, "A Counterfactual Analysis of Event Causation"; Wayne A. Davis, "Swain's Counterfactual Analysis of Causation".

7. Unless one supposes that at the closest world where I don't make that handwave I don't wave my hand at all, whereas worlds where I wave it a little faster or higher than I actually did are more remote. But no tenable standards of world-closeness would let one suppose that.

happened to be a wave but could instead have been a nod. I take no stand on this. I want only to illustrate how judgments about the essences of events are relevant to counterfactuals about them and thus, if Lewis is right, to event-causation statements.

23. *The search for data about event essences*

A search for missing climbers was conducted by seven men and one woman, using ropes and flashlights and whistles, on the west side of the mountain, from dusk on Friday through to dawn on Sunday. Could that search have involved fewer people, occurred later, spread onto the north slope . . . ? That raises the question of which features of the search were essential to it.

To ask how that search could have been different is not to ask how else the missing climbers might have been searched for. They could have been sought a month later, on a different mountain, by seventy children carrying butterfly nets, but that does not imply that the search that *was* conducted could have had all those features. On the other hand, the search that was carried out may not have been essentially a search: perhaps that very event could have differed in ways that made it not a search but an endurance test.

How can we decide when and where and how a particular search could have occurred, whether it could have been something other than a search, and so on? Some of our plain talk looks relevant, but if it is not handled with care it leads to funny results, as happened when Davidson first discussed the essences of events. He may have been sarcastically attacking the very notion of individual essences, but let us consider the passage as though it were meant not to mock but to help. It was a reply to this challenge by Chisholm:

> Consider that entity which, according to Davidson's analysis, Sebastian is said to stroll. Could some other person have strolled it? Could Sebastian have strolled it in Florence instead of in Bologna? Or, had he not strolled it, could he have done something else with it instead? It would be unphilosophical, I think, to reject such questions—if one assumes that there really is a certain concrete thing that Sebastian strolls.[8]

Challenged by this to say which of a stroll's properties are essential to it, Davidson answered:

> Suppose that . . . each night someone, chosen by drawing a card, takes a stroll at 2 a.m. Then we might say that had the cards fallen

8. Roderick Chisholm, "States of Affairs Again", p. 182.

> out differently, another person might have taken that stroll. Or, if Sebastian takes a stroll each night at 2 a.m., we might say that if he had been in Florence that night instead of in Bologna, then the stroll that he did take in Bologna would have taken place in Florence.[9]

If this is an unargued proposal about what "we" as theoreticians might say about the essence of the stroll, I have nothing to say; I am looking not for proposals but for evidence. Taken rather as a remark about what "we" as ordinary people might naturally say, it seems false. The form of words " . . . then another person would have taken *that stroll*" is too strained and unnatural to be a plausible slice of conversational life.

Davidson may have been thinking of pronouns. One might well say: "Sebastian took a stroll; if the cards had etc., someone else would have taken *it*." Does that imply that the very same stroll could have been taken by someone else? If so, then in the following case—

> Every Wednesday morning, the members of the squad vote on what practical joke to play on the corporal that day. Last Wednesday's joke was a hotfoot, but if PFC Jones had voted the other way it would have been a fake air-raid alarm

—we must say that a certain event was a hotfoot but could instead have been a fake air-raid alarm. No careful thinker will be willing to draw that conclusion just on the strength of an "it" that connects with "last Wednesday's practical joke", without at least asking whether the "it" is a pronoun of coreference. What else could it be? Well, it could be a pronoun referring to a different instance of a previously involved universal, as in "He hit his wife yesterday, and then he did it again today".[10] Or it could be a pronoun of laziness—a mere replacement for a noun phrase that has occurred earlier, as in "Sam gave his paycheck to his wife; Jack gave it to his mistress", where "it" merely replaces "his paycheck". In my practical-joke example, I think we have a pronoun of laziness.

It doesn't matter whether I am right about that. The main point is that if event essences are to be taken seriously, we need linguistic data other than mere unsifted uses of pronouns that hook up with event names. We need some way of telling when such pronouns genuinely corefer; our ordinary speech and thought do not provide one.

---

9. Donald Davidson, "Eternal vs. Ephemeral Events", p. 197.

10. Chisholm holds that in that sentence the "it" is a pronoun of coreference, because he thinks that events *are* universals, not particulars. For more along those lines, see Charles Landesman, "Actions as Universals".

If we were much given to counterfactualizing about particular events, that would throw light on what we ordinarily think or assume about the essences of events. But what led us to inquire about essences was the hope of getting help from that quarter in evaluating counterfactuals! The point is that counterfactuals that clearly are about particular events have at most a tiny place in our everyday thought and talk. I imagined someone saying "If that handwave had not occurred, the auctioneer wouldn't have thought you were bidding", but that would be a strange thing to say. It sounds strained, awkward, improbable, and if someone did say it we would guess that he was stiltedly trying to say, "If you hadn't waved your arm like that, he wouldn't have thought you were bidding", which is not a counterfactual about a particular event.

We clearly counterfactualize about particular events, it seems, only in speaking about how the later stages of time-taking events could have been otherwise: "If the temperature had been a bit higher, *the storm would not have reached the coast*"; "If it hadn't been for that bad call, Jordan wouldn't have lost her composure and *the game would have gone very differently*". Perhaps from those we do get some negative result about the nonessentiality to a particular event of many of the features of its later parts; but I don't know how to make this more precise, and I cannot get from it any insights that help me with the counterfactual analysis (by which I mean, from now on, "the counterfactual analysis of event causation"). Other counterfactuals that seem to be about particular events and to yield stronger results about what is accidental to them, may well not be what they seem. For example: "If Argentina had not cheated in the semifinal, *the final would have been between England and Germany*. Someone who said this would almost certainly be using "the final" to name a type, not a particular game; he would not be trying to say that the very game that was played between one pair of teams could have been played by a different pair.

24. *Three approaches to the essences of events*

Ordinary speech and thought provide no evidence, independently of the counterfactual analysis, about the essences of events. This is confirmed by how three philosophers have defended views about the essences of events—the only such views that I know of.

Peter van Inwagen compares the essences of events with the essences of substances. It is widely believed that a substance's origin is essential to it: I could have become a farmer, but I could not have had parents other than my actual ones. Perhaps a "necessity of origins" thesis applies to events also, van Inwagen suggests, and he interprets this as meaning that no event could have differed in its causal ancestry. He writes:

> I do not know how to justify my intuition that this criterion is correct, any more that I know how to justify my belief in the causal-genesis criterion for substances. But, of course, arguments must come to an end somewhere. I can only suggest that since substances (like human beings and tables) should be individuated by their causal origins, and since we are talking about events that, like substances, are particulars, the present proposal is plausible.[11]

It would be good to find some arguments for or against this proposal, but I have none. Someone has pointed out that it implies results like this:

> Think of all the causal chains leading to the death of Socrates, spreading outwards and backward in time for centuries. Consider a world that is extremely like ours, but which differs from it in respect of the identity of some one event, in one of those causal chains, about a century before Socrates died. According to van Inwagen, that is a world where Socrates' death—the actual one that did occur—does not occur.

This is offered as so implausible as to discredit van Inwagen's position, but I have no idea what force to give it because I still have *no* sense of how to divide the properties of events into essential and accidental.

If I wanted to attack van Inwagen's thesis, I would rather challenge his argument. There are two points at which one might burrow in. Our Kripkean intuitions that *substances* necessarily have their origins are not beyond question and might be challenged. Furthermore, even if they are right, that might be because of some features of substances that events do not share. Granted that items of both kinds are particulars, they differ in ways that might be relevant: substances last through time and do not have temporal parts, whereas events stretch through time and do have temporal parts.[12] If the "necessity of origins" thesis was plausible for substances only because they last through time, van Inwagen's analogy would fail.

Anyway, accepting van Inwagen's thesis would not greatly help us to evaluate the counterfactual analysis of event causation. One consequence of the former is also entailed by the strongest version of the latter, namely:

---

11. Peter van Inwagen, "Ability and Responsibility", pp. 208f.

12. The early part of the picnic occurred on the lawn; the later part occurred indoors. But the entire drink table was present first on the lawn and then in the house. More about this later.

If e_1 caused e_2 then if e_1 had not occurred e_2 would not have occurred.

That is in the spirit of one half of the counterfactual analysis, though as it stands it is too strong for Lewis's stomach: he thinks—and van Inwagen must deny—that the antecedent could be true and the consequent false, because it could be that if e_1 had failed some other event would have caused e_2 instead. As for the other half of Lewis's analysis, namely the conditional

If (if e_1 had not occurred e_2 would not have occurred) then $C(e_1,e_2)$,

van Inwagen's thesis has nothing to say about any version of that, which is why I don't think it can help us to evaluate the counterfactual analysis.

The second of the three views about event essences is Lombard's opinion that no event could possibly have occurred earlier or later than it actually occurred. Here is his argument:

> At possible world Alpha a certain object changes twice in a certain way, once at t_1 and again at t_2. Those two changes—call them e_1 and e_2 respectively—are as alike as possible given that they occur at different times. Now consider a possible world Beta, which is as like Alpha as it can be consistently with this difference: at Beta e_1 occurs at t_2 and e_2 occurs at t_1. If an event's time of occurrence is not essential to it, Beta is possible; but really it is not possible; and so an event's time of occurrence is essential to it.[13]

Lombard gives no reason for his crucial claim that if an event's time of occurrence is not essential to it then Alpha and Beta are distinct possible worlds, and his own subsequent discussion undermines it. In itself, that discussion is admirable. Rather than merely appealing to our intuitions to agree that Beta is not possible, Lombard cogently argues that it is not, as follows. He contends that events are supervenient on substances, properties, and times, so that two worlds that are (i) indiscernible in respect of what substances they contain and what those substances are like at each moment must also be (ii) exactly alike in respect of all truths about events occurring at them; it has been stipulated that Alpha and Beta satisfy (i), so if they are both possible they also satisfy (ii); but they have been stipulated as being unalike in one event respect, which clashes with (ii), so they are not both possible. That excellent reason for saying that Alpha and Beta are not both possible worlds destroys Lombard's claim that his essentiality-of-time thesis is the only basis for saying that they are not both

13. Adapted from Lawrence Brian Lombard, *Events: a Metaphysical Study*, pp. 213f.

possible; and without that he is left with no argument for that thesis.

I have been looking for *independent* grounds for judgments about the essences of events—independent, that is, of the counterfactual analysis. If we had such grounds, we could use them to help us evaluate counterfactuals about particular events, and those evaluations would help us to test the counterfactual analysis. The form of such a test would be this: On the one hand, our knowledge of event essences and of the world lets us sort out true from false among counterfactuals about events; on the other hand, our firm, nonnegotiable opinions about what causes what let us sort out true from false among event-causation statements; and we compare the two sortings to see if they conform to the counterfactual analysis of event causation. But we haven't been able to get going with any independent judgments about event essences. The facts about "what we might say in ordinary speech" are utterly jejune, van Inwagen's analogy with substance essences is not compelling, and Lombard has no good argument for his thesis about event essences. We are getting nowhere—not because we are driven this way and that, but rather because we can't get any wind into our sails.

There remains the less ambitious course of basing judgments about the essences of events *on* the counterfactual analysis of event causation: start with our firm beliefs about what causes what, put them into their counterfactual form in accordance with the analysis, and draw conclusions about what the essences of events must be like if we are not to be convicted of too much error in our causal beliefs. That is the third of my three approaches, and it is the one that Lewis adopts.[14]

In his original defense of the counterfactual analysis, Lewis helped himself to "the set of worlds at which e occurs", that is, "the proposition that e occurs"; but he knew that this was a mere promissory note, and in his paper "Events" he undertakes to make good on it. In that paper, he rightly does not rest much on naked intuitions about how particular events might have differed. Nor does he or could he get help from either of the two theories we have looked at. Rather, he sets out to discover what the essences of events *must* be like if we are to be mainly right in our pretheoretic causal opinions and the counterfactual analysis is to be true.

If the judgments about essences that are reached in this way are not answerable to some other standard as well, doesn't that make this whole project trivial, and its conclusions irrefutable? No. For it might be that no account of event essences could reconcile the counterfactual analysis with the majority of our beliefs about what causes what; so Lewis has the nontrivial task of showing otherwise.

14. David K. Lewis, "Events".

25. *Counterparts and modal continuants*

What kind of thing are we doing when we attribute an essence to a particular or assert a counterfactual about it? What does a particular item existing at one world have to do with other worlds? When the particular is a substance, Lewis answers this in terms of *counterparts*. I shall expound this notion, applying it to people.

Lewis holds that no particular—and thus no person—can exist at more than one world, but he is willing to divide counterfactuals about named people into true and false by reinterpreting them a little. Someone meditating on the Attica prison rebellion might say: "If Cuomo had been in charge, there would have been no deaths or injuries". This may be true because it means something about possible men who are counterparts of Mario Cuomo: they are sufficiently like him (in the right ways) for us to talk about how *they are* in the language of how *he might have been*. So the Cuomo conditional is true if, and only if, there are no deaths or injuries in the Attica prison incident at the closest world where a counterpart of Mario Cuomo is in charge.

Don't think that on this account of it the conditional is not really about Cuomo. Lewis's analysans does say, about Cuomo, that *he* has counterparts of which such and such is true. This is not mere word-play. If I were told that twenty people resembling me in character and personality had been convicted of crimes of violence, I wouldn't calmly dismiss this as not being in any way about me.

Lewis is an extreme realist about worlds; he holds that other possible worlds are chunks of rock and space, just as ours is, and that to call a world "actual" is merely to say that one exists at it. That gives him one reason for denying that any substance can exist at more than one world.

A second reason weighs more with me. It is the fact that judgments about the essences of substances seem not to fall sharply into true and false, but rather to lie on a *smooth* scale from undeniable to intolerable; much of the middle ground is controversial, with no apparent means for resolving the controversies. If counterpart theory is true, that is just what one would expect, for the theory says that the answer to a question of the form "Could x, which is not actually F, have been F?" depends upon whether we are willing to describe certain possible F things in the language of "how x could have been". It is for us to decide what similarities should be accorded that kind of weight (says counterpart theory), and our decisions could vary across speakers and across times. That would explain the sliding slack in our thoughts about how a substance could have been different. If counterpart theory is false, however, and counterfactual questions about particulars have objectively right answers, it is puzzling that we should be so lost and adrift in our attempts to find out what the answers are.[15]

Counterpart theory, divorced from realism about worlds, is merely the thesis that judgments about how a given particular could have been different have values on a sliding scale of acceptability rather than dividing cleanly into true and false, and that these values are themselves relative to contexts. That thesis seems to me indisputable, and I don't understand why anyone doubts it. For Lewis, of course, counterpart theory is more than that, but it does include that.

The work done by *counterpart* can be done instead by *modal continuant*. I shall explain.

According to counterpart theory, "Hobbes" names a man who exists only at the actual world, and "Hobbes might have been F" assigns to him some counterparts who are F. According to modal continuant theory, "Hobbes" names a class of items, no two—or almost no two—existing at a single world, and "Hobbes is F" means, strictly, that the actual world member of Hobbes is F, while "Hobbes might have been F" means, strictly, that some member of Hobbes is F. Thus, some members of the class wrote nothing and died young, whereas the member of it that exists at our world wrote *Leviathan* and died old; or, in the vernacular, Hobbes could have written nothing and died young but in fact wrote *Leviathan* and died old.

Modal continuant theory provides for indeterminacy in our thoughts about essences: the membership of a given class is sharp, but there may be fuzz around the question of which class is picked out by a given name. We may have a complete description of a woman philosopher at a certain possible world, and thus know exactly which classes she belongs to, and yet not be clear about whether any of those classes could acceptably be called "Hobbes", and thus not be clear about whether Hobbes could have been a woman—or, more exactly, about whether it is acceptable to say "Hobbes could have been a woman".

There is a simple route between the two theories: what one theory calls Hobbes is what the other says is the class of Hobbes's counterparts (he being one of them). Lewis has remarked that the modal continuant idea "is an equivalent reformulation of counterpart theory", though he holds that it is parasitic on the latter.[16]

The two differ only in *where* they bring in the indeterminacy that gets into counterfactuals about named particulars. Modal continuant theory implies that statements of the forms "If . . . , Hobbes would have been——" and "Hobbes might have been . . . " are cloudy because there is indeterminacy about which item is referred to by

---

15. For some related remarks, see David K. Lewis, *Counterfactuals*, pp. 38–43.

16. Postscripts to "Counterpart Theory and Quantified Modal Logic", p. 41.

"Hobbes". Counterpart theory gives "Hobbes" a definite referent and brings in indeterminacy further down the line when we get to modals and counterfactuals.

Lewis's realism about worlds won't let any event occur at two worlds. He handles counterfactuals about events—unlike ones about substances—in terms of modal continuants. He could have said that the death of Socrates occurs only at the actual world and has counterparts at other worlds, but instead he associates Socrates' death with a class of zones, no two existing at one world. According to him, if it is true (in the vernacular) that Socrates' death could have been less painful than it was, this is because at some member of the class of zones picked out by "Socrates' death" Socrates dies less painfully than he does at the actual world. (Strictly, some counterpart of Socrates dies less painfully, but I shall usually omit that complication.)

Why does Lewis handle events in this way, after criticising it as parasitic and having no advantages when applied to substances? There are technical reasons that I shall not go into here. In addition, a certain drawback of modal continuant theory for substances may be a merit when it comes to events. I mean the implication that ordinary names are somewhat indeterminate in their reference, so that our uncertainty about how Hobbes might have been different reflects an uncertainty about what item "Hobbes" refers to. A theory implying that our ordinary *event* names are indeterminate in their reference has less need to apologize, for it is plausible to suppose that phrases like "Hobbes's birth" and "Hobbes's reconciliation with Cromwell" have referential slack that is not shared by "Hobbes". I shall give evidence for that in due course.

The choice between counterparts and modal continuants is not essential for anything I want to say about Lewis's theory, but it had to be faced because it affects Lewis's formulations.

26. *The essences of events*

Any class of zones no two of which belong to a single world is "formally eligible" to be an event, according to Lewis, but it won't actually be an event unless it satisfies some other constraints. Lewis undertakes to say what these are, guided by his need for something that will, when combined with the counterfactual analysis, respect enough of our opinions about what causes what.

Some of the further constraints come under the general rubric that "the essence of an event must not be too rich", i.e. that the class of zones that an event comprises must not be too small. That is because an event with a rich essence will be "fragile", meaning that it could easily not have occurred. An unduly fragile event would, by the counterfactual analysis, be one that has too many causes. The extreme of richness is an event e that contains only one zone. If there were such an event at some world, then, for almost *every* event c occurring at that world, it would be true that *If c had not occurred, e would not have occurred*. So e would have had among its causes virtually every other event at its world. Lewis reasonably does not believe that any event is as fragile, as easily caused, as that.

We need not go to that extreme to see the dangers of undue richness. For example, even if Socrates' death involved his heart's slowing down at a steady rate, we don't want to say that it essentially did so. For if it did, any truth of the form "If c had occurred, Socrates' heart would have slowed down somewhat erratically" would generate a truth of the form "If c had occurred, Socrates' death would not have occurred", which, by the counterfactual analysis, entails that c caused Socrates' death. Thus by making the death's essence too rich we would make the death too fragile, thereby implying an implausible statement about a cause of it.

Events with unduly rich essences would not only be caused too easily; it would be too hard for them to cause anything. Build a few dozen trivial aspects of Socrates at the time he died into the essence of his death, and you will not only confer truth on falsehoods such as "Plato's wiping of Socrates' brow caused his death" but will also imply the falsehood of innocent truths like "Socrates' death caused Plato to grieve".

Lewis puts constraints on the structure of event essences, as well as limiting how rich they can be. They must not be mainly extrinsic: no event is essentially the start of widowhood (p. 263). Nor may they be disjunctions of "disjuncts that are overly varied", such as would be the essence of "the supposed disjunction of one event that is essentially a walking and another that is essentially a talking" (p. 266). These requirements, like most of the restrictions on richness, are vague and impressionistic, but Lewis is open about that and apparently untroubled by it. He would say, I think, that it accurately reflects the considerable indeterminacy in our thoughts about what items we are willing to countenance as events.

27. *Ordinary names for Lewis's events*

A certain feature of Lewis's account strikes me as more important than, apparently, it strikes him. He writes:

> Events made in the image of nominalisations are right for some purposes, but not for mine. When I introduce nominalisations to denote events . . . , it will not be analysis of natural language but mere stipulative definition. (p. 241)

> While it is clear enough what it would mean to specify events essentially [namely, to *say* what their essential properties are], often that does not seem to be what we really do. At any rate, it is not what we do when we specify events by means of our standard nominalisations. (p. 251)

This concedes that our event names are radically indeterminate as to reference. The phrase "Socrates' death" might but need not name an event that is essentially a death, might but need not name one that essentially happens to (a counterpart of) Socrates, and so on. And this indeterminacy of reference, added to the counterfactual analysis, infects the truth-values of event-causation statements.

The estrangement between Lewis's events and ordinary event names makes itself strongly felt in what he says about pairs of events whose members are neither identical nor fully distinct. Compare the event I call General, at each member zone of which Socrates dies of poison but not always of hemlock, with the event that I call Specific, at each member of which Socrates dies of taking hemlock. These are not identical, because Specific has a richer essence, which means a smaller membership; they obey different counterfactuals and thus, according to Lewis, different event-causation statements. Still, although they are not identical, they are not outright distinct either, Lewis says, because one "implies" the other. He needs this tertium between identity and distinctness in order to protect the counterfactual analysis. It is clear both that Specific is not General and that if General had not occurred Specific would not have occurred; but we don't want to say that General caused Specific, Lewis holds, and he blocks this result by saying that an event can only cause an event that is outright distinct from it.

Should we agree that General didn't cause Specific? I don't know, because I have never before met these two putative events, or anything like them, and don't know how to behave in their presence. I recognize them as products of Lewis's theory, but not as parts of my everyday conceptual armory. When Lewis enlarges the scope of the "different but not distinct" relation, I am more lost still. Even if neither of e_1 and e_2 implies the other, he says, if some event implies both then they are still not distinct. Thus, if there is a death of Socrates that is essentially from hemlock but only accidentally a death, and one that is essentially a death but only accidentally from hemlock, these are not distinct if there is a death of Socrates that is essentially a death from hemlock, since that would imply them both. When I try to relate this to the event concept that I use in everyday life, I get hopelessly lost.

The fog clears when Lewis also argues for a tertium between identity and distinctness for reasons that concern spatiotemporal parts of events. The actor's big shout of "Blow, winds, and crack your cheeks!" includes his small shout of "winds". The big shout is obviously not identical with the small one, and if the small one hadn't occurred the big one wouldn't have either; yet it seems wrong to say that one causes the other. Here again Lewis says that one event causes another only if they are outright distinct, and no event is distinct from its parts. Here we can easily identify the two events in question, independently of the theory, and can agree that neither causes the other. This is in striking contrast to the other kind of case, where the events that are said to be neither identical with nor outright distinct from one another occupy the same portion of space-time. We have no untheoretic way of referring unambiguously to either of *them*: we can pick them out only in the language of "essences", by the rules laid down in Lewis's theory; which means that we have no independent purchase on them to help us to evaluate what Lewis's theory says about them.

Lewis mentions but does not defensively discuss this looseness of fit between ordinary event names and the items that he calls events. He *does* discuss an indeterminacy that he says is present even in "essential specification", that is, even when we specify an event by saying what its essential properties are. He rightly compares *that* indeterminacy with a kind of vagueness or openness of texture that we are familiar with in our daily lives:

> Often we find it tolerable to leave some indeterminacy in our specifications of things. Where exactly does the outback begin? Nobody knows; not because it's a secret, but because we've never bothered to settle exactly what "the outback" denotes. And yet we know, near enough, what we're talking about. It might be the same way with our best feasible approximations to essential specifications of events. (p. 251)

Lewis needs no lecture from me on this topic, but it may be helpful to some if I explain why the "outback" kind of example, though it illustrates how events relate to their "essential specifications", does not provide an analogue to the indeterminacy that Lewis must say obtains between events and their ordinary names.

Statements using "the outback" can be divided into three classes: (i) purely true, (ii) true on some permissible readings and false on some, and (iii) purely false. But we could shrink the truth-value gap either by charitably counting all of (i) and (ii) as true, or by uncharitably counting all of (ii) and (iii) as false. Neither policy is needed, but each is feasible, and neither would make much difference because the members of (ii) are all *nearly* false and all *nearly* true. If someone who says "We camped in the outback" is not speaking falsely, then they did camp in *or near* to the outback. If "Charles is bald" is not definitely true, then it is false or *nearly* false. That is how it is with the indeterminacies of daily life, and with the ones that Lewis says beset the essential specification of events, which is why it matters so little if we don't all draw the "outback" or "bald" line in quite the same place.

The situation with ordinary event names, on Lewis's account, is not like that. Consider this episode from a discussion of two events, each of which is a loud utterance of "Hello" by John, a weak one that is accidentally loud and a stronger one that is essentially so:[17]

> The real reason why we need both events, regardless of which [ordinary event name] denotes which, is that they differ causally. An adequate causal account of what happens cannot limit itself to either one of the two. The first event (the weak one) caused Fred to greet John in return. The second one (the strong one) didn't. If the second one had not occurred—if John hadn't said "Hello" so loudly—the first one still would have, in which case Fred would still have returned John's greeting. Also there is a difference on the side of the causes: the second event was, the first wasn't, caused *inter alia* by John's state of tension. (p. 255)

This passage can persuade us of what caused what only because it picks out the two events not by ordinary nominals but through Lewis's theoretical device of essential specification. Lewis says that either event might properly be named by either "John's saying 'Hello' " or "John's saying 'Hello' loudly" (he is not finicky about imperfect nominals). Now, consider someone who asserts "John's saying 'Hello' caused Fred's reply". He could permissibly mean that Fred wouldn't have replied if John hadn't said "Hello" so loudly or that Fred wouldn't have spoken if John hadn't said "Hello" in some fashion, and it might be that in one meaning the remark is flatly false and in the other perfectly true. This swing between full-fledged truth and total falsity is not a matter of borderlines.

So we are not free to accept Lewis's theory and say that his events are the ones we refer to by our perfect nominals, the indeterminacy in our reference being of the familiar "outback" kind. Lewis doesn't say this, but neither does he in any other way connect his theory with everyday thought and talk. If the two don't intersect at statements of the form "e_1 caused e_2" where e_1 and e_2 are named by perfect nominals, where do they make contact?[18]

---

17. It would be better to replace "weak"/"strong" by "poor"/"rich". The event that Lewis here calls "strong" is, in his own terminology elsewhere, the more "fragile" of the two.

18. I shall later argue that there is indeterminacy in how our event names relate to events, but not of a kind that could generate previously unsuspected swings from truth to falsity. Because my views about indeterminacy *arise out of* facts about how we do use ordinary event names, they could not divorce events from their names as Lewis's theory does.

Lewis's "Events" paper, rather than directly defending the counterfactual analysis of event causation, explores what that analysis implies, helping us to estimate the price of accepting it. The job could hardly be better done; and what it shows, I submit, is that the asking price for the analysis is a fairly complete divorce from the event-causation judgments that we actually make in thought and speech. That is too high.

That line of argument rests on Lewis's own work. All I have done is to put the spotlight on certain features of it, and then run it in the contrapositive direction.

28. *Essences and times*

Try combining the counterfactual analysis of event causation with Lombard's thesis that no event could have occurred at any time other than when it actually did. Lewis rejects that combination:

> It is one thing to postpone an event, another to cancel it. A cause without which it would have occurred later, or sooner, is not a cause without which it would not have occurred at all. Who would dare to be a doctor, if [Lombard's thesis] were right? You might manage to keep your patient alive until 4:12, when otherwise he would have died at 4:08. You would then have caused his death. For his death was, in fact, his death at 4:12. If that time is essential, his death is an event that would not have occurred had he died at 4:08, as he would have done without your action. That will not do. (p. 118)

In an earlier publication of mine, I transformed this passage into something that I claimed to be fatal to the counterfactual analysis of event causation.[19] I appealed to "the asymmetry fact" about our concept of event causation: It is the fact that, to put it crudely, we tend to regard hasteners as causes but not delayers. For evidence that something like this is true about our thought, and to get a little clearer about what truth it is, consider:

> You are told that *a nurse gave a patient a massage, and if she had not done so he would have died at a time other than the one at which he actually died.* From that alone, you have no basis for saying whether the massage caused the patient's death. If you had to hazard an answer, you might as well toss a coin. But if you are told that the patient died earlier than he would have without the massage,

19. Jonathan Bennett, "Event Causation: the Counterfactual Analysis".

> that gives you some reason to guess that it caused his death; and if you learn instead that he died later than he would have without the massage, that makes it almost certain that the massage did not cause his death. That illustrates *the asymmetry fact* about this corner of our conceptual scheme.

This, I argued, makes trouble for the counterfactual analysis of event causation, because it implies that there are more worlds at which a given particular event occurred earlier than it actually did than worlds at which it occurred later; and that is contradictory. It implies that when we have an event e_1 occurring at t_1 at world w_1, and an event e_2 occurring at t_2 at world w_2, the question of how much chance there is that e_1 is e_2 depends on whether the pair $\{t_1,t_2\}$ exemplifies the earlier-than or rather the later-than relation. That is absurd, because any pair of times that exemplifies one of those relations also exemplifies the other.

This whole line of argument as presented in my article is quite strong, though the above sketch may not do it justice. But there are three things wrong with it, and when they are remedied there is nothing left.

(i) My argument focuses on the idea of a "hastener": the claim was that, if e causes x to acquire property P at a certain time "rather than later or never", then we are apt to regard e as a cause of x's acquisition of P, whereas we are less likely to think this if e causes it to be the case that x acquires P at a certain time rather than earlier. Really, this hastener-delayer contrast cannot be applied in the multitude of cases where it is certain that, whether or not x acquires P at T, it will (re)acquire P later. For example, a tuning fork sits on the piano, and several times a day somebody flicks it, making it vibrate. I flick it at T, causing it to vibrate for a period starting just after T: it seems clear that the flick I give it (an event) causes that vibration (another event). But I don't cause it to *vibrate then rather than later or never*; that formulation was appropriate for the special case where the change is of a kind—like dying—that a thing can undergo at most once. All I do with the tuning fork is to cause it to *vibrate then rather than not vibrating then*.

(ii) Even in those special cases, it is not clearly true that an event that delays x's acquiring P is not a cause of its acquisition of P. If a massage saves the patient's life and he dies years later in an accident, the massage is a cause of his death: the accident has among its causes his being in a certain place a moment earlier, and the causes of that include the massage that he got all those years before; and transitivity takes it from there. The two causal premises are correct on either a counterfactual or an NS analysis; all they require is that we be working with a causal relation that is extremely weak because it is transitive and involves no salience conditions. (Those sources of weakness overlap but do not coincide. Transitivity pushes some but not all salience out of the concept.)

(Lewis agrees with me about this and points out that his example about the doctor is different. In it, the doctor's intervention brings it about that the patient dies only a little later, and it is meant to be a death from the same kind of process as would have killed the patient without the intervention. Lewis holds that in these circumstances the intervention doesn't cause the death, though if the patient survived for years and then was killed by a bus the doctor's intervention would have caused the death. I'm not persuaded that he is right about the former case. He is not entitled to offer the "Who would dare to be a doctor. . . . ?" move as support for it, for he agrees that any action through which a doctor saves a patient's life, enabling her to live for much longer and die differently, is also a cause of her eventual death. Indeed, who would dare to be a doctor?)

That refutes one half of the asymmetry thesis, and when you lose half of an asymmetry you lose it all. Of course there is a temporal asymmetry in what we are ordinarily prepared to *say* about causes, but that can be relegated to pragmatics. Of all the events that cause x's acquisition of P, one that did so by preventing x from acquiring P earlier will be lengthily, remotely, unsaliently related to its eventual acquisition of P, and that will make us hesitate to *say* that it caused the acquisition, because considerations of salience have a strong effect on what we are comfortable about *saying* in the language of causation.[20]

(iii) Underlying point (ii) is a point about transitivity. The counterfactual analysis of event causation was supposed to involve something like this:

> e_1 causes e_2 ≡ there is a sequence of events $e_1, \ldots, e_2$ each member of which, after e_1, depends counterfactually on its immmediate predecessor,

with "counterfactual dependence" explained in the obvious way. According to this account, counterfactual relatednesss is relevant only for *immediate* cause-effect pairs—ones that are causally related but not through intervening causal chains. Now, suppose that e_1 occurs at t_1, and e_2 occurs at t_2, which is little later than t_1. We want the counterfactual analysis to help us decide whether e_1 is an immediate cause of e_2. The analysis will tell us to look at nearby worlds where e_1 does not occur at t_1, to see whether at any of them e_2 occurs at t_2. To do this we

20. For the destruction of one half of the asymmetry and the pragmatic explanation of why it was plausible in the first place, I am indebted to Alastair Norcross and Frances Howard.

must know some things about the essences of the two events, but not about their temporal components, if any. The temporal limits are set by the framework within which the search is conducted—namely, the t_1–t_2 time-slices of the relevant worlds—rather than by anything temporal in the essences of the events.

Thus, the theory does not require its adherent to choose among the various views about how time relates to the essences of events. Down at the ground level, where counterfactuals do the basic work before sitting back and letting transitivity take over, the only question is whether, if e_1 had not occurred *then*, e_2 would not have occurred *then*. The question of what other times either event could have occurred at is one that the theory need not face: it need take no stand, for example, on Lombard's thesis. That, of course, is sheer gain for the counterfactual analysis of event causation, but it does not get the analysis out of the other difficulty that I have found in it, namely its remoteness from the everyday life of our concept of event causation.

The relational and counterfactual analyses have both let us down. To improve on them, we need to know more than we do about how in general our event concept works. When we do, I shall return to event causation, in Section 52.

V

KIM'S SEMANTICS

29. *Kim's semantics for event names*

Jaegwon Kim, one of the most interesting and influential writers on events, has advanced a metaphysical view about what events are and a semantic thesis about which pairs of expressions refer to a single event.[1] The semantic question, he has said, is not "the most important problem about the concepts of event and event-description", implying that "the ontological and logical nature of events" matters more (p. 203). He did start with it, however, and I shall follow suit. I shall argue that Kim's semantic doctrine is quite wrong, considered as a view about events, and seems plausible only to those who conflate events with facts.

Kim's *metaphysic* of events, which is also Leibniz's, is probably true. (Its only considerable rival is a theory of Quine's that is pretty certainly false.) Yet few students of events have been won over to it, because everybody has assumed that if Kim is right about what events are then he must be right about how their names work; and it is widely and rightly thought that his account of event names has no chance of being correct. I shall show that we can have the metaphysics and dump the semantics.

Following Kim, I shall focus on event names that are derived from sentences built out of a noun phrase, a verb phrase, and a temporal adverb, as "the walk that John took at midnight" is derived from "John walked at midnight".[2] It is a trivial matter to extend this to

---

1. Jaegwon Kim, "Events and their Descriptions" (pp. 198–215); "Events as Property Exemplifications" (pp. 159–77). Page-number references to Kim in the main text of this chapter will be those two papers. The main outlines of Kim's views about events and their names were reached independently by Alvin Goldman.

2. "John's walk at midnight" is short for "John's walk *that occurred at* midnight". Don't think of it as containing "at midnight" as an adverb; that way confusion lies.

sentences involving two noun phrases and a dyadic verb phrase, yielding nominals like "the quarrel that Emma had with Mr Knightley at the hunt ball"; further extensions may be harder to manage, but not for reasons that matter to philosophy.

Kim's view about which pairs of nominals (of his favored form) refer to the same event is most easily stated by reference to the sentences from which the nominals are derived. It is the view that if N_1 is derived from S_1 and N_2 from S_2 then

> N_1 and N_2 refer to the same event (if either refers to any event) if and only if the noun phrases in S_1 and S_2 refer to the same substance, their verb phrases connote the same property, and their temporal adverbs pick out the same time.

Thus, if John is my cousin and the thunderstorm occurred at midnight, "the walk that John took at midnight" refers to the same event as "the ambulation that my cousin underwent at the time of the thunderstorm". But the phrase "the stroll that John took at midnight" refers to a different event, even if at midnight John was strolling; it comes out as different because "strolls" does not connote the same property as "walks"—those two predicates are not even coextensive. In short: $[S_1,P_1,T_1]$ refers to the same event as $[S_2,P_2,T_2]$ if and only if S_1 is S_2, P_1 is P_2, and T_1 is T_2.

Most of Kim's critics have homed in on the requirement that P_1 be P_2, but the other two conditions should also be controversial. If we understand the names "the walk across Auckland that David did at T" and "the walk across New Zealand that David did at T" as having, respectively, the forms

> [(D, A), walks-across, T] and [(D, NZ), walks-across, T]

they name different events by Kim's criterion, because they name different pairs of "substances". Yet Auckland sprawls across an isthmus, from the Pacific Ocean to the Tasman Sea, so someone who walks across that isthmus at T engages in a single walk that crosses Auckland and crosses New Zealand. There are temporal analogues of this: the walk that I took last Wednesday and the walk that I took last week. Still, the property-identity clause in Kim's semantics is challenging and interesting, and I shall follow tradition in concentrating on that.

This says that two event names $[S,P_1,T]$ and $[S,P_2,T]$ refer to the same event if and only if P_1 is P_2. This implies that David's walk across Auckland cannot be his stroll across Auckland, that Bernard's cross-Channel swim cannot be his journey to Calais, that Mary's theft of the bicycle at noon yesterday cannot be the crime that Mary committed yesterday, and so on. Although this is implausible on the face of it, Kim says, it is supported by data about the ordinary uses of event language—data about what seems intuitively to be true of the forms "e_1 did (not) cause e_2", and "e_1 is (not) the same as e_2". Let us first look at his chief causal argument.

30. *Kim's causal example*

Kim is impressed by sentences like "The collapse was caused, not by the bolt's giving way, but by the bolt's giving way so suddenly" (p. 167). He thinks that this could be true and that it affirms "The collapse was caused by the bolt's giving way suddenly" while denying "The collapse was caused by the bolt's giving way", from which he validly infers that the bolt's giving way is not its giving way suddenly. So "the bolt's giving way" and "the bolt's giving way suddenly" name different events, Kim concludes, because replacing one by the other can lead from truth to falsity.

But those are names of facts, not of events: the adverb "suddenly" makes one of them an imperfect nominal, which compels us to hear the other as imperfect also. If we replace them by perfect nominals, we get something like "The collapse was caused not by the bolt's failure but by its sudden failure", which doesn't sound right at all.

Kim is right that his two imperfect nominals do not corefer: they refer to different *facts*. He has adapted the sample sentence from one of Davidson's, which is explicitly about facts: "The collapse was caused, not by the fact that the bolt gave way, but by the fact that it gave way so suddenly and unexpectedly." Davidson says that this expresses a "rudimentary causal explanation", in which the word "caused" should not be understood as "the 'caused' of straightforward singular causal statements, but is best expressed by the words 'causally explains'."[3]

That gives Kim an opening. He remarks that he can let the word "caused" in his sample sentence mean what it ordinarily means, rather than treating it as a cover for something else:

> Where Davidson says, with regard to sentences like
>
> > The collapse was caused, not by the bolt's giving way, but by the bolt's giving way so suddenly
>
> that here "was caused" should be understood in the sense of "is

---

3. Donald Davidson, "Causal Explanations", pp. 161f. Incidentally, Kim's example, whether understood as causal or as explanatory, is defective. The bolt's giving way suddenly cannot explain or be an NS condition of x unless the bolt's giving way also explains or is an NS condition of x. Let's take Kim's example to say that f_1 was not, whereas f_2 was, a salient enough cause of x to be worth mentioning.

> causally explained", and that explanations "typically relate statements, not events", I would take [the sentence] more literally, and be inclined to take it as evidence that . . . the bolt's giving way and the bolt's giving way suddenly are different events.

Since there is nothing wrong with fact causation, we can agree with Davidson that the "bolt" phrases name facts without paying the price—which Davidson and Kim seem to agree is a fair one—of saying that the statement is not strictly true but can be turned into a truth by replacing "caused" by "causally explained". So there is no support here for Kim's semantics of events.

31. *Facts and events in Kim*

In that argument, Kim offers as names of events two expressions that really name facts, and what his argument shows is that those are indeed *two* facts. Most of Kim's data concern facts rather than events. Indeed, he gives the back of his hand to that distinction:

> I am using this blanket term ["event"] to comprehend not only what we ordinarily call "events" but also such entities as "states", "states of affairs", "phenomena", "conditions", and the like. Perhaps "fact" is more appropriate [as a blanket term], although it too has disadvantages. (p. 213)

One gets the impression that, if events are different from facts, Kim's topic is the latter and not the former. That is also strongly suggested here:

> By "a description of an event" I have in mind what might more properly be called a . . . propositional description of an event; thus, logically, the linguistic units in which I am interested are statements, and not nominal phrases such as definite descriptions (e.g. "John Smith's most unforgettable event") purporting to make unique reference to individual events.[4]

There is a gap in this declaration of interest. Kim tells us that he is interested in so-called event-descriptions that are complete sentences, and his examples show that he is also concerned with imperfect nominals, which is understandable, since they are so close to complete sentences. He also explicitly banishes the likes of "John Smith's most unforgettable event" and, presumably, "the terrible thing that hap-

---

4. Ibid. See also Jaegwon Kim, "Causation, Nomic Subsumption, and the Concept of an Event", p. 333.

pened to the *Titanic*" and "the naughty thing that Tom did at the picnic". Now, what about sentence nominals that have derived nominals at their core? What about "the loss of the *Titanic*" and "Mary's theft of the bicycle" and "Brutus's assassination of Caesar"? In ignoring these, Kim is staying silent about the vast majority of event names that occur in ordinary speech and thought. So we cannot be sure that he is pitching camp entirely on the "facts" territory. Still, there is no denying that, when Kim refers to "events" through phrases derived from sentences, the phrases are virtually always imperfect nominals.

Here again Kim tries to win us over to his semantics for "events" by appealing to our intuitions:

> It is not at all absurd to say that Brutus's killing Caesar is *not the same as* Brutus's stabbing Caesar. Further, to explain Brutus's killing Caesar (why Brutus killed Caesar) is not the same as to explain Brutus's stabbing Caesar (why Brutus stabbed Caesar).[5]

Davidson's comment on that is worth pondering:

> I turn . . . to Kim's remark that it is not absurd to say that Brutus's killing Caesar is not the same as Brutus's stabbing Caesar. The plausibility of this is due, I think, to the undisputed fact that not all stabbings are killings. . . . But [this does not show] that this particular stabbing was not a killing. Brutus's stabbing of Caesar did result in Caesar's death; so it was in fact, though not of course necessarily, identical with Brutus's killing of Caesar.[6]

Presumably Kim had that in mind when, writing later about what he took to be the many agreements between his views on events and Davidson's, he admitted:

> True enough, Davidson and I disagree about particular cases of individuation of events; for example, whether Brutus's stabbing Caesar is the same as Brutus's killing Caesar. (p. 167)

Notice the switch from Kim's imperfect nominals to Davidson's perfect ones, followed by Kim's switch back again. Neither of these writers, nor anyone else until now, seems to have noticed this click-click change of terminology that enables Kim to say true things about facts and Davidson to counter by saying true things about events.

If that is not obvious, it may be because of two special features of the stabbing/killing example. One is that it involves perfect *gerundial* nominals such as "Brutus's killing of Caesar", which are more slippery than derived nominals. The other is that there is a prima facie reason,

---

5. Jaegwon Kim, "On the Psycho-Physical Identity Theory", p. 232n.

6. Donald Davidson, "The Individuation of Events", p. 171.

apart from Kim's semantics, for questioning whether the stabbing is a killing—namely that the stabbing is confined to the time when the knife moves, whereas the killing may seem to extend forward to the time of the death. This second point raises issues that I shall discuss in Chapter XII.

In my next section, I shall offer an analogous example that has neither of those special features, showing how to construct indefinitely many counterexamples to Kim's semantics of event names. Then I shall consider Kim's options in trying to defend his theory against these counterexamples, and I will conclude that there is no escape and that all the energy and persuasiveness of Kim's view comes from its being applied only to fact names and not to event names.

32. *The intuitive data about event identity*

Kim holds—to put it in shorthand—that $[S,P_1,T]$ names the same event as $[S,P_2,T]$ only if the property picked out by P_1 is the property picked out by P_2. This is radically at variance with how our actual event concept works. I have mildly argued for this, suggesting that Kim wouldn't believe it either if he had distinguished events from facts, but now I shall push the argument further.

Naked event identity statements are not prominent in everyday talk about events, so that it is hard to check Kim's thesis against our sense of what careful speakers would be apt to say of the form "e_1 is [not] e_2". There are simply not enough data of that kind. As I pointed out in Section 4, however, we have another resource, because we can derive an identity statement from premises involving predication and counting, which do occur a lot in ordinary speech and thought. Abstractly, it goes like this: if we can establish that something is F (pred) and that at most one thing is F (count), that entitles us to the name "the F"; repeat for G and we have "the G"; then we need only to know that *The F is G* (pred) to be able to infer that *The F is the G*, which is an identity statement.

Here it is again, with an example. Bertram assaulted Candice by kicking her on the kneecap. He did it only once, so that our normal answer to "How many kicks did he give her?", as to "How many assaults did he make on her?", would be "One". So we have a couple of event names: "the kick that Bertram gave Candice" and "the assault that Bertram made on Candice". Now, if Bertram said that his kick was only a joke, Candice might reply, "That kick wasn't a joke—it was an assault!" So there was one kick and one assault, and the kick was an assault, from which it follows that *the kick was the assault*. Thus we get a naked event identity statement, offered not as a likely slice of conversational life but rather as entailed by predications on events and counts of events that *obviously* could be true. On the other hand, kicking is not the same as assaulting, so Bertram's kicking Candice is not the same as his assaulting her; in short, the fact-distinguishing statements that Kim offers are also *obviously* true.

If Kim is to resist, he must either deny that Bertram gave Candice a kick that was an assault or deny that he gave her only one kick. He takes the latter course: he accepts the intuitive predications, but rejects the intuitive countings. His treatment of predication on events also needs to be examined, however, and I shall take it first.

33. *Constitution and character*

Suppose that at noon David kisses Eva just once, doing it tenderly, on her cheek. According to Kim's semantics, the following name three events:

(a) the tender kiss that David gave Eva at noon
(b) the kiss that David planted on Eva's cheek at noon
(c) the tender kiss that David planted on Eva's cheek at noon.

Each has the form [(David,Eva), P, noon] with different values of P—"kissed tenderly", "kissed on the cheek", "kissed tenderly on the cheek"—and because the P's are different the named events are different. Now, let us ask whether event (b) was tender—we could as well have asked whether (a) was planted on Eva's cheek.

If Kim said No, it would have to be on the grounds that the only predicates that are applicable to an event are ones that are logically included in the subject term. That would lead to some rebarbative conclusions, which are perhaps all versions of the same thing. (i) There are no contingently true monadic predications on properly named events. (ii) Many of our plainest and (we had thought) safest statements are literally false and can be rescued only by reinterpretation: their rejection of him was cruel; the next breaker will be bigger; the clambake was enjoyable. (iii) The kiss that David gave Eva was not planted on any part of her; a walk might be at no specific speed; a climb might be neither vigorous nor gentle nor middling; a surgical operation might be neither skilful nor clumsy and not directed to any particular part of the body.

This would be all right if our topic were facts. The fact that David kisses Eva is not, for any x, the fact that he kissed her on x; the fact that someone walked is not, for any n, the fact that he walks at n miles per hour; the fact that the surgeon operated is not, for any adverb, the fact that he operated adverbly. And we can comfortably accept that when a fact is referred to by an imperfect nominal, whether gerundial or that-P, the name that is used expresses its whole intrinsic nature: "the fact that David kissed Eva" names a fact about which the whole intrinsic truth is that it is the fact that David kissed Eva; there is nothing more that could be said about it, except about relations in which it stands—who knows it, what it caused, and so on. So, if a fact is named through an imperfect nominal, there cannot be a true contingent statement about its intrinsic nature.

Kim's ostensible topic is events, however, and he says that the events he is talking about are "particulars". Leibniz to the contrary, there cannot be a particular that can be referred to only by an expression that conveys its whole intrinsic nature, i.e. that cannot be the subject of true contingent monadic predications. So Kim has to answer Yes, (b) was tender, and (a) was planted on Eva's cheek, and, more generally, an event name need not involve all the attributes of the named event. That is just what he does say: he allows that (a) and (b) have many characteristics that can be read off from the facts about how and in what circumstances David kissed Eva on that one occasion. In short, (b) the kiss David planted on Eva's cheek is not (c) the tender kiss that David planted on Eva's cheek, although (b) is also tender. What is going on here?

Well, Kim distinguishes the property that constitutes a given event (its *constitution*) from those properties that it merely has (its *character*, as I shall say):

> Events themselves have (exemplify) properties; Brutus's stabbing Caesar has the property of occurring in Rome, it was intentional, it led to the death of Caesar and caused grief in Calpurnia, and so on. . . . The properties an event exemplifies must be sharply distinguished from its constitutive property (which is exemplified, not by an event, but by the constitutive substance of the event). . . . Events can be redescribed by the use of different predicates expressing the properties of (exemplified by) them; what cannot be done is to redescribe them by tampering with their constitutive properties. (p. 170)

Notice the technical point: an event's constitutive property is possessed not by it but by its constitutive substance. For example, the supposed event named by "David's tenderly kissing Eva" has in its constitution not *being a tender kiss* (a property of events) but rather *kissing tenderly* (a relation between people).

I think that Kim holds that any property in an event's constitution generates a corresponding property in its character: an event that has *walking* in its constitution will have *being a walk* in its character. (The alternative is to say that the constitution of an event corresponds to a blank in its character, so that the constitutionally tender kiss that David gave Eva was not tender and was not a kiss.) So we get the result that, although only two of our events have kissing tenderly in their constitutions, all three have tenderness in their characters. Quite generally, the picture is of a lot of events occurring at the same zone, all with the same character and differentiated from one another only by differences in which part of the shared character corresponds to something in the constitution.[7]

Stated thus abstractly, this is a tenable position, free of error and absurdity,[8] but there is nothing to attract us to it unless we are told more about how character differs from constitution. So far, we have been told only that (i) two events that coincide in space-time and have the same character are two because their constitutions are different, and that (ii) what determines whether a given event name picks out a given event is how it relates to the event's constitution, and the rest of the event's character has nothing to do with it. That doesn't tell us what a constitution is, only what it does.

Recall, however, that Kim's denials of event-identity partly rest on what he takes to be facts about causal statements, e.g. the supposed fact that "The collapse was caused, not by the bolt's giving way, but by the bolt's giving way so suddenly" could be true. Let us take another example (I'll give it with imperfect nominals, in Kim's fashion, switching to perfect nominals when I have to): "What got him down was not (so much) her refusing him but (more) her refusing him rudely." Kim takes this to mean that his depression was caused by her refusing him rudely, and not by her refusing him, which implies that these are two events, not one. But now we know that these two events differ only in their constitutions, not in their characters: *the refusal that did not get him down (so much) was just as rude as the other*, but it lacked the other's depressive powers because rudeness was not in its constitution. So, if someone asks, "Why did her refusal of him get him so depressed?", we cannot truly answer, "Because it was rude". Presumably even the question, "Why did her rude refusal of him get him so depressed?" should be answered not by saying, "Because it was rude", but rather, "Because it was constitutionally rude".

In a nutshell: differences of constitution *and they alone* create differences in respect of causal power. This puts flesh on the bones of

---

7. I am here confining the characters to the nonmodal properties; Kim might have room to distinguish the events in terms of which counterfactuals are true of them. I don't know whether he would, though. He denies that constitutions are essences.

8. On this matter I disagree with Bernard D. Katz, "Kim on Events", pp. 430–32 and 438f.

the term "constitution": it tells us that an event's constitution is the repository of all its causally effective attributes. That, however, should make us suspicious. All the popular theories of event causation, including the one Kim endorses, agree with clamorous common sense that the causal powers of any event depend upon what it is like, what properties it has, what its character is. Yet that is what Kim must deny.[9]

This is yet another trouble that evaporates if Kim's topic is facts. For then, instead of having many events with different constitutions and the same character, we have a multiplicity of facts about a single event, and the causal statements that interest us say how one fact causally explains another. Her being tired is explained by (or is a consequence of) her sprinting homewards but not by her going homewards; there is nothing paradoxical about that.

Of course Kim is right to say that (a) is on Eva's cheek and (b) is tender; I am not denying that. Rather, I am pointing out the great price he has to pay for this bit of "normality" in his position.

34. *Cardinality*

Kim's views about counting under event sortals are fiercely at variance with what people ordinarily say about how many events of a given kind occurred at a given zone. If Bertram kicked Candice only once, most of us will infer that he gave her only one kick, but Kim must say that he gave her many—his clumsy kick, his hard kick, his kick on her shin, and so on. Similarly with the kisses. Kim's denials of identity force him to say that there were many kisses between David and Eva at that moment.

Kim defends this by saying that there was a single kiss that had all these others as parts, and that when we say say, "David gave Eva only one kiss" and thereby express something true, this is because we mean that he gave her only one maximal kiss, only one that was not part of any larger kiss. (pp. 170f)

He notes that reputable philosophers have said similar things in other areas, especially this:

> If the desk on which I am writing lost a few molecules, there would still be a desk in my room; that desk is presumably here now; but it is not the largest desk in the room, because it contains fewer molecules. So there are now hundreds of desks in my study—one maximal desk and all the others parts of it.

9. This point is made against Kim by Alexander Rosenberg, "On Kim's Account of Events and Event-Identity".

Without endorsing this, Kim rightly says that philosophers have been led to it by sober reflection on familiar facts, and he wants this to make us patient with his view that although David kissed Eva only once there were many submaximal kisses between them.

If Kim is merely reminding us that some respectable philosophical theories imply strange things about how many Fs there are, I have no comment to offer. I think he means more, though, and offers the line of thought about desks as an illuminating analogue of his view about the kisses. If so, I disagree.

The line of thought about desks has this genuine analogue for events:

> When David kissed Eva, the kiss could have lasted a hundredth of a second less long and it would still have been a kiss, or a fiftieth of a second etc.; so there were many kisses going from David to Eva—the temporally maximal one and a lot of briefer kisses, its temporal parts.

That parallels the thesis about the desks: in each case an item that is *maximal in extent* has others of the same kind as *less extensive parts.* But Kim is adding that each of these temporally distinguished kisses is itself really a number of kisses—a *qualitatively maximal* one and its many *qualitatively less rich parts.* His thesis, then, far outruns any legitimate analogy with the line of thought about desks.

Furthermore, that comparison helps us to see that the language of "part" and "whole" really has no place here. Events have extensive magnitude: they are spread out in space and time, and so they can have spatiotemporal parts. Kim wants to credit them with parts that are not smaller or briefer but qualitatively thinner than they are: *a passionate kiss that David gave Eva* is supposed to have *a kiss that David gave Eva* as a part. This misuses the language of part and whole as applied to extended items such as chairs and kisses. It is as wrong as it would be to say that the largest brown desk in my study has the largest desk in my study as a part.

It would be legitimate, however, if the topic were facts. The fact that David kissed Eva passionately has as a part the fact that David kissed Eva, and this part is not less extensive than the whole but rather is less rich, less detailed, more abstract. Said with gerundial nominals, it still passes muster: David's kissing Eva passionately has his kissing her as a part.

35. *What sorts of facts are Kim's "events"?*

In certain ways, Kim's "events" behave like super-Russellian facts. Recall that, highlighting aside, if two sentences express the same fact they are interderivable either (i) *a priori* or (ii) by substitution of coreferring Russellian names. This is not quite true of Kim's S-P-T constructions, on his account of them. He clearly treats the S and T positions in a Russellian way, and usually he treats the P position as Russellian also.[10] This gives a Russellian treatment to items that are not referring expressions at all—for example, to the words "blue" and "yesterday" in "my favorite garment's turning blue yesterday". This, according to Kim, could name the same "event" as "my only silk shirt's acquiring the color of sapphires on the day of the hailstorm". This detracts a little from the suggestion that Kim's theory of "events" goes best when seen as a theory about facts, because now the items in question seem to have a "coarseness" that far outruns that of Russellian facts as ordinarily understood. It doesn't detract much, however, because this super-Russellian aspect of Kim's theory is not well motivated, even by his own lights, as I now explain.

Given that Kim wants his "events" to be relata of an explanatory relation, one might think that he would make them wholly Fregean[11] or at least explain why, when, and how they can be Russellian in respect of this or that contained name, e.g. by calling attention to the noun-infinitive form. That is not what happens.

On the contrary, he presents the case for saying that explanations need Fregean rather than Russellian items as relata, remarking that what explains the fact that Socrates died may not (equally well) explain the fact that Xantippe's husband died, because it may omit the information that Socrates is Xantippe's husband. But rather than concluding that "Socrates' dying" and "Xantippe's husband's dying" name different events (so-called), Kim comments

> These are unacceptable results; if any useful meaning is to be attached to the talk of a statement's describing an event or phenomenon, it seems clear that one and the same event is described by "Socrates died" and "Xantippe's husband died". Not only is this intuitively correct but no useful theoretical purpose seems to be served by denying it. . . . (p. 202)

On the contrary, the theoretical purpose has just been exhibited! It is the purpose of making the names figure transparently in explanations, so that an explanation will not suffer if one expression is replaced by another that has the same referent. This reason for not giving a Russellian treatment to the S component in an "event"-name applies with

---

10. Kim has his own way of distinguishing his "events" from V-facts and thus of preventing them from melting into one. See his "Events and their Descriptions", pp. 208ff.

11. As Davidson remarks in "The Individuation of Events", p. 171.

equal or greater strength to the P and T components.[12]

As for the remark about what is "intuitively" plausible: if Kim expressed that not in terms of what is "described" by a pair of sentences, but rather in the material mode—"It is intuitively correct to say that Socrates' dying is the same as Xantippe's husband's dying"—he would see that intuition does not clearly go his way. Of course Socrates' death is the death of Xantippe's husband; but that is a truth about a genuine event, properly so called, and not one of the factlike items to which Kim nearly always addresses himself.

So much for the Russellian aspect of Kim's "events". In another way, however, they are even more delicate—even less able to survive substitutions—than are perfectly Fregean facts. In effect, they behave in some respects like highlighted facts, and Kim's justification for this connects with highlighting or something like it.

Highlighting aside, if P is *a priori* interderivable with Q, then f_P is f_Q, but that is not sufficient for the identity of Kim's "events". Suppose that "incestuous" and "close relative" have meanings such that necessarily a marriage is incestuous if and only if the parties to it are close relatives of one another. Then consider these:

Oedipus's and his close relative Jocasta's marrying one another;
Oedipus's and Jocasta's incestuously marrying one another;

with the same temporal adverb tacked onto each.[13] These have the same informational content, so they name the same unhighlighted fact; but Kim must say that they name distinct events, because the relations connoted by the verb phrases are different: in one it is *marrying one another*, while in the other it is *incestuously marrying one another*. The difference is just that some information expressed in the S part of one name is expressed in the P part of the other.

Kim points out[14] that there is a motivation for distinguishing logically equivalent facts that have, like the above two, different "structures". He contrasts these two:

Reagan, who is the 40th president, is Nancy's husband
Reagan, who is Nancy's husband, is the 40th president,

---

12. Kim writes to me: "What you say here is right only if we view explanations as logical inferences involving sentences, and not consider what these sentences are about. I would say, contra you, that whatever explains why Socrates died also explains why Xantippe's husband died, why Plato's teacher died, etc. For these are the same fact (or event, in my parlance)."

13. The example comes from Alexander Rosenberg, *op. cit.*, p. 330. Rosenberg's specific purposes are different from mine, but our general thrusts are the same.

14. In his "Events and their Descriptions" and in a personal communication.

and points out that one might explain either of these without explaining the other. I agree, and I would put this in the same general category as the phenomena of highlighting: a certain content is presented, with some of it tagged differently from the rest, creating a difference between foreground and background, so to speak.

In making his "events" super-Russellian in some ways and super-Fregean in others, Kim is responding sensitively to a wide range of linguistic data to which my discussion has not done justice. But these complexities do not alter my view, for which I think I have made a good case, that Kim's theory of "events" is at its best when understood as a theory of facts.

Kim might be disagreeing with that here:

> My events are "particulars" and "dated". That they are dated is obvious. I am not clear what "particulars" are; but events in my sense have locations in space, namely the locations of their constitutive substances. . . . And my events are not "eternal" objects; they do not exist in all possible worlds; they exist only if the existence condition is met, which is a contingent matter of fact. If this doesn't show that something is "concrete" or "particular", what does?[15]

This could be a reply to the charge that Kim's so-called "events" are facts, because it seems wrong to suppose that facts are concrete, are particulars, are located, and so on. Let us look more closely.

(i) Facts are not "eternal" objects and do not exist at all possible worlds. At a world where bananas are purple, there is no such thing as the fact that bananas are yellow.

(ii) Since facts are not *universal* as properties are, they are *particular* (adjective) in the most basic sense of that word. In Kim's remarks, some other sense seems to be at work, a sense in which something's being a particular (noun) is tied to its being located. Let us turn to that.

(iii) Although facts don't occupy spatiotemporal zones, they can be uniquely associated with zones. Each of Kim's S-P-T items may be a fact *about* the zone delimited by S-T. Kim may say that his "events" are not merely about zones but are *in* them—are *in* places *at* times—but he has not laid any basis for saying this. If he tried to make good on it through examples, expressing himself (as he nearly always does) through imperfect nominals, he would have to say things like: "Brutus's killing Caesar occurred at the Capitol on the Ides of March"—and that, since it is strange and possibly defective English, is no basis for an intuitively compelling argument.

15. Jaegwon Kim, "Events as Property Exemplifications", p. 165. See also a remark by Alvin Goldman, quoted in Hector-Neri Castañeda, "Intensionality and Identity in Human Action", p. 237.

(iv) I don't know whether Kim intends "concrete" to add anything to "particular". If he doesn't, then I have nothing to add either. If he does, then I need to know *what* he means by "concrete". I shall be using it soon in its true, best sense.

VI

THE TRUE METAPHYSICS OF EVENTS

36. *What are events?*

According to Kim, an event is the instantiation, at a time, of a property by a substance, or of a relation by a pair of substances, or . . . etc. That is not to say that every such instantiation is an event; Kim thinks that many are not, though he avowedly has no firm doctrine on how to draw the line.

This way of looking at events is reminiscent of what Aristotle says about changes:

> There are three classes of things in connection with which we speak of change: the "that which", the "that in respect of which", and the "that during which". I mean that there must be something that changes, e.g. a man or gold, and it must change in respect of something, e.g. its place or some property, and during something, for all change takes place during a time. Of these three it is that in respect of which the change takes place that makes it one generically or specifically, it is the thing changed that makes the change one in subject, and it is the time that makes it consecutive: but it is the three together that make it one without qualification.[1]

Kim and Aristotle emphasize the thing that is the subject of the event, but no harm would be done by dropping that emphasis. Instead of saying that an event is the instantiation of a property *by a thing at a time*, we can say that an event is the instantiation of a property *at a zone*. The zone will often be delimited by a substance and a time, but perhaps not always.[2]

---

1. Aristotle, *Physics* Book V, Chapter 4 (227b21ff).

2. I hold that in each case a property is instantiated *by the zone*. It is often more natural to speak of it as instantiated *by something in the zone*, but I believe that wherever a space-occupying thing x has property P at time T, that is because at a deeper metaphysical level the zone defined by x and T has a corresponding property P*. That opinion is developed in my *A Study of Spinoza's Ethics* (Hackett: Indianapolis, 1984), Sections 22, 25, and will be touched upon in Section 47 below.

(Some philosophers think that a zone could be completely occupied by a mass of gold and a coin, these being distinct from one another; and there are reasons for this. This threatens trouble with my move from substance-at-time to zone, but it may not be serious. Consider: some properties must be had by both coin and gold or by neither (e.g. melting, falling); some can be had by the coin but not by the mass of gold (being squashed out of shape); perhaps there are some that could be had by the gold but could not be had by the coin. Those are all harmless. If I am in trouble, it is because there is a property that could be had by both the coin and the gold but could be had by one while the other lacked it. The instantiation of that property at a zone would be ambiguous as between an event with the coin as subject and an event with the gold as subject. If there are any such properties, which I doubt, I must either shift from "zone" back to "thing at time" or deny—as I am inclined to anyway—that there are two things at that zone. Perhaps there is only one thing, a portion of coin-shaped gold, and statements about "the coin" should strictly speaking be rephrased—e.g. "This coin came into being yesterday" really means "This gold became coin-shaped yesterday and has remained so ever since".)

Don't build the time into the property. If an event were S's having the property P-at-T, then the event would exist from S's beginning, or at least from T, through to the end of S's existence. For example, Watteau's first journey to Paris existed or occurred in 1702 and only then, but Watteau had the property goes-first-to-Paris-in-1702 all his life, or at least from 1702 onwards. So the event is not the instantiation of a dated property, but rather a dated instantiation of a property—Watteau's instantiation in 1702 of the property goes-to-Paris.[3] There are many instantiations of that property, and several of them were Watteau's; the one we are talking about is the one of his that occurred in 1702.

These instantiations are particulars. There is another theory of events, devised by Chisholm, according to which events are universals. Chisholm takes as his starting point such locutions as "She swam a mile yesterday, and she did it again today"; wanting to construe them literally, he supposes that the "it" refers to some item that the woman did both yesterday and today, and it seems that the item has to be a universal event or action, one that can occur or be performed more than once.[4] Provocative and interesting as this is, I must pass it

3. For warnings against the wrong readings of Kim and scepticism about the right one, see Judith Jarvis Thomson, *Acts and Other Events*, pp. 105f, 113f.

4. For defenses of this theory and criticisms of it, see in order: Roderick Chisholm, "Events and Propositions"; Donald Davidson, "Events as Particulars"; Chisholm, "States of Affairs Again"; Davidson, "Eternal vs. Ephemeral Events"; Major L. Johnson, "Events as Recurrables".

by as needing too much space to discuss properly. It is clear, anyway, that doctrine about these recurring items does not challenge, even prima facie, the idea that there are nonrecurring events.

A phrase of the form "the instantiation of P by S at T" might refer to the fact that P is instantiated by S at T. Kim sometimes seems to construe it like that: I have shown that what he says about the semantics of "event" names fares best if his "events" are taken to be facts. Now set semantics aside, and look just at the statement that an event is the instantiation of a property at a time. We can reasonably interpret this as meaning something that is true—not about facts but about events. We get that pleasing result if we interpret Kim as meaning that each event is an *instance* of a property, or what Donald Williams has called a "trope".[5] The fall that stone S underwent at time T is not the fact that S falls at T, but rather one particular instance—namely the by-S-at-T instance—of the property *falling*. If we combine this with the move from substances-at-times to zones, then the event is the instance of the property that occurred at a certain zone. (I help myself to the notion of a property, assuming that it excludes all the pathological "sayables" such as grueness and bleenness. How that exclusion is to be effected is a problem for all of us and is not special to the metaphysics of events. I can throw no light upon it.)

I used to object to the notion of a quality instance or trope, along these lines: "This stone is a particular substance; its shape is a universal property, flatness. The friends of tropes are trying to introduce a third item that is particular rather than universal but is a property rather than a substance, namely the flatness of this stone. This is a gratuitous, pointless addition." Some friends of tropes would reject this protest on the grounds that they base their metaphysic on tropes and then develop the notion of particular substances out of them. In a metaphysical scheme such as that, the notion of a trope, whatever it is, is not a gratuitous *addition* to properties and substances. For my purposes, though, a shallower reponse is enough. Try the objection again, but this time taking a property that is more naturally thought of as constituting an event: "This stone is a particular substance; its way of moving is a universal property, *falling*. The friends of tropes are trying to introduce a third item that is particular rather than universal, but is a property rather than a substance, namely the fall of this stone. . . ."—at which point the objection peters out. One cannot confidently continue ". . . and this is a gratuitous, pointless addition". An enemy of tropes must either oppose events as well, contending that there are no such things, or find a good rival account of what events are.

The only considerable rival is the thesis that each event is a

5. For references, see the first footnote in Section 6 above.

triple, a class whose members are a substance, a property, and a time. When Kim mentions this as a possibility, he does not ponder it at anxious length, as one might expect him to do with a rival to the view that events are tropes.[6] That is because he does not see it as radically alternative to his own theory, but rather as a different "line" along which "the theory can easily be developed".[7] There seems to be no underlying theory that could be "developed" along either of two "lines" depending on whether events are said to be tropes or triples. In fact the "triples" account is quite different from and much worse than the other.

One's first thought about it is is that if each member of a triple exists then so does the triple, which implies that *Mondale's election in 1984* exists because there is a triple whose members are Mondale, getting-elected, and 1984. Kim meets this easily: he says that although in the theory under consideration each S-P-T event is a triple, an S-P-T triple counts as an event only if S has P at T.

Many things that one can say about events are not literally true of triples, but Kim could deal with these by reinterpretation. Triples don't occur, but Kim can say that "x occurs" means that x's first member has its second member at its third. Triples don't cause other triples, but Kim can say that "x causes y" means that x occurs because y occurs. This escape route will never run into a blank wall—a statement that defies reinterpretation—for any statement about an event must be expressible somehow in terms of the class of the event's constituents, and it can always be maintained that the vulgar say one while the learned think the other.

That might be legitimate if the "triple" theory had enough merits or if the rival notion of a trope or property instance were indefensible. But that is not how things stand, and it is a defect in the "triples" approach that it has to rewrite so much of what we ordinarily say about events. Above all, the statement that *events occur in space-time* seems to be a rock-bottom truth that a good metaphysic should imply to be strictly and literally true, but, if events are triples, this too comes out as false except on some contrived reading under which "the location of {S,P,T}" is understood to refer to the zone delimited by S and T. (Or the locations come out wrong. If a class has a place, it must be the sum of its members' places; try on that basis to locate F.D. Roosevelt's declaration of war against Japan in the same part of space-time as the

6. This point is made by R.M. Martin, "Events and Actions: Comments on Brand and Kim", pp. 188f.

7. Jaegwon Kim, "Events as Property Exemplifications", p. 161. At one stage, Goldman thought that this *was* the theory. In "The Individuation of Actions", p. 773, he wrote: "Our account reduces act tokens to persons, act properties, and times."

triple whose members are FDR, the property of declaring war, and December 7, 1941!) We should not submit to this when we can escape it through the theory that events are tropes. When we assign a zone to a trope we are not making something up to save a theory: it is strictly and literally true—who could doubt it?—that when a sparrow falls that instance of *falling* exists at the zone at which the sparrow falls.[8]

Leibniz took events to be tropes and attributed the view to Locke also, with some reason. Locke wrote this:

> Substances alone of all our ideas have particular or proper names, whereby only one particular thing is signified. Because in simple ideas, modes and relations it seldom happens that men have occasion to mention often this or that particular, when it is absent. Besides the greatest part of mixed modes, being actions that perish in their birth, are not capable of a lasting duration, as substances that are the actors.[9]

Leibniz evidently took the "modes" that Locke equates with "actions that perish in their birth" to be tropes, which he called accidental individuals or (more often) individual accidents. Here is what he writes in the corresponding part of the *New Essays:*

> *Locke's spokesman:* Of all our various ideas, only the ideas of substances have proper, i.e. individual, names. For it seldom happens that men need to make frequent references to any individual quality or to some other accidental individual. Furthermore, individual actions perish straight away, and the concatenations of states of affairs that occur in them do not persist as in substances.
> *Leibniz's spokesman:* In certain cases, though, there has been a need to remember an individual accident, and it has been given a name. . . . For example, the birth of Jesus Christ, the memory of which we celebrate every year; the Greeks called this event [*evenement*] "Theogony", and gave the name "Epiphany" to that of the adoration of the Magi.[10]

Quinton writes that "a trope . . . is a kind of minimal event"—minimal in the sense that it lacks "qualitative complexity", but I take the term more broadly than that. Any property instance is a trope, in my usage,

---

8. The main point in the present paragraph is made by Terence Horgan, "The Case Against Events", p. 30.

9. John Locke, *An Essay Concerning Human Understanding* III.vi.42, quoted with omissions.

10. G.W. Leibniz, *New Essays on Human Understanding*, p. 328. The concept of an individual accident does other work also in Leibniz's thought; see Kenneth C. Clatterbaugh, "Leibniz's Doctrine of Individual Accidents".

and I set no upper limit on the complexity of properties: if something could have P_1 and P_2 at the same time, then there is a property that is the conjunction, so to speak, of P_1 and P_2. So tropes can be as complex as you like. That is clearly Leibniz's position: he cites a birth and an act of adoration (and the passage of an angel) as individual accidents, and there is nothing minimal about those.

Leibniz's metaphysic of events has occurred to several recent writers in addition to Quinton. Donald Williams suggested explicitly that tropes are the items that are sometimes called "events"; and the same approach has been developed by Hugh McCann and is just beneath the surface in Kim's writings.[11] As well as having no considerable rivals, this view about what events are is hardly even controversial.

37. *The supposed link with semantics*

Kim's work on events has been much criticized, but the critics have been objecting to his semantics of event names; if they thought this put them in opposition also to his metaphysic of events, that was their mistake. I shall explain.

A single event is named by "Leibniz's coach ride on November 24, 1676", by "Leibniz's journey on November 24, 1676", and by "Leibniz's journey between Delft and The Hague". The event in question was a certain instance—namely the one that had Leibniz as its subject on November 24, 1676—of a certain complex property. It is not the property of taking a coach ride or of journeying or of journeying between Delft and the Hague, though it includes those. The metaphysical thesis that Leibniz's journey was an instance of property P has not the faintest tendency to imply the semantic thesis that any name of Leibniz's journey must contain a name of P or a predicate that connotes P. There is plenty of room for us to accept the former of those while rejecting the latter.

In discussing this, I shall speak of the property that "constitutes" a given event e, meaning the property P such that *the whole intrinsic truth about e is that it is an instance of P.*

I don't know exactly what property constitutes any event, but I shall pretend to know for one example. Suppose that e is an instance—in a certain pebble S at a time T—of the property of falling with an acceleration of 32 ft/sec^2 while rotating .68 times per second on an axis at right angles to the line of fall. I see no reason that e

11. See especially Jaegwon Kim's "Events as Property Exemplifications"; Hugh J. McCann, "Individuating Actions: the Fine-Grained Approach".

should not be named by expressions that do not name or connote that complex property—for example by "the fall that S underwent at T".[12]

Objection: "You spoke earlier of a kick that was an assault. If it was a kick, it was an instance of *kicks;* if it was an assault it was an instance of *assaults;* since the properties are different, how can you escape saying that the instances are different?" Easily! There is some property P such that the whole truth about the event under discussion is that it was an instance of P. This property is not being-a-kick or being-an-assault, but each of those is a part of it. In mildly formal terms: there are two relations Con and Has, such that for any event e there is just one property P such that Con(e,P), and every property P* such that Has(e,P*) is part of P. I mean "part of" in such a way that necessarily whatever has P has all its parts.

If the property that constitutes the event doesn't have to be named or connoted in the event name, how *does* it have to relate to the latter? If we think—as most of us do—that "Henry's anger at Iris" couldn't name the same event as "The slap that Henry gave Iris", even if the slap and the anger both occurred in Henry at the same time, there is presumably some account of why these two names cannot corefer. The explanation, I think, must come from there being a relation R between properties such that:

> If e is an event constituted by property P and exactly occupying zone z, and N names an event that exactly occupies z, and N contains a name of (or a predicate connoting) property P*, then N names e if and only if P* has relation R to P.

If R were identity, we would have Kim's semantics as well as his metaphysics. From the evident truth of Kim's metaphysics and the evident falsity of his semantics, I infer that R is weaker than identity. Just what relation it is will be considered later.[13] We don't have to answer that question, however, to know that Kim's metaphysic is consistent with more than one view about the semantics of event names. How *could* a purely metaphysical thesis about Fs, unaided, imply a semantics for names of Fs?

---

12. A similar point is made in Lawrence Brian Lombard, *Events*, pp. 54f, though he does not put it in terms of coreference of event names.

13. I here ignore external event names like "what we were just talking about", "the event that dominates my thoughts", "what Alexa did when I gave her the spoon", and "the immediate cause of the retreat". Once we understand names that do involve parts of the constitutive properties of the named events, it should be easy to extend our understanding to external event names.

38. *"Identity criteria" and circularity*

The conflation of metaphysics with semantics is responsible for most of what philosophers have written about "identity criteria" for events. There is so much about this in the literature that I cannot ignore it entirely. I shall try to clear things up a little, but I do not offer a comprehensive treatment.

Never mind interworld questions about the identity of events—that is, questions about how a particular event could have been different. That is the topic of essences, and I have done with it.

Nor am I concerned here with "diachronic" questions about identity. As applied to any kind F, those are questions about the possible shape of an F's life span. They boil down to two. For Fs that last through time, do not have temporal parts, and can alter: What changes in the world count as alterations in an ongoing F, and what count as the ending of one F and the start of another? For Fs that stretch through time, have temporal parts, and cannot alter: How must two items existing at different times be interrelated to count as parts of a single F? Since events stretch through time and have temporal parts, only the latter kind of question applies to them. In its general form—"What has to be the case for two events, occurring at different times, to count as parts of a single event?"—the question is a meagre thing that admits only of jejune answers. When "event" is replaced in it by "forest fire", "conference", "riot", and so on, there is more to be said; and I shall come to that in Section 49.

With those two matters set aside, we confront questions about "synchronic identity", which have been the main topic of the befogged literature on "identity criteria for events". When philosophers discuss "criteria of event identity", they are looking for a relation R such that:

For any event e_1 and event e_2, $R(e_1,e_2) \equiv e_1$ is e_2

is true for every e_1 and e_2. If that were the whole problem, we could let R be identity and call it a day. In fact, a further demand is usually made, especially by those who want a "criterion" in the sense of a principle that could help us to decide whether e_1 is e_2 in particular cases. Clearly the value R = identity yields a principle that could not do that. Some philosophers seem to think of "criteria" as belonging to metaphysics, not epistemology; so they do not regard "criteria of identity" as essentially helps to getting any question answered. Yet they too worry about "circularity". I suppose that when *they* say that a given "identity criterion" is "circular" they mean that it is trivial, empty, unsubstantive.

The only values for R that have been suggested are similarity relations, yielding event-identity principles of the form: If e_1 exactly resembles e_2 in respect K, then e_1 is e_2. The full principle is always a biconditional, but the other half of it—If e_1 is e_2 then e_1 exactly K-resembles e_2—can be omitted as trivially true. The former conditional gives the form of what David Lewis calls a "nonduplication principle": it says that no two events can be exactly alike in respect K.

(Notice the wording of the consequent of that schema: "e_1 is e_2". I don't say "e_1 is identical with e_2", because one is tempted to use "identical" as though it related two things, as in the absurd phrase "identity of indiscernibles". Davidson often writes like that, as when he discusses ". . . what it could mean to say that two events are one" and says that one event is "identical with another"; and in one place, to be discussed in Section 42, this seems to have led him into real error. Here is another philosopher in bad trouble from the same source: "Identical events must have the same property essences. They must, of course, share all their other properties as well. But, their sharing of those other properties in common will be . . . a matter of contingent fact only." Even the innocent "same" can make mischief. This appeared once in one of the journals: "P and Q may be the same proposition though there is a proposition R that is entailed by one of them but not by the other." Moral: don't handle identity in relational language; stick with the simple copula.)

Some years ago Davidson propounded the nonduplication principle: *No two events can be exactly alike in respect of what their causes and effects are.*[14] He has recently renounced this, but it needs to be looked at because so much of the events literature has focused on it. It has been attacked as possibly false, because it entails that at most one event has no causes and no effects, whereas really there might be many such.[15] Judith Thomson has gone further, adducing pairs of events that are obviously distinct and claiming to prove that they have the same causes and effects.[16] My present concern, however, is with the charge that Davidson's principle is "circular".

This means that we would be driven around in a circle if we used Davidson's principle as an aid to discovering which events are identical with which. That is because the principle is equivalent to this: If e_1 has exactly the same causes and effects as e_2 then e_1 is e_2. If we try to establish (1) instances of the antecedent of this, and conjoin them with (2) the principle, using modus ponens to infer (3) instances

14. Donald Davidson, "The Individuation of Events", p. 179.

15. Myles Brand, "Identity Conditions for Events", p. 332.

16. Judith Jarvis Thomson, *Acts and Other Events*, p. 70. I shall discuss this work of Thomson's in Section 62.

of the consequent, our procedure will be "circular" in the sense that we cannot achieve anything under (1) unless we already have some results under (3).

It is generally agreed that some nonduplication principles do generate circular procedures and are therefore useless. Notable among these is the one that says that if x exactly resembles y in every respect then x is y, where exact resemblance is understood to include x's sharing with y the property of being identical with y. That could not possibly help us to advance our knowledge. Baruch Brody disagrees. That supersafe conditional can be decisive in solving philosophical problems, he claims, but he does not succeed in showing this, at least where events are concerned.[17]

For a class as vast as that of *events*, any true identity conditional is bound to be conceptually or logically true. This condemns it to being circular in that its antecedent logically involves its consequent, just as every deductively valid argument is circular in that its premises implicitly contain its conclusion. If a principle is "circular" in that way, that threatens to put some limits to its utility: to the extent that *If P then Q* is logically true, so far it is plausible to say that learning that P involves learning that Q and so cannot be a means to learning that Q.[18] This fact, which is part of the enormous problem of how logically valid inferences can bring new knowledge, does not condemn all identity principles to equal uselessness; there are differences of degree. Still, when some such principles are criticized as unhelpful or "circular", this can only be in contrast with possible others that are *less* open to that charge.

Davidson has said that his "same causes and effects" conditional is not "formally" circular, because its antecedent contains no explicit identity statements. Some of his unappeased critics have replied that the circularity is implicitly there, for reasons having to do with an alleged link between quantification and identity. This seems to be a mistake, but I am unwilling to give this tangled, complex, barren issue the space that a proper discussion of it would need, so I acknowledge its existence and pass on.[19]

A better basis for the charge of circularity is one arising from

---

17. Baruch Brody, *Identity and Essence*, pp. 65–70.

18. I say "to the extent that . . ." because I follow Quine in thinking that being conceptually true is a matter of degree. W.V. Quine, "Two Dogmas of Empiricism" and "The Problem of Meaning in Linguistics", both as interpreted in Jonathan Bennett, "Analytic-Synthetic".

19. For references and discussion, see Lawrence Brian Lombard, *Events*, pp. 41–48; Myles Brand, "Identity Conditions for Events", p. 332.

something I said in Section 4 above. The principle could be useful only to someone who was competent in determining whether or not its antecedent is true in a given case. That involves, among other things, competence in making judgments of the form "$C(x,e_1)$ & not-$(C(x,e_2))$; and every such judgment is a double predication of the kind that involves the concept of identity. If we need a crutch to help us think about event identity, then how can we know that some event x caused e_1 and that *that same event* x did not cause e_2?

Although Davidson thinks that all causes and effects are events, the accusation of circularity does not depend on that. Just so long as the causes and effects of any given event include some events, we would be caught in a circular procedure if we tried to use Davidson's principle as our *initial* fingerhold on event identities.

That trouble would disappear if no causes and effects were events, just as there is no circularity in the standard principle for identity for classes whose members are not themselves classes: *If x's members are exactly y's members, then x is y.* This is all right, because it introduces the identity of classes in terms of the identity of class-members. But since Davidson and his critics think that the causes and effects of events are themselves events, the causal identity principle is comparable rather with this definition of class identity: *If x's subclasses are exactly y's subclasses, then x is y.* Considered as a definition or explanation of class identity, this is objectionably circular, because it explains class identity in terms that presuppose class identity, namely the identity of the subclasses that are quantified over in the definiens.[20] (The apparent health of set theories in which every class-member is also a class is a problem for customary ideas about circularity; but I shall not explore it.)

There need be no circularity if we look to Davidson's conditional for help, not in getting our first grip on any event identities, but only in moving from some that are already secured to others that have been in doubt. The situation might be like this:

> We are in the clear about many event identities, but stubborn pockets of difficulty persist. We can mop up some of these with help from causal nonduplication principle, because sometimes we know that e_1's causes and effects coincide with e_2's even though we are—or would be if we didn't have the principle—unsure whether e_1 is e_2.

In that case the use of the principle would be innocent, but I cannot see that any of our problems about event identity are so shaped that the principle can help us in that way.

---

20. See N.L. Wilson, "Facts, Events and Their Identity Conditions", pp. 303f.

39. *What is a criterion of identity?*

Having done my dutiful best by the circularity issue, I must now admit that the very terms of the debate are suspect. We are supposed to have a problem about "the identity of Fs" that a nonduplication principle might help us to solve, but what sort of problem can this be?

Consider the following two situations. (1) You and I are at an auction where, for the past hour, we have been having a bad time. I whisper to you, "One bullet would fix the situation! The man who has been bidding against me for the past hour is the one whose pipe smoke has been annoying you", and you reply that you don't agree. (2) Someone says to two philosophers: "Consider a situation in which Marcel shouts across a crevasse to Jeanne 'Are you all right?' and she shouts back 'Yes!' Was her response the same event as her shout, or a different one?" One philosopher says, "The same—the response *was* the shout", and the other says, "I don't agree".

In each case, two people give different truth values to an identity statement, but the two cases are enormously unalike. For one thing, in (1) the disagreement is local, giving no basis for predicting whether or how we might disagree about other identities, whereas in (2) there is a tiny fragment of a global disagreement—the philosopher who identifies Jeanne's response with her shout will also identify Marcel's inquiry with his shout, while the other won't, and so on, endlessly.

It is plain what the source of that difference is. It is that in (1) the disagreement is empirical and could be settled by careful and lucky observation, whereas the disagreement in (2) is conceptual or semantic. The disputants in (2) base their opinions on the slim evidence provided by the statement of the example; their disagreement still stands even if the example is purely fictional; they could not be brought to agree by observing the episode on the mountain.

Even in case (1), of course, it will be relevant that two men can't fully occupy the same region of space at the same time; so one might say that a principle of identity is at work here too. Sometimes, indeed, a local empirical identity question might be answered with the overt, explicit help of such a principle. It might happen that I know that John and Henry are both playing football this afternoon, but not whether they are playing in the same game; I then discover whether they are playing at the same time on the same field, invoke the identity principle that *if game* x *is played on the same field at the same time as game* y *then* x *is* y, and infer whether they are playing in the same game. But that identity principle doesn't hold for all games, let alone for all events. It is not at all like what philosophers have tried to offer for events generally.

What, then, have they been after? They have not been concerned with local questions such as: "You heard a thunderclap, and so did I; I wonder if it was the same one?" but rather with some global problem about event identity. I introduced it as the question of "which events are identical with which", but that is rubbish. If it means "Which events are identical with themselves?" the answer is too easy, as also if it means "Which events are identical with something else?"

Look again at the example I numbered (2). The crucial point about it is that it involves a disagreement about the coreference of event names, or about how much of the world is picked out by event names of the form "The . . . that x gave (uttered, produced, did, underwent, etc.) at T". Differing opinions about that produce differing opinions about whether "The shout that Jeanne uttered at T" refers to the same event as does "The response that Jeanne uttered at T". As that implies, any statement of F-identity will stand or fall with a corresponding statement about coreference of event-names. For example, the game John is playing in is the game Henry is playing in if and only if the names "the game John is playing in" and "the game Henry is playing in" refer to the same game. Although the two are tightly linked, however, they do not mean the same (the latter is about names whereas the former is not), and they cater to two different intellectual needs: the need of someone who has a question about the nonlinguistic world and uses linguistic means to express it, and the need of someone who has a question about how words relate to the world. Discussions of "event identity" in the literature are either (i) semantic discussions of coreference of event names or (ii) metaphysical discussions of nonduplication principles or (iii) a confused mixture of those two.

40. *Two possible answers*

It is important to see how different (i) and (ii) are and how wrong it is to jumble them together. So far, only two determinate nonduplication principles for events have been offered. One of them is Quine's thesis, to be discussed shortly, that two events cannot have the same position in space-time. We shall see that this does encourage a certain view about the coreference of event names, but that is a freak, an idiosyncrasy, and not evidence of some general alignment between nonduplication principles and semantic theses.

The only other clear nonduplication principle that has been offered is Davidson's, according to which two events cannot have the same position in the causal network. That does not naturally lead to any semantic conclusions, which is why disputants about coreference of event names can agree—as many do—in accepting Davidson's causal principle; differences of attitude to it cannot affect their semantic disagreement. The causal identity principle is thus a wheel that turns whatever the semantic wheels are doing: it could be accepted by all the semantically quarrelling parties without bringing peace any nearer.[21]

Coming at the matter from the other side, there have been just two determinate views about the coreference of event names: Kim's and a Quinean one that I shall discuss shortly. The latter, as I have said, happens to get support from Quine's nonduplication principle, but Kim's rival view is not supported by any underlying metaphysic.

If we want a nonduplication principle that implies Kim's thesis about the coreference of event names, it will have to be this:

> If the substance(s), property or relation, and time that constitute e_1 are the substance(s), property or relation, and time that constitute e_2, then e_1 is e_2,

or, edging over a little in the direction I prefer:

> If the property-zone pair that constitutes e_1 is the property-zone pair that constitutes e_2, then e_1 is e_2.

That is not all that we need, but it is bad enough. This supposed nonduplication principle involves the technical notion of *constituting*, which has to be explained; and Kim's explanations have the effect of turning the supposed nonduplication principle into a thesis about coreference of event names—the one way we are given of determining what the constituents are of a given event is by reading them off from one of its canonical names. Thus, where we were looking for a nonduplication principle that might lead us to semantic conclusions, we find only a semantic thesis that does all the work unaided.

In separating nonduplication principles from issues about coreference of event names, I am not attacking either. Davidson's causal principle, for example, might be a significant metaphysical thesis, none the worse for not hooking up with semantics. Perhaps I should add, though, that so far nobody has done anything interesting with it, apart from Brand's and Thomson's attempts to show that it is false. It is not put to work even in Davidson's famous argument that every mental event is a physical event. The argument has the premises "Every cause of a physical event is a physical event" and "Every mental event is a cause of a physical event". Those entail the desired conclusion, without help from the causal nonduplication principle.

A final word: There is more to metaphysics than nonduplication principles. The metaphysical view about events that is accepted by

---

21. This has been noted by Monroe C. Beardsley, "Actions and Events", pp. 270f. See also Jaegwon Kim, "Events as Property Exemplifications", p. 164.

Leibniz and me, and perhaps by Locke and Kim, namely that events are tropes, yields no nonduplication principle except this trivial one: If the trope T_1 such that e_1 is T_1 is the trope T_2 such that e_2 is T_2 then e_1 is e_2. This is resplendently true, but not useful. It says only that two events cannot be exactly alike in respect of the tropes that they are identical with.

VII

CONCRETE EVENTS

41. *Quine's metaphysic of events*

A view of Quine's about what events are comes closer to implying a semantics for event names. Quine says "Each [event] comprises the content, however heterogeneous, of some portion of space-time, however disconnnected and gerrymandered."[1] He means that each event comprises the *whole* content of a zone—everything that occurs or is the case at it. Although this has some implausible consequences, it has found favor in some quarters.[2]

It is the thesis that *there are only concrete events*. The word "concrete" is the antonym of "abstract", and philosophers these days use the latter to mean "eternal", "necessarily existing", "not causally potent", "not existing in space-time", and so on. I use it in a good sense, warranted by etymology and by the traditional meaning of the word, as in Locke's "abstract idea". An item is "abstract" in my sense if it omits detail. Facts, for example, divide into abstract and concrete. The fact that my study is now warm and sunlit is highly abstract (relative to my study), because it leaves out so much of the whole truth about how my study is now. There are plenty of less abstract facts about how my study is now; and there is one fully concrete one, but don't ask me to express it in words. Some philosophers will say that all facts, *qua* facts, are "abstract"—meaning perhaps that facts are not in space-time. I don't think they know clearly what they mean by this, but I shall not argue the point. My way of using "abstract" and its antonym has been explained and is legitimate, even if the alternative is some coherent way of using the terms and not (as I believe) a muddled mess.

---

1. W.V. Quine, *Word and Object*, p. 171.

2. It is cautiously endorsed by J.J.C. Smart in "Further Thoughts on the Identity Theory", p. 160; and, as will be reported later, Davidson has also recently come around to it.

To repeat: according to Quine, every event is concrete (relative to the smallest zone that contains all of it), whereas most theorists of events think that some events are abstract relative to their zones, that is, they do not exhaust the whole of what goes on at their smallest containing zones. From now on I shall drop the language of "relative to its smallest containing zone" and simply speak of events as "abstract" or "concrete".

From Quine's thesis it follows that no two events can exactly occupy the same zone. A few years after Quine first said this, John Lemmon arrived at it independently, in comments on an early paper of Davidson's.[3] Lemmon was looking for a nonduplication principle for events, and he came up with "If e_1 occurs exactly where and when e_2 occurs then e_1 is e_2". That is to say that no two events occur in exactly the same place at exactly the same time, which is a consequence of Quine's metaphysic and may be equivalent to it.

Quine countenances events that are wildly "disconnected and gerrymandered", but in the meantime let us keep within intuitive bounds by thinking only of events with fairly neat and natural spatio-temporal shapes. Indeed, to make this metaphysic easier to contrast with Kim's, let us stick with events that exactly coincide, for as long as they last, with things such as people and rocks and atoms and alligators—items whose names occupy the S position in Kim's S-P-T names.

Where Kim's metaphysic maps events onto S-P-T triples, Quine's maps them onto S-T pairs. Or, if we generalize each a little, Kim maps events onto zone-property pairs, while Quine maps them onto zones. Since a Quinean event is constituted by all the properties that are instantiated at the zone, it is uniquely determined by the zone, with no need to mention properties at all.

According to the Leibniz-Kim view, an event is a property instance. One could say that Quine's events are also property instances, the property in each case being the conjunction, so to speak, of all the properties that are instantiated at the zone. I am not sure whether Quine would be willing to put it like that. What he says is that an event is "the content" or "the material content"[4] of a zone. He does not explain this use of "content". It cannot mean "whatever physical object is contained in the zone, i.e. is contained in that spatial region at that time", because Quine uses his ideas about events and zones as a basis for explaining what physical objects are. So perhaps he would accept the idea that an event is a concrete trope. Either way, it would be in the spirit of his work to slice through this question and say that nothing is lost if events are identified outright with zones.

---

3. E.J. Lemmon, "Comments".

4. W.V. Quine, "Events and Reification", p. 167.

42. Some nonproblems about event location

When Lemmon presented his Quinean suggestion that two events could not be colocated in space-time, Davidson questioned "whether we have adequate criteria for the location of an event". One of his arguments about this is puzzling: "If a man's arm goes up, the event takes place in the space-time zone occupied by the arm; but if a man raises his arm, doesn't the event fill the zone occupied by the whole man? Yet the events may be identical." This seems to attack not the half of Quine's thesis that says that if e_1 is exactly colocated in space-time with e_2 then e_1 is e_2, which is controversial, but rather its trivially true converse. It has been suggested to me that Davidson was not making that mistake and that he meant his remark rather as a *reductio ad absurdum* of the idea that events have locations at all. If so, I find it unpersuasive.

Davidson also implies that Quine's metaphysic may have trouble from

> . . . the following argument: if an event is a change in a certain object, then the event occupies at least the zone occupied by the object during the time the event takes place. But if one object is part of another, a change in the first is a change in the second. Since an object is part of the universe, it follows that every event is a change in an object that takes place everywhere (throughout the universe).[5]

This trades on an ambiguity in "if one object is part of another, a change in the first is a change in the second". It is true if it means that any change in the first also occurs in the second, but it is troublesome only if it means that any change in the first completely occupies the second. Quine's metaphysic does not say that a single zone cannot have two events rattling around in it somewhere, but only that there cannot be two events each of which completely fills it.

Davidson writes: "If a man drives his car into his garage, how much of the garage does the event occupy?", but what does he mean by "*the* event"? For a Quinean, every event consists in all the doings in some zone; so any spatially small event is contained in a Chinese box of ever larger ones—all the doings in the space of the car at T, all the doings in the space of the garage at T, and so on right up to the vast event that consists in all the doings in the universe at T. There simply isn't any problem for the Quinean metaphysic here.

The only clearly intelligible general questions about event location are semantic ones. For example, we can make sense of Davidson's question about the car if it means: "What is the location of the event

---

5. Donald Davidson, "Criticism, Comment, and Defence", pp. 124f.

referred to by 'the man's driving of his car into his garage'?" That question allows that there is an event that coincides with the car, another that coincides with the garage etc., and merely asks which of them is picked out by a certain name.

When supposed problems about "the location of events" are understood in that way, they shrink and fade. Here are three of them, all concerning event names involving two substances.

(i) If an event name refers to two substances, what determines whether it is located in both of them or in only one? Granted that "the fight between Dempsey and Firpo" names an event that spreads through both men, what about "Dempsey's fight with Firpo?"

(ii) When an event name involves two substances and a relation between them that cannot obtain unless certain events occur outside of them, are those linking events part of the named event? For example, does "his telephone conversation with her" name an event some of which occurs along the wires?

(iii) When an event name involves a relational property of the named substance, does the named event occur partly or wholly in the other relatum? For example, does "the start of Xantippe's widowhood" name an event that occurs partly or wholly in Socrates?

There may be conventional answers to some questions of those types, though in many cases we would have to stipulate. Nothing important hangs on this. If anyone prefers to use many-substance event names in one way rather than another, he can do so without fear of colliding with any stern semantic regularities. None of this has any bearing on metaphysics, or any other interest either.

43. *A Quinean semantics of event names*

At the end of Section 37, I asked: "How *could* a purely metaphysical thesis about Fs, unaided, imply a semantics for names of Fs?" It couldn't, and the question was rhetorical. Still, a semantics might be implied by a metaphysic conjoined with some plausible further thesis that bridges the chasm between them. No such bridge presents itself for Kim's metaphysic: to get from that to Kim's semantics, we need the wildly implausible principle that the whole intrinsic nature of any trope can be recovered from every name of it. And I can think of no other bridge that would convincingly take us from Kim's metaphysic to any other semantics either.

With Quine's metaphysic, the story is different, for the following bridge principle has some plausibility: *Any S-P-T event name refers to an event that exactly occupies the zone defined by S and T*—that is, an event that spreads throughout the S-T zone but no further. Add this to

Kim's metaphysic, and you still have a choice about what event is referred to by a given S-P-T nominal, for there may be many events exactly occupying a zone; but with Quine's metaphysic it is a different story—the bridge thesis ties the name to a zone, and Quine's metaphysic ties the zone to a single event.

However, the bridge thesis is not really defensible for a Quinean or for anyone else. Sometimes it seems clear that an S-P-T nominal refers to an event that spreads through only a part of S at T, spreads through S for only a part of T, or both. For example, it seems perverse to suppose that "FDR's headache on December 30, 1943" and "FDR's toe-wiggling exercises on December 30, 1943" name events that are exactly colocated in space-time and thus, according to the Quinean, name the same event. Even if the worry and the exercises started and stopped together, we are reluctant to say that they occurred in the same place: on the most generous ideas about where events occur, the exercises did not spread up to the waist, we feel, or the worry down to it, so that far from coinciding in space they do not even touch. That seems right, but I cannot find a decent general principle that covers it. Davidson was presumably trying for one when he proposed to pin an event down to "the location of the smallest part of the substance a change in which is identical with the event",[6] but that is no help to a Quinean. It presupposes that we know which event is in question, and for a Quinean that is knowing which zone is in question, leaving no work for Davidson's principle to do. I doubt if that principle can be useful to anyone else either.

There may be no way of making precise the intuitive idea of a spatial region that snugly contains the whole of a named event. The following case seems incapable of satisfactory treatment: The cargo in a ship has been badly stowed, and at time T one bale slides across the hold, thus changing the cargo's center of gravity. Where is *the shift of the cargo's center of gravity*? It is in the world, in the ship, in the hold—but what is the smallest space that contains it all? If it coincides with the shifting bale through T, then the shift in the center of gravity took place in a zone that wholly excluded the center of gravity. If it coincides with the line travelled by the center of gravity through T, then the shift in the center of gravity may have been caused by an event that sent no energy into the zone where the shift occurred. There seems to be no third alternative.

In discussing Quine's view of events, I shall confine myself to examples for which the false bridge thesis seems to be about right. Thus, I shall not infer from the Quinean metaphysic that FDR's headache was his toe exercises, but I shall infer certain other identities.

6. Donald Davidson, "The Individuation of Events", pp. 175f. Essentially the same idea can be found in Lombard, *Events*, pp. 122f.

Here are a couple of implausible event identities that a Quinean probably has to accept, there being no plausible line of escape through a plea that the relevant event names, despite containing the same S component, pick out different zones.

(1) Throughout time T, a whole ox S is roasted over hot coals while turning on a spit. The pair S-T marks off a determinate zone through the whole of which the ox rotates and is roasted, and neither the roasting nor the rotation, I stipulate, slops out over the edges of the zone. Thus, each of the perfect nominals "S's rotation at T" and "S's loss of rawness at T" names an event. Most of us think that they refer to different (abstract) events, involving different subsets of the totality of properties that S has at T. The Quinean, on the other hand, says that since each refers to a concrete event, one that that completely fills the zone defined by S-T, they both refer to the same event, which is to say that *S's rotation at T is its loss of rawness at T.*

(2) A woman S swims throughout a period of time T, when she also catches a cold. On the assumption that the swim exactly fits the zone delimited by S-T and that the onset of the cold does likewise, the Quinean says that the swim was the onset of the cold. In this case there is perhaps a little room to manoeuvre, because it is not absurd to say that the onset of the cold occupies less of the swimmer's body than does her swim, but all the points I shall make would survive a switch to an example involving a new disease that *does* coincide with the swim because it permeates the entire body. So the plea that really the cold is spatially smaller than the swim is just a delaying tactic. Let us ignore it.

44. *Defending the Quinean semantics*

Is the ox's rotation its loss of rawness? Is the swim the onset of the swimmer's cold? We shall get no answers by looking at the naked event identities that we are apt to assert or deny in everyday life: there are few of those, and they are all peculiar. But the concept of identity is also at work in double predications and—I now emphasize—in substitutions. That is, evidence about our event concept is provided by our willingness to assert Fe_1 on the grounds that Fe_2 (premise: e_1 is e_2) or on our willingness to assert Fe_1 while denying Fe_2 (conclusion: e_1 is not e_2). Let us shine this light on the Quinean identity of the swim with the onset of the cold.

Some obvious truths about the swim would not be obviously true about the onset of the swimmer's cold. Take a particular swim that did coincide with the onset of a cold, and that was (i) famous, (ii) a record for the distance, (iii) circular and three miles long, and (iv) healthful.

These are not among one's favorite things to say about the onset of a cold! This may seem to threaten catastrophe for Quinean semantics, but the Quinean can make certain defensive moves, and there are lessons to be learned from them.

(i) The Quinean might say that "The F became famous" means that the F caused people to have knowledge and thoughts whose content was "There was a . . . F", with the blank filled in appropriately. That implies that " . . . became famous" is an opaque context, so that "The swim became famous" could be true and "The onset of the cold became famous" false, even if the swim was the onset. Unfortunately for the Quinean, however, the premise is false. Suppose that some soldiers were ordered, as a punishment, to raise and lower a flag a hundred times, and that a photograph of them doing it became widely and mistakenly admired as a slice of battlefield life. In such a case, it seems true to say that *their punishment became famous*, even though it did not cause widespread thoughts of the form "There was a . . . punishment".

The Quinean has an alternative defense, however. He can say that "The onset of the cold became famous" is true, but it feels false because it *suggests* that the item in question became famous *as* the onset of a cold. This is coherent and may be true, but beware! Indulgence in claims of the type "P is true, and if nearly everyone thinks it false that is because of falsity in what it suggests rather than in what it outright says or means" is dangerous to your intellectual health. They are wonderful for protecting semantic claims against counterevidence, but, just because they are so easily available, they ought not to be used unless there is a lot of independent evidence for them.

(ii) The notion of opacity can help the Quinean to deal with "The swim was a record". He can say:

> To call an event a record is to say that it somehow surpasses any previous member of a certain class of events. It is a record *qua* member of that class—a record *qua* three-mile swim by a five-year-old girl, say. What the relevant class is must be stated or implied in the statement or through the context. Now, the statement "The swim was a record" plainly implies that it is supreme in some class of swims; that could be true even though "The onset of his cold was a record" is false, for the latter means that the event in question was supreme in some class of onsets of colds.

That seems to be right, but how far does it go? It holds for "a record" and the almost synonymous "unprecedented"; it also seems right for "slow"—the swim was slow for a swim but not for a swim by a five-year-old. But the range and variety of descriptions that will need help from "*qua*" is suspicious; too many of them are forced on us by Quinean semantics and are not independently motivated or justified. For example, if we were not under pressure from Quinean semantics, would we say that "The swim was graceful" means that it was graceful for a swim? I doubt it.[7]

(iii) Here is what the Quinean can say about "The swim was circular and three miles long":

> The onset of the cold was also circular and three miles long: that event plainly did have that spatial shape and size, just as it plainly did stretch for two hours along the temporal dimension. Nobody would care about the shape and size of an event that he was thinking of as the onset of a cold, just as nobody would care about the taste when cooked of an animal that was eating him, or about the weight of a house he was painting. So "The onset of his cold was circular etc." would be a bizarre thing to say—an answer to a question that no-one would ask—but it would not be false.

That is probably right. On any theory of events, the cold-onset we have been discussing has an overall circular shape just so long as it occurs inside the body of the swimmer and lasts as long as the swim. To block this conclusion, we would have to deny the event any location in space-time, which would be to go drastically further than merely rejecting the Quinean view.

So far, we have three different treatments. The suspect statement is (i) true in what it says, false in what it suggests; (ii) false, but the event-identity is safe because the context is opaque; (iii) true and doesn't even suggest anything false, but is merely something we wouldn't ordinarily have reason to say. I have no quarrel with (iii), but the other two invite comment. They point to the fact that the Quinean semantics can be defended only by making lavish use of the plea of opacity and of the claim that apparent falsehoods are truths that we dislike because they suggest or weakly imply something false; and that entitles us to suspect it of special pleading. I don't have to press that charge in a general way, however, because there is something sharper and more definite to be said about the Quinean treatment of event-causation statements, focusing on (iv) the statement that the onset of the cold was healthy.

---

7. In his "Events and Reification", p. 167, Quine offered to back off from his account of events to something like Kim's, because it might be that the ox's rotation is fast and its loss of rawness slow. He did this rather airily, suggesting that it was a small concession and not exploring where it might lead. But he now agrees with me that he ought not to have yielded an inch for *that* reason; he could have left the ontology alone and invoked the notion of a syncategorematic predicate—a noun-dependent adjective—as he would in explaining how a competent swimmer can be an incompetent pianist.

45. *The Quinean treatment of event causation*

(iv) The sentence "The swim was healthful" means that the swim caused in the swimmer's body certain events, states etc. that were conducive to his health. I shall abbreviate this to *The swim caused his health*. Here is what the Quinean must say about this: "The onset of the cold did cause the swimmer's health. That may seem obviously false, but really it is true in what it *says* and false only in *suggesting* that the event was healthful because it was the onset of a cold." There is a strong argument for some claims like this.[8] An event-causation statement relates two items: its truth depends on what the items are, not on how they are named. When the items are facts, there is not much gap between what they are and how they are named or expressed, because any standard name or expression of a (Fregean) fact conveys the whole truth about its intrinsic nature. We have seen, however, that event names are different: one can refer to an event through some of its intrinsic properties, while keeping quiet about the rest. So a statement of the form "e_1 caused e_2" might be true although the features of e_1 that gave it this causal power are not even hinted at in the nominal by which e_1 has been named. Mary's theft of the bicycle upset her father—not because it was hers, or a theft, or of a bicycle, or any combination of those, but because she did it noisily and disturbed his sleep.

To explain why "The onset of the cold caused the swimmer's health" *seems* false, the Quinean can say that normal civilized discourse is guided by principles of economy and informativeness which require that, other things being equal, one should not say "The G event caused the H event" unless G and H have some overlap with the causally relevant properties. Because of this, we tend to hear "The onset of his cold caused his health" as weakly implying that the former event's *being the onset of a cold* helped it to have that causal role; but this is only implied, not outright said. Somewhat similarly, "The man who was executed yesterday had committed a terrible crime" implies, but does not say, that he was executed for that crime.

Still, it is one thing to say that event-causation statements can be true in what they say (about what caused what) and false in what they suggest (about why), and it is quite another to say that this obtains as often as Quinean semantics must say that it does. I shall argue that it does not. My argument will assume that we want some kind of relational analysis of event-causation statements: I cannot see how to combine Quinean theory with a counterfactual analysis.

Let us set the scene. Event-causation statements on Kim's ac-

8. In this paragraph, I am much indebted to Davidson's "Causal Relations".

count of them are extremely informative and therefore highly likely to be false. According to Kim, a statement of the form $C(e_1,e_2)$ is not true unless the causally relevant features of the events are actually expressed in the events' names. Thus, Kim will count "John's greeting caused Fred to be annoyed" as false if the annoyance arose from the fact that John greeted Fred loudly; he is not willing to say that the statement is true by virtue of an unmentioned feature of e_1, namely that it was loud.

In most of Davidson's work on events he has been willing to say such things, and so he has counted as true many event-causation statements that Kim thinks are false. Event-causation statements are less informative, and thus have a better chance of being true, on Davidson's than on Kim's view of them.

Quine's metaphysic makes event-causation statements still less informative and still more likely to be true. Where Davidson will assert $C(e_1,e_2)$ on the grounds that some perhaps unmentioned feature of e_1 has a certain causal power, Quine must be willing to assert it on the grounds that some perhaps unmentioned feature of *the zone occupied by* e_1 has a certain causal power. On the Quinean theory, event-causation statements say only that there is some causal flow from one zone to another, i.e. that undeclared features of two zones are causally relevant to one another in a certain way.

Our actual event concept does not work like that. When we say things of the form $C(e_1,e_2)$, although we do not mean them to be as informative as the grammatically corresponding fact-causation statements (Kim), we do mean them to do more than merely report the locations of two way stations on an episode of causal flow (Quine). I should remark, incidentally, that this consideration does not depend on any particular choice of example; it cannot be countered by defensive moves along the lines of "The swim isn't exactly colocated with the onset of the cold", and indeed it cuts right through the semantics and gets down to the underlying metaphysical thesis that only one event can exactly occupy a zone. Combine that with any semantics you like, and the result will still be that $C(e_1,e_2)$ reports only a causal connection between a pair of zones.

That consequence is obviously false, which makes it puzzling that anyone should adopt the Quinean position as conservative or descriptive metaphysics, that is, as true for the event concept that we actually have. Yet that is what Davidson seems to have done in a recent volte-face.[9] What brought him around? Well, he reports coming to see that Quine's metaphysic does not pose special problems about events' locations and ought not to be shunned for that reason; but he doesn't say what positive virtue he now sees in it.

9. Donald Davidson in "Reply to Quine on Events".

Perhaps he is still influenced by an argument that he adduced years ago. Circling warily around the Quinean metaphysic, he wrote that it might be supported by this argument concerning a metal ball that rotates while getting warmer: "The warming of the ball during T is identical with the sum of the motions of the particles that constitute the ball during [T]; and so is the rotation", from which it follows of course that the rotation is the increase in warmth.[10] This is not a good argument. If we are already assuming that there are only concrete events, the argument has no work to do. If we are not assuming that, why should we accept the premise that the ball's rotation (or that its warming up) is the sum of *all* the motions of the particles? Until the Quinean metaphysic has been established, we cannot rule out this:

> A single substance may at a given time be the subject of distinct motions. When a particle moves southwest, there is a southward motion and, in the same zone, a westward one, the total motion of the particle being the sum of these two. Thus, the ball's rotation is the sum of motions that do not alter how the moving particle relates to its neighbors, while its warming up is the sum of motions that do alter that. Even if each motion of either kind coincides spatiotemporally with a motion of the other kind, that is only colocation and not identity. So the sets of motions are distinct, and Davidson's argument has two false premises.

So we are still looking for a considerable independent reason for believing Quine's metaphysic. I don't believe that there is one.

46. *Events and physical objects*

Unlike Davidson, Quine has not offered the thesis that there are only concrete events as a truth of conservative metaphysics. He has never cared half as much about the niceties of our actual conceptual schemes as he has about the schemes that will best bring the world under intellectual control. So he would have no immediate reason to be troubled by the intuitive implausibility of his view of events or to go through the moves I have supposed "the Quinean" to make so as to reconcile his metaphysic with what intelligent people in the street think and say.

Quine's metaphysic of events, then, is offered as revisionary, or rather as excisionary: Quine's position is notable not for saying that

---

10. Donald Davidson, "The Individuation of Events", pp. 178ff. My ensuing criticism of this was made by Myles Brand, "Identity Conditions for Events", p. 333.

there are concrete events, total goings-on at zones, but for ignoring all the others, the abstract events more than one of which could exactly occupy the same zone. His position seems to be that there are serious reasons for an interest in concrete events and none for caring about the rest. I don't agree with the latter half of that, of course, but now I want to consider the former. Do concrete events have a special importance that makes them worth attending to?

To see why Quine thinks so, we must attend to the idea of *physical objects, understood as four-dimensional*. That is not how we ordinarily understand them. In our normal way of thinking, any physical thing *stretches* through space and *lasts* through time: proper parts of a thing's space contain only proper parts of the thing, whereas proper parts of its time contain all of it. The Trans-Canada Highway is stretched through space: some of it is in BC, some in Alberta, and so on, its spatial parts being laid end to end to make the spatial whole. Someone who says "The TCH is on the other side of town" means that a certain (spatial) part of it is there, but if someone says that Vermeer's "Girl in a Red Hat" is in the National Gallery, we don't take this as a *façon de parler* for the statement that a temporal part of the picture is there, some of its earlier parts being in Delft.

That difference creates another, namely that four-dimensional objects don't move. The table, we say, was moved from the yard into the kitchen; but of a four-dimensional table we should say rather that one temporal part of it was in the yard and a subsequent part in the kitchen.

The four-dimensional view of objects, though abnormal, may be philosophically profitable. Some philosophers think that it is. They believe, in my opinion rightly, that we can add depth and firmness to our thinking about the occupants of space by taking them to relate to time in the same way as to space—that is, taking them to be four-dimensional. Such philosophers may then have an interest in likening physical objects to events. A time-taking event has temporal parts, which are often referred to as such in ordinary speech: The first half of the baptismal service was solemn and moving, but the rest was farcical. And although we talk about events as though they moved, a little reflection gets us to admit that they do not. We may say "When the rain started, we moved the picnic from the yard to the kitchen", but we know that really an early part of the picnic occurred in the yard and a later part in the kitchen.[11]

Several writers have said or implied that the only difference between events and physical things is that two events can, while two physical things cannot, fully occupy a zone,[12] and if that is right then

11. See Fred I. Dretske, "Can Events Move?".

12. Anthony M. Quinton, "Objects and Events", pp. 201f; Myles Brand, *Intending and Acting*, p. 56.

concrete events must be physical objects. Davidson has denied this, however, apparently on the ground that even concrete events have a different number of dimensions from physical objects:

> Occupying the same portion of space-time, event and object differ. One is an object which remains the same object through changes, the other a change in an object or objects. Spatiotemporal areas do not distinguish them, but our predicates, our basic grammar, our ways of sorting do. Given my interest in the metaphysics implicit in our language, this is a distinction I do not want to give up.[13]

This rather obscure passage could be relying on the claim that events have temporal parts whereas objects do not. Another way of reading it will be discussed shortly.

What about the view that physical objects, when viewed as four-dimensional, can be identified with events? This line of thought was memorably expressed by Reichenbach: "A thing is a monotonous event; an event is an unstable thing", was developed at some length by Russell,[14] and lies behind Quine's treatment of events. He is interested only in the events that he thinks can plausibly be identified with physical things, when these are viewed as four-dimensional, and he assumes that all such events are concrete.

Well, it seems clear that if four-dimensional objects are events they cannot be as abstract as we ordinarily understand events to be. We cannot identify any temporal part of the swimmer with her swim, if "her swim" names a different event from "the onset of her cold".[15] But I don't see why they must be perfectly concrete. The following seems to me possible:

> Some of what goes on at zone z makes it the case that z is fully occupied by a physical object, and, in addition to that, there are other goings on at z as well. That is, the concrete event that fully occupies z—i.e. the totality of what goes on at z—does not all go into making it the case that there is a physical object at z; and so it should not be identified with the physical object.

That may be splitting hairs, though, and I shall not pursue it.

There is a different objection, which may have been Davidson's in the passage last quoted. It is that the nearest a concrete event gets to being an object is being the totality of everything that happens to the

---

13. Donald Davidson, "Reply to Quine on Events", p. 176. Cf. his rejection of Lemmon's idea that concrete events are zones: "It would be wrong to say that a space-time zone is a change or a cause (unless we want to alter the language)" ("The Individuation of Events", p. 178n).

14. Bertrand Russell, *The Analysis of Matter*, Chapters 23 and 27.

15. Thus Judith Jarvis Thomson, *Acts and Other Events*, p. 125.

object or being the object's entire history for the period in question; and it is a grammatical error to identify an object with its history. (This echoes a criticism that has been levelled against Lewis's introducing possible worlds thus: "I believe in the existence of entities that might be called 'ways things could have been'. I prefer to call them 'possible worlds' ", and then two pages later referring to one of the possible worlds, namely the actual one, as "I and all my surroundings". It has been objected that he can't have it both ways, and one of his critics has compared identifying the cosmos with the way the cosmos is with "saying that Socrates is identical with the way Socrates is, which is plain bad grammar".[16] The point seems to be right, as far as it goes. But it does not damage the idea that whatever can be said about an object can be expressed in predications on the corresponding concrete event, nor does it conflict with the view, which I accept, that someone who is interested in physical things viewed four-dimensionally has reason to attend to the concept of a concrete event.

47. *The immanence thesis*

One special point of contact needs a section to itself.

If there are only concrete events, then, as I have pointed out, event-causation statements merely say that some unspecified kind of causal flow went from one zone to another. That was a defect in the Quinean view considered as true for our actual event concept, but in our present context, where concrete events are being treated as aids to thinking four-dimensionally about physical objects, it is a different story. Here is why.

Anyone who tries to analyze the notion of a time-occupying physical thing such as an *atom* in terms of relations among its temporal parts must face a dilemma. If the analysis has this form:

> An atom stretching through a year is an aggregate, closed under relation R, of atoms each stretching through a minute,

or, more generally, if one analyses the concept of a thing with a certain temporal extent in terms of the concept of a thing with a lesser extent, it seems to follow that *every* philosophical problem raised by the analysandum is equally raised by the analysans, so that the whole procedure will be worthless. (I owe this point to James Cargile.) On the other hand, if the analysis says something of the form:

16. David K. Lewis, *Counterfactuals*, pp. 84, 86; Peter van Inwagen, "Indexicality and Actuality", p. 406. See also Robert Stalnaker, "Possible Worlds", p. 68.

An atom stretching through a year is an aggregate, closed under R, of Fs that have no temporal extent,

one must explain what sort of item an instantaneous F is. No one has ever been able to explain this, whether "F" stands for "atom" or not. We seem to have no notion of temporally unextended occupants of space.

A way out of this dilemma presents itself if the analysis of temporally extended things in terms of their temporal parts is embedded in a larger analytic endeavor. It has seemed to some philosophers—Plato, Spinoza, Newton (for a while), Eli Hirsch, me—that we can be helped to understand the notion of a thing *in* space if we analyze it in terms of qualitative variation *of* space. The basic idea is that for there to be an atom in a given region of space is for that region to be *thus* rather than *so*. This project of understanding the contents of space in terms of the attributes of spatial regions is neutral with respect to time: it could be deployed in terms of regions at instants or regions throughout periods. But if it is combined with the analytical project I have been discussing in these pages, or if for *any* reason we are thinking of the atom as being temporally extended and thus as having temporal parts, then the natural and perhaps inevitable procedure is to analyze the notion of an atom in terms of attributes of *spatiotemporal zones*.

So now we replace "atom that lasts through time" with "atom that stretches through time". We dig down into that with help from "spatiotemporal zone that has certain characteristics", and we explain what the relevant characteristics are with help from the notion of "sequence of R-related spatiotemporal zones". In this analytical scheme, neither horn of the original dilemma is any longer present as a visible threat.

What relation is R? I don't know the whole answer to that, but I am fairly sure of one part of it, which comes from the *immanence thesis*. This says that a thing's state at a given time depends predominantly on what that same thing was like a little earlier: its surroundings will have made some difference, but the greater causal contribution must have come from the thing itself.[17] In short: the dominant causal flow into the thing at any time comes from that thing at earlier times.

The statement that the dominant causal flow into x-at-t_2 is from x-at-t_1 means something like this: Differences in how the world outside x was at t_1 would have made less difference to how x was at t_2 than would comparably sized differences in how x itself was at t_1. As that clearly implies, the notion of "dominant causal flow" requires a

17. I am here agreeing with Sydney S. Shoemaker, "Identity, Properties, and Causality".

quality space with a metric, so that sizes or amounts of difference can meaningfully be compared.

Now, if we want to analyze the concept of a thing in space in terms of properties and relations of zones, our analysis must incorporate the immanence thesis. It must say that two zones count as lying on the spatiotemporal track of a single atom only if there is a dominant causal flow from one of them into the other. Let us pretend to have a God's eye view of the whole of space-time in all its variety, and let us ask which tracks through it are so related that the facts about them can be expressed as facts about atoms in space. To answer this, we must look for the paths of dominant causal flow, the sequences of zones that satisfy this condition on S: Each noninitial member of S is affected more by earlier members of S than by zones outside S. If the immanence thesis is correct, the tracks of atoms will be a subset of the paths of dominant causal flow. (Shoemaker sees the immanence thesis as an obstacle to the idea of physical objects as four-dimensional aggregates with temporally smaller parts. I agree rather with Armstrong, who says that "Causality does seem to furnish a powerful enough cement to bond together different phases of the same thing", thus using the immanence thesis to strengthen his view about how physical things are four-dimensional aggregates of briefer things.[18])

In this context, the uninformative event-causation statements to which I have called attention start to look good. Their main connective is not merely "causes" or "is causally relevant to" but rather "is strongly or dominantly causally relevant to". But something like that is usually at work when we make causation statements—we don't bother to *say* $C(f_P,f_Q)$ unless f_P is a salient or dominant cause of f_Q. What the present context does that is really new is to give us a reason for a special theoretical interest in causal statements whose relata are zones rather than something more fine-grained.

That is enough about Quine's metaphysic of events considered as revisionary or excisionary. Let us return to the exploration of the event concept that we actually have.

18. See David M. Armstrong, "Identity through Time", pp. 75–78.

VIII

THE TRUE SEMANTICS OF EVENT NAMES

48. *The search for middle ground*

A semantics of event names that fits our actual, informal, considered ways of talking must be intermediate between Kim's and the Quinean semantics.[1] If Leander caught a cold throughout the time (T) when he swam the Hellespont, then a Quinean must say that these three nominals:

> the complete swim that Leander took in the Hellespont at T,
> the crossing of the Hellespont that Leander made at T,
> the onset of Leander's cold that occurred at T,

name *one* event, whereas Kim, if he applies his views about the semantics of "event" names to perfect nominals, must say that they name *three*. Most of us think the right answer is *two*. So the truth lies in the middle. But where?

Myles Brand proposes the following nonduplication thesis for events: No two events can *necessarily* fully occupy the same zone.[2] Where Quine implies that if e_1 coincides with e_2, then e_1 is e_2, Brand says only that if e_1 *necessarily* coincides with e_2, then e_1 is e_2. This has an "intermediate" sound to it, but there seems to be no way to apply it to particular cases.[3] How could we know that the swim was necessar-

---

1. I label as "Quinean" the semantics of event names that loosely follows from Quine's metaphysics of events *construed as true of the event concept that we actually have and use daily.* Quine himself, of course, does not so construe it.

2. Myles Brand, "Identity Conditions for Events", and *Intending and Acting*, pp. 65–73.

3. Thus George N. Schlesinger, "Events and Explicative Definitions", pp. 217f. Schlesinger also argues that Brand's principle is uninteresting because it is derivable from a triviality.

ily colocated with the onset of the swimmer's cold except *through* knowing whether the swim was the onset? This is how, according to Brand:

> [My] identity conditions permit the occurrence of distinct events in one spatiotemporal region. Esther Williams swimming the channel and EW catching a cold, despite being spatiotemporally coincident, are distinct. For it is possible that EW swim the channel and not catch a cold at that time; and it is possible that she catch a cold and not swim the channel then. (p. 66)

This substitutes the manageable but irrelevant question "Where and when could she have swum?" for the relevant but intractable question "Where and when could her swim—the one she actually took—have occurred?"[4] One can see the trouble coming when Brand purports to refer to events with imperfect nominals.

The most popular kind of intermediate position is built on the idea that two event names that pick on the same zone refer to the same event if an entailment runs between their predicates.[5] That would give "Leander's swim" the same referent as "Leander's swim across the Hellespont" and would give "Mary's theft of the bicycle" the same referent as "Mary's removal of the bicycle" and as "Mary's reckless theft of the bicycle", none of which coreferences are valid in Kim's semantics; but it does not give the same referent to "Leander's swim" and "the onset of Leander's cold" or to "sphere S's loss of radioactivity" and "sphere S's journey from Washington to Oswego", even if these pick out the same zone.

This intermediate theory, satisfactorily, can also say that the expressions "Mary's crime" and "Mary's taking of the bicycle" name the same event, because it is linked in the right way with "Mary's theft of the bicycle" and the relation ". . . refers to the same event as . . ." is transitive. So far, so good.

But this proposed sufficient condition for coreference is too generous: a slight push collapses it back into Quinean semantics. Consider the predicate "performs while losing energy"—or, for short,

---

4. This is pointed out by Edward Wierenga and Richard Feldman, "Identity Conditions and Events", pp. 81f.

5. This was suggested by Alvin A. Goldman in "The Individuation of Action", p. 772, but the position it leads to undermines some of Goldman's and Kim's arguments, as Goldman has remarked to me in a personal communication. The idea is also endorsed in Judith Jarvis Thomson, "Individuating Actions"; Monroe C. Beardsley, "Actions and Events: the Problem of Individuation"; Hugh J. McCann, "Individuating Actions: the Fine-Grained Approach".

"lerforms". Now, Callas performed while losing energy, so the nominal "Callas's lerformance" names an event. According to our supposedly intermediate theory, the very same event is named by "Callas's performance" and also by "Callas's loss of energy", and so her performance is her loss of energy. If we admit that, all the unwanted Quinean event identities will troop in with it.

Many applications of this argument required invented words or event names derived from conjunctive predicates of the form ". . . while . . ." or ". . . and . . .". But what's wrong with such predicates, or with invented words? Presumably English *could* contain "lerform" with the meaning I have given it, and I don't see why the referent of "Callas's performance" should depend on facts about what other verbs English happens to contain.

Anyway, similar results can be achieved without help from conjunctive phrases or invented words. For example, since reading something necessarily includes both perceiving it and understandingly taking it in, the theory implies that "King John's perception of Magna Carta" refers to the same event as "King John's understanding intake of Magna Carta", since each corefers with "King John's reading of Magna Carta". That implies that King John's understanding intake of Magna Carta might be impeded by the stye in his eye or that his perception of Magna Carta might be helped by his knowledge of Latin, and these are consequences that only a Quinean could love.

Some friends of this kind of middle stand have sought to prevent it from turning into Quinean semantics by adding to it what I call "the adverbial idea". This makes the coreference of event names depend not just on whether an entailment runs between their predicates but also on whether the parent sentences of the event names have a principal verb in common and differ only in how or whether they adverbially modify it (or on whether the event names have a principal event-sortal noun in common and differ only in how, if at all, they adjectivally qualify it; but the verb/adverb version is the popular one and I shall stay with it).

The adverbial idea does block the "lerformance" and "reading" examples, which is good, but it blocks too much else. For example, it won't let us say that "the theft that Mary committed" refers to the same event as "Mary's removal of the bicycle". In any case, it is hard to believe that the reference of event names depends so entirely on accidents of wording. Sometimes one verb means about the same as a different verb modified by an adverb—as with "strolls" and "walks casually"—and the adverbial idea infers from this that the corresponding nominals name different events, so that "John's stroll" names one event and "John's casual walk" another. Also, there could be two verb-adverb (or noun-adjective) pairs that have the same content, distributing it differently between the two members of the pair, and then, according to the adverbial idea, two logically equivalent event names could refer to different events.

According to the friends of the adverbial idea, the differences between predicates that it focuses on are not superficial and accidental, but rather correspond to differences between properties. For example, Beardsley (p. 266) distinguished the "basic event property" from "dependent event properties", saying that the former is connoted by "the main verb" and the others by adverbs. McCann (p. 497) also claims to classify properties in terms of whether they share a verb: he says of the properties singing, singing loudly, and singing the Marseillaise that "the distinctive feature of these properties is that in them the verbal [meaning: verb-al] element is the same".

It makes no sense to talk of the verb-al element *in* a property, and I see no evidence that properties correspond to predicates tightly enough for Beardsley's purposes either.[6] Perhaps some distinction between properties is pivotal in the semantics of event names and also guides the opinions of Beardsley and the rest about the examples and is what they are basically talking about. Such a distinction, if there is one, might align with the division of labor between verbs and adverbs in English. But that division cannot *define* the distinction; we need a less superficial way of drawing the line, and I haven't found one.

49. *Surveying the relevant data*

I shall contend that there isn't one and that, although the truth about how event names work lies between Quine and Kim, it does not lie at a point—or even on a narrow band—between those extremes. Rather, I shall contend that there is a considerable spread, an indeterminacy, which is of the essence of our event concept and is perfectly innocent in itself, but dooms the search for a precise intermediate position.

Since I'll have to defend this on the basis of the relevant linguistic data, I should first remind you of what those are.

Existence statements about events are not relevant. Kim and the Quinean and everyone in between can agree that there was an explosion in the cellar if and only if some gases heated and rapidly expanded in the cellar; that there will be a quarrel between us before the day is over just in case we will quarrel with one another before the day is over; that there has never been an election in Ethiopia just in case people have never been asked and enabled to vote for anyone in

6. This point is made by Jay Alan Smith, "Goldman on Act Individuation", p. 239.

Ethiopia. There is nothing here that engages with our present problem. We want to know how far the reach of a perfect nominal stretches beyond that of the corresponding imperfect nominal (Kim: no further; the Quinean: far enough to grab everything that obtains at the zone); and existential statements about events use perfect nominals in a way that does not use any of that extra reach.

Naked event-identity statements would be relevant if we could trust our intuitions about them, but we cannot, since they play so small a part in our natural repertoire of uses of our event concept.

Then there are statements based on the *counting* of events. These are plentiful and central in our lives: we care about such truths as that I have needed three appointments with my chiropractor, there will be ten dismissals in the firm this month, the one who does best in seven games is the winner, she enjoyed two of her three divorces, this summer there were twice the usual number of forest fires in the state, he has been able to afford only one trip to Europe, and they are sulking at one another because their quarrels have outnumbered their reconciliations. This is promising, because the counting of events seems directly relevant to our present topic, which I recently crystallized into a question to which the Quinean, we, and Kim answered One, Two, and Three respectively. Here, one might think, we have struck pay dirt. Well, let us see.

We have three ways of counting events, illustrated respectively by (a) "There have been two forest fires in the state this month", (b) "He ran two laps", (c) "There are two conferences in the hotel today". I shall discuss these in turn.

(a) If a sizable region contains a fire, then it contains many: there is a fire in this bush, and in that, and in that other—the whole forest is raging. So we cannot count fires in a determinate way. To give sentence (a) a determinate enough sense to make it worth asserting, we must take a single fire to be a *zonally maximal fire*—one that fills a fiery zone entirely surrounded by coolness. By that standard, two synchronous fires must be separated by space that is not fiery at that time; and two fires in the same place must be separated by time when that place is not fiery. Here is how, in general, to count fires: *There are n fires in zone z if and only if z contains n zones such that: something burns at each of them, and every spatiotemporal track between any two of them runs through a zone at which nothing burns.* That is a general pattern for counting uproars, traffic jams, storms, invasions, and many other kinds of event.

This kind of counting fits Quine's views, but not Kim's. Kim must say that the very same forest is filled by many synchronous fires—ones constituted by "burning adverbly" with different adverbs. Still, there is a defensive move he can make. I have acknowledged that things we say about numbers of fires (riots, etc.) are really about *zonally maximal* fires, etc.; and Kim can add that things we say about numbers of Fs, for any event sortal F, are really about *qualitatively maximal* Fs, i.e. ones that are not qualitative parts of richer Fs.

(b) If you run two laps nonstop, they are not zonally separated in the manner of forest fires. Rather, the *amount* of an activity is measured in terms of *numbers* of associated items—the amount of running you did is given by the number of times that you went around the track. This is analogous to a statement reporting a quantity of stuff in terms of a number of measures of it: five laps' worth of running is analogous to five gallons of beer.[7] We could even fuse them together: if a gallinking of beer were defined as the drinking of a gallon of beer, we could say *how much* beer someone drank by saying *how many* gallinkings he performed.

This kind of counting of events has no significant bearing on either Kim's views or Quine's.

(c) The counting of conferences, weddings, games of chess, etc. is clearly not of type (b), and it is not of type (a) either because here zonal separation is not part of the story. It is not *needed*, because a proper part of a conference (wedding, etc.) is not itself a conference (wedding, etc.), and sometimes it is not *present*. For example, two conferences can overlap in space-time: a roomful of people discussing philosophical logic may all be participating, there and then, in the annual conferences of the ASL and of the APA. Two chess games could coincide exactly. Have a pair of masters play two games at once, not using physical pieces, and using a code—it is easy to devise—in which each signal conveys two moves but not because one part of the signal indicates one move and the rest of it indicates the other. And, on the other hand, many events of these kinds can be temporally discontinuous: a single conference, unlike a single forest fire, can occur half last month and the rest next week.

How, then, do we count conferences? Well, there is at least one conference in the hotel today if and only if people there relate to one another in a certain complex manner R, which has to do with overlap of interest and concern and with a relevantly shared causal history (so that R relates them not only to one another but also to things outside the hotel now). That there is a conference going on in the hotel now may follow from facts about how people are behaving and interrelating in rooms A, B, and C, and it may also follow from facts about the goings on in rooms D, E, and F. The question of whether those two

7. For an interesting development of the comparison between things/stuff on the one hand and events/activities on the other, see John Wallace, "Some Logical Roles of Adverbs", p. 704; and Alexander P.D. Mourelatos, "Events, Processes, and States". I was alerted to type (b) counting of events by Major L. Johnson, Jr., "Events as Recurrables", p. 225.

trios of rooms are the scenes of different parts of one conference or of two conferences depends on how the people in one set of rooms relate to those in the other set; specifically, it depends upon whether the relation R holds across the sets of rooms as well as among the rooms within each set. In short, how many conferences a zone contains depends upon *how many sets of people it contains that are closed under a certain relation R*. The broad outlines of that account apply to the counting of weddings, football games, and many other kinds of event—including, apparently, every event kind that does not fall into either of my first two categories. I have not found any way of dividing (c) into large and sharply demarcated subspecies.

Of course Kim's views conflict with these data as well as with those in category (a): he must proliferate conferences and kisses, as well as fires and uproars. I have nothing to add to what I have already said about this.

Category (c), however, introduces something new, namely a conflict with Quine's views when they are offered as conservative metaphysics. A single zone could be fully occupied by two chess games, their distinctness being secured by differences in the moves and in the outcomes: each ends with a move by Karpov, but in one case it gives him checkmate (a victory) and in the other it produces stalemate (a draw). These are two games, and yet Quine must say that their zone is fully occupied by only *one* event. A conservative Quinean, such as Davidson has lately become, must say that the games are not events but aspects of a single event. This bizarre result is a further reason for rejecting Quine's metaphysic as anything except revisionary.

So the data about counting provide some evidence against Kim's semantics and stronger evidence against the Quinean's. But they provide no guidance on where the truth lies between those extremes. For that, we had better look to the one remaining kind of datum, namely the facts about predications on events. These offer a rich store of serious linguistic data: we make plenty of room in our lives for statements such as "The revaluation of the currency was devastating", "The lobotomy was clumsily done", "The rehearsal made the interview less difficult for him", "The concert was more enjoyable than the rodeo". We have already made some use of such data, finding (Section 44) that the Quinean has to endorse as true more predications than most of us could stomach, defending that position with many pleas of opacity and *suggestio falsi*. We also saw (Section 33) that Kim can get as many predications as he needs only by implying that most of them—the ones that give the characters but not the constitutions of the event—are irrelevant to the event's causal powers. These results are evidence that the truth lies between Kim and the Quinean, but they do not locate it more precisely than that. We are still searching.

50. *The true semantics of event names*

Any event name has a parent proposition: P is the parent proposition of N if P does not involve the event concept and if it is necessary that *[N] exists if and only if P.* Thus, for example, that we quarrelled last night is a parent of "the quarrel we had last night"; that many vehicles were brought nearly or entirely to a halt by how crowded they were on the available road is a parent of "the traffic jam"; and so on.

Now, for "[N] is F" to be true, [N] must exist, and it must be F. So "[N] is F" is true only if

> the parent proposition of N is true, and . . .

. . . something further, something F-related, is the case. This "something further" must be connected with the truth of the parent proposition by more than merely being true of the same zone. If the zonal link were enough—as the Quinean semantics says it is—you could receive a *demotic insult* just because she insulted you while wearing a peasant dress; there could be a *noisy fire* just because trees burned quietly while the threatened animals screamed; an *illegal fight* could occur just because some men fought while having heroin in their pockets; there could a *healthy quarrel* because the parties to it jogged while quarreling. A more than merely zonal connection is needed, then, but what is it?

I submit that there is no general, systematic answer to this question. The truth lies between Kim and the Quinean, but there is no precise point between them such that it lies there. Consider:

Two men fought with knuckle-dusters, on a public street after 10 p.m. Was their fight illegal? The answer will be Yes, I think, if there is a law specifically against fighting or against fighting with knuckle-dusters or against fighting on a public street after 10 p.m. Suppose, however, that the only relevant law forbids wearing knuckle-dusters or forbids being on the streets after 10 p.m.; would either of those make *the fight* illegal? Most people that I ask are not confident of either answer.

(a) If you answer No to the last questions, then consider this: Suppose there is a law that proscribes more than just fighting in the streets at night but less than being in the streets at night—say, a law against interacting with other people on the streets after 10 p.m. Does that make the fight illegal? If you say Yes to this, your previous No will be hard to maintain. If you again say No, you will presumably be implying that the interaction between the two men was not the fight between them. I wish you luck with that!

(b) If you answer Yes, a general law against wearing knuckle-dusters or being on the streets at night does make the fight illegal, then consider this: If there were a law against the possession of heroin, and the men fought while having heroin in their pockets, would that make their fight illegal? You will have trouble saying No to this, given your previous Yes. If you answer "Yes" this time too, you have no clear obstacle to the conclusion that the fight was illegal just so long as the combatants were breaking some law while they fought. That stance, generalized, leads to the Quinean position.

Think of various different states of affairs in which a zone is occupied by a fire and is also the scene of a lot of noise, and consider in which of them you are willing to say that *the fire* is noisy. If the noise is from the crackling of flames: Yes. If the noise is all from the trapped animals: No. What if the noise is all from the falling of the burned branches?

She insulted me, and something about the situation surprised me. Scenario one: I was surprised that she insulted me. Scenario two: I was surprised that at that time she was painting her fingernails green. Scenario three: I was surprised that she smiled, which she did while insulting me. In the first case, the insult was surprising; in the second it wasn't; but in the third?

I submit that the questions I have left unanswered have no determinate answers, though no doubt special contexts could be created that would make one answer or the other seem right. Our concept of a particular event has a large dimension of vagueness, letting it sprawl across much of the continuum of possible views running from Kim to the Quinean. The concept is richer than Kim allows and poorer than the Quinean implies, but there is no answer to the question of exactly where between those two the truth lies. If we want a sharply drawn circle that the concept contains, we shall not find a larger than Kim's; if we want a sharply drawn circle that contains the concept, we shall not find a smaller than the Quinean's. The middle territory is the domain of vagueness, or indeterminacy, where what is said can properly reflect differences of context, interest, personal style, and so on.

Here is another example, involving the attribution to an event of a causal property. A parachutist is spiralling downwards: relative to the straight line from his parachute to the ground directly below, the jumper is moving down that line while also swinging in a circle around it. Because he is circling (and only because of that), he feels dizzy; because he is descending (and only because of that), he feels sick. Now tell me: Does his descent cause him to feel dizzy? If "his descent" names a movement, a trope, which is an instance of a property that has *spiralling downwards* as a component, then indeed his descent causes him to feel dizzy, not because it is a descent but because it has a circular aspect. If, on the other hand, the trope named by "his descent" is an instance of a property that has *descends* as a component but not *circles*, then the answer is No. Isn't it clear that neither answer is decisively correct? I conjecture that it would be fairly easy to elicit either answer from an intelligent audience, if one went about it in the right way, and I take that to be evidence that in this and related matters there is a good deal of indeterminacy.

In short, the meanings of ordinary perfect nominals don't lie at any determinate point on the Quine-to-Kim continuum. The facts that give truth to predications on a perfect nominal include much more than just the fact actually expressed by the nominal (so Kim is wrong), and they must be connected with the expressed fact by some closer link than merely being about the same zone (so the Quinean is wrong). That is as far as we can go with any general account of the matter; from there on, it depends on local context and unprincipled intuitions.

51. *Events and their companion facts*

The position I have adopted consists of two separable elements. (i) *The trope thesis.* Any event name refers to an instance of a property that includes but may not be identical with the property expressed by the predicate in the event name. Thus, "Leibniz's journey at T",2if it names an event at all, names a T-dated instance of a property of which *journeying* is a proper part. To state it generally: any S-P-T event name refers to an event that is the instance that S has at T of a property P*, which usually includes other properties as well (contra Kim), but does not ordinarily include every property that S has at T (contra the Quinean). The whole of P* must be had by S at T, so the identity of the named property (i.e. the property an instance of which is named) is a contingent matter: to know what property constitutes the event picked out by any given S-P-T nominal, you must understand the name and inspect the zone. (ii) *The indeterminacy thesis.* Although there are limits to what the named property could be, the question of what it is has no determinate answer; in this respect, our language of events contains a lot of slack. I have no proof of this, and I offer it merely as a conjecture, to explain how indecisively and variably certain kinds of example are handled. The discussion in this and the ensuing sections will depend not upon (ii) the indeterminacy thesis, but just upon (i) the trope thesis.

Indeed, I need to keep (ii) out of sight for a while, as I now explain. I want to say, on the strength of the trope thesis, that event names correlate with facts in the following way. Every S-P-T event name refers to a trope, an instance (possessed by S at T) of a property P* of which P is a part. Corresponding to this there is a unique fact, namely the fact that S has P* at T or, more generally, the fact that P* is instantiated at a certain zone. I shall call this fact the "companion" of the event named by the S-P-T name. Now, it is not strictly true that each event name has a unique companion fact, because the indeterminacy thesis implies that a single event name may be used by different speakers or at different times to pick out somewhat different tropes and that one speaker at one time may hesitate between several candidates for the role of P*. Still, we get a correlation if we work not with "event name" but rather with "event name on a particular occasion of use by someone who has sharply made up his mind what event he is using a given name to refer to". I shall not bother saying all that every time, but please understand me to mean it.

It would be convenient if the correlating relation were identity—that is, if we could drop the idea of an event's companion fact and say that what an S-P-T name names is always a fact, so that events are a species of facts. We shall see, however, that that is not so: we are sometimes taken from truth to falsity by replacing a perfect nominal by the imperfect nominal that names the companion fact; this shows that the two nominals don't have the same referent, from which it follows that the event named by one of them is distinct from the fact named by the other.

However, the obstacles to identifying events with their companion facts are fairly superficial; they do not show that facts and events are items of deeply different metaphysical kinds. The upshot of much of what I have argued so far in this work and of some that is still to come is that it would not be deeply false to say the following.

Events are facts of a kind: many facts are not events (e.g. ones that are not about zones), but every event is a fact.[8] The illusion that each event has a companion fact that is distinct from it has its source in our two ways of naming facts. We think of facts as "events" when we are naming them with perfect nominals and as "facts" when we are naming or expressing them with imperfect nominals. But they are the very same items, however named; the difference is all in the naming. *An imperfect nominal names the fact it expresses; a perfect nominal names a fact that includes the fact it expresses.* When an imperfect nominal names a fact, the only role of the extralinguistic world is to make it the case that there is such a fact; it makes no difference to what fact is named, for the identity and whole intrinsic nature of the named (Fregean) fact are determined by the meaning of the expression that names it. Perfect nominals, on the other hand, are like descriptive names of physical things; the meaning of the name tells you something about the item named, but there is more to be

---

8. N.L. Wilson said, "There is no such thing as an event distinct from a fact" ("Facts, Events and their Identity Conditions", *Philosophical Studies* (1974), at p. 317), but I have no sympathy with his reasons for this, or for his terminology, which almost precisely reverses the proper sense of "event" and "fact".

learned about it by consulting the world; reference outruns meaning. The phrase "this afternoon's avalanche", if it refers at all, refers to something of which the fact that *snow slid massively down a hillside this afternoon* is a part. What is the rest of it? Well, it may be the fact that 20,000 tons of snow slid massively down a 30° hillside slope at an average speed of 45 miles per hour, engulfing nine people . . . , etc. The "avalanche" phrase does name a fact, but which fact it names depends not only on what it means but on what is the case at the zone that it picks out. Thus, for example, "John's walking quietly home at midnight" names *the fact that John walks quietly home at midnight*, whereas "John's quiet, homeward, midnight walk", in a given particular use, will name something like *the fact that John walks quietly home at midnight, swinging a stick, following a route across campus, along Euclid Avenue, then along Sumner to Dorset, . . .* and so on. In sum: perfect nominals do name facts, but not the ones that they express. Since the firmest anchor we have for the term "event" is our use of perfect nominals, we should conclude that events are facts of a special kind, named in a special way.

As I have said, that paragraph is not strictly true. If a perfect nominal corefers with the imperfect nominal that names its companion fact (so that the event *is* the companion fact) then the two nominals should be intersubstitutable in all transparent contexts, and they are not. Still, the false paragraph is nearly true. Such structure as our event concept has comes almost entirely from our uses of perfect nominals, and the cardinal truth about those is that a perfect nominal takes one to a fact that is, though abstract, richer and less abstract than the fact it expresses, i.e. the one named by the corresponding imperfect nominal.

I shall illustrate this by reexamining Vendler's work. He explains certain semantic data by supposing that perfect nominals refer to events and imperfect ones to facts. I accept that explanation, but now I want to deepen it. In Vendler's hands (and in mine, up to now) the explanation has assumed that facts and events belong to distinct ontological categories. But really there is not much explanatory value in *that*, whereas we can strengthen Vendler's explanation of the data if we bring in the thesis that most of the features of our event concept arise from the way perfect nominals take us to richer facts than the ones they express. In sum: by seeing that the difference between facts and events is *shallow*, we can *deepen* the use of it to explain Vendler's data.

The data concerning adjective versus adverb, tenses, modalities, etc. are purely syntactic, cannot be explained semantically, and have no bearing on metaphysics. They are aspects of the grammatical fact that a perfect nominal is fully a noun, while an imperfect one is a noun that "preserves the regimen of a verb" (OED) or "has a verb alive and kicking inside it" (Vendler). Setting all that aside, we are left with three data: (i) about articles, (ii) about predicates that attach to perfect nominals but not to imperfect ones, and (iii) about predicates that give a much wider meaning when attached to a perfect nominal than when attached to the corresponding imperfect nominal. I shall explain these with help from my basic thesis: *An imperfect nominal names the fact that it expresses; a perfect nominal picks out a fact richer than the one it expresses.* I use "pick out" as a term of art for the relation between a perfect nominal and the companion fact of its referent. I cannot quite say that the one "names" the other, for the reason I have given; but I do maintain that the main role of a perfect nominal is to take us to, help us to focus our thought upon, and inform us about, a certain rich fact.

I shall also use the basic thesis to explain something that Vendler does not mention and that seems inexplicable on his account of the matter, namely (iv) that all predicates that attach to imperfect nominals attach also to perfect ones.

(i) *Articles.* The definite article serves to signal that only one item falls under the description that follows it. The indefinite article does nothing but mark the absence of a definite article; it could be dropped from the language without loss of expressive power, as it often is in the plural in English ("She brought some apples"; "She brought apples"). In short, the whole truth about articles is that the definite article is a singulariser; so we have explained why articles can be prefixed to perfect but not to imperfect nominals when we have explained why perfect but not imperfect nominals can function as sortals, that is, general terms with more than one instance.

Imperfect nominals are systematically debarred from serving as sortals, since none of them can name more than one item.[9] However often Henri sang the Marseillaise last week, "Henri's singing the Marseillaise last week", if it names anything, names the fact that Henri sang the Marseillaise (at least once) last week. Imperfect nominals of the form "fact that [S]" are typically prefixed by "the", but in that context "the" does not have a singularizing role—as witness the fact that we don't have "a fact that P". A perfect nominal, on the other hand, does not express the fact that it picks out but merely functions like a description of it. Now, if you thin out a description that picks out just one item, the result may apply to more than one item; and so a successful definite description of a fact may contain proper parts that apply to several facts, i.e. are fact sortals, just as an event name contains event sortals as proper parts.

9. The sortal "positive square root of 4" can name only one item, but it does not belong—as every imperfect nominal does—to a grammatical class no member of which can name more than one item.

For example, the perfect nominal "performance of the Marseillaise that Henri gave around 2 p.m. on October 29, 1986" has the force of something like "fact that amplifies the fact that Henri performed the Marseillaise around 2 p.m. on October 29, 1986". I here use "amplifies" as a technical term: f_Q "amplifies" f_P in my sense if and only if there is a zone z such that (i) f_P obtains throughout z and (ii) f_Q is the conjunction of the fact that f_P obtains throughout z and every fact that has R to that one, where R is the relation of connectedness that stakes out the domain of the truth somewhere between the Quinean and Kim. Actually, the truth is a little more complex, but that will do to make my present point, which is that a description of the form "fact which amplifies the fact that P" could be satisfied by more than one fact. If Henri sang the Marseillaise at about 2 p.m. on that day and again at about 3 p.m., then the description "fact which amplifies the fact that Henri performed the Marseillaise around 2 p.m. on October 29, 1986" applies to only one fact, but "fact which amplifies the fact that Henri performed the Marseillaise on October 29, 1986" applies to two facts. That is the ultimate source of the truth that in the case as described, Henri gave two performances of that song on that day. I offer this as explaining why perfect nominals admit of plurals, are sortals, can take articles.

(ii) *Untransferrable predicates.* Certain contexts that take perfect nominals will not happily take imperfect ones: "Mary's theft of the bicycle" is all right in the context ". . . took less than a minute", while "Mary's stealing the bicycle" is not. Countless other predications on perfect nominals are infelicitous or worse when transferred to imperfect ones: "His organization of the conference was skilful", "Her rendition of the song was deafening", "Their passage through the straits took seven hours", "His fall from the clifftop was visible from a mile away".

Vendler explains this range of data by saying that the predicates in question attribute properties that events can have and facts cannot. I don't say that that is wrong, but I complain that it doesn't tell us why there is this difference between the two categories, and (to anticipate) it makes a mystery of the fact that all predications on imperfect nominals can just as well be made on perfect ones. We can do better, with help from the idea that what a perfect nominal chiefly does is to take us to a fact that is richer than the one it expresses.

I suggest this: any predication on a perfect nominal is equivalent to—and gets its truth from the truth of—a predication on the companion fact, but the predicates in the two cases are different. That is, "[EN] is [Pred]" is equivalent not to "[FN] is [Pred]" with the same predicate, but rather to "[FN] is [Pred*]", where Pred* is systematically related to Pred in some way that needs to be explained. I don't have a full account of that systematic relation, but I can give examples that should make my view plausible.

All predications that say where and/or when an event occurred are covered by the principle that "[EN] occurs at zone Z" is equivalent to "[FN] has the form '. . . at Z' ". Thus "John's sneeze occurred at noon" is equivalent to "The fact which has relation F to {John, sneezing, noon} has the form 'John sneezed . . . at noon' "; similarly for attributions of place. It is easy to adapt this to attributions of subjects to an event, as in "The sneeze that occurred at noon in my study was by John".

"[EN] took less than a minute", according to this general approach, must be equivalent to "[FN] is of the form '. . . for less than a minute' ", so that "Mary's bicycle ride took less than a minute" means that the companion fact is of the form "Mary rode a bicycle . . . for less than a minute". I don't have a neat formula that captures all the cases, and even with my chosen examples there is some wishful thinking. For example, "Mary's ride took less than a minute" is not made true by the fact that Mary rode a bicycle . . . while holding her breath for less than a minute, and I don't know how to rule that out cleanly and precisely. (I did have "Mary's theft took less than a minute" and "Mary stole . . . for less than a minute", but one reader understandably took the latter to mean that Mary returned the object within a minute. Plenty of linguistic oddities stand in the way of handling this matter cleanly.) But I still suggest that a predication on an event name is equivalent to a statement about the intrinsic content of the companion fact.

Then we can explain why those predications cannot be applied to imperfect nominals. We can say "Their quarrel was savage", using a perfect nominal to say something about the intrinsic content of a certain fact; we could, so to speak, force meanings onto statements of the form "[Imp.nom.] was savage", making them say something about the content of the named fact, but anything we said of that kind would either be necessarily true (because the imperfect nominal had savagery in its meaning) or necessarily false (because it didn't). The point is that the quarreling doesn't involve savagery and isn't a fact of the form "They quarrelled savagely . . .". Just because "their quarrelling" is an imperfect nominal, it names the very fact that it expresses; what you see is what you get. Since such statements will always be either necessary or impossible, we have no ordinary use or need for them, which is why we haven't provided for them in our language.

(iii) *Differences in breadth of meaning*. Imperfect nominals can be used in contingent statements about how facts relate to other items, especially to minds. All of these relational predicates can be applied to perfect nominals also, but that always produces a broader meaning than does the same predication on an imperfect nominal. My present standpoint lets us explain this more satisfyingly than Vendler does.

Consider for example: " . . . surprised us". The truth of any report of surprise ultimately rests on something of the form "x is surprised that P". Now, in the sentence "Mary's stealing the bicycle surprised us", the only fact that has been referred to is the fact that Mary stole the bicycle, which is thus the only candidate for the role of P. So we get only the reading "We were surprised that Mary stole the bicycle". In the sentence "Mary's theft of the bicycle surprised us", however, a richer fact is picked out, along these lines: "Mary stole the bicycle in less than a minute, at about noon yesterday, deftly, cruelly, in the knowledge that she could have stolen a better bicycle, . . ." and so on. All that is needed for the original sentence to be true is that we be surprised that P for some P that is a constituent in this rich fact. It could be the fact that she stole the bicycle, but it might instead be the fact that she handled a bicycle deftly, or the fact that she acted cruelly, or . . . and so on.

(iv) *Free transferability the other way.* Every predicate that can be applied to an imperfect nominal is also applicable to perfect ones, and it is hard to see why this should be so if the two sorts of nominals take us to different ontological categories, and this difference is used to explain why some predicates can be applied to perfect nominals but not to imperfect ones. From my standpoint, however, this is just what we should expect. There is no reason why a predicate that can properly be attached to an imperfect nominal—a phrase that expresses the fact that it names—should not also be attachable to an expression that names a fact of which it expresses only a part.

IX

EVENT CAUSATION AGAIN

52. *Getting it right*

Back in Section 21 we were stuck: we got the wrong answer if we tried to elucidate $C(e_1,e_2)$ in terms of only the intrinsic properties of e_1 and also if we allowed unrestricted access to all its relational properties. The former made too many event-causation statements false; the latter made too many true. I now propose a solution to the difficulty. In this, I shall use the form "F(x)" to name x's companion fact.

I propose that $C(e_1,x)$ means that *some part of $F(e_1)$ is a cause of* x. That means that an event-causation statement is an existentially quantified fact-causation statement: $C(e_1,x)$ means that *there is a fact* f_1 that is part of $F(e_1)$ and is a cause of x. It is a routine matter to work out the analogous account for statements of the form $C(x,e_2)$.

By analysing event causation in terms of fact causation, we escape the bind about intrinsic versus relational properties of the event, which was the fatal difficulty in Section 21. Of course we then have to cope with fact causation; I prefer an NS analysis of it, but I shall not go through all that again.

Let us see how the analysis works on a specific example, namely the statement: "The remark that Isabelle made in French at dinner last night caused the guests to leave early." I take this to be true if and only if the guests were caused to leave early by the obtaining of some part of the fact that at 10:37 p.m. precisely, Isabelle said, in perfect Parisian French but in a tone of voice reminiscent of Elizabeth Taylor, looking all the while in a fixed way at Hubert, "La propriété, c'est le vol" . . . with some more as well, building it up to the whole of the companion fact of Isabelle's remark. So the original event-causation statement is true if the guests left because Isabelle spoke in French or because she spoke in Parisian French or because someone spoke in French or because Isabelle spoke before midnight or because a woman spoke at 10:37 or because Isabelle said that property is theft or because she reminded them of Elizabeth Taylor . . . and so on. If nothing of this kind is true, the event-causation statement is not true either.

Another example: If someone says "The insult caused an uproar", referring to an insult that Schopenhauer launched in the direction of Hegel, the statement will be true if people behaved unroariously because someone insulted someone in Heidelberg at T or because Schopenhauer insulted someone in Heidelberg or because someone insulted Hegel in the middle of a lecture or because in the course of insulting Hegel Schopenhauer used three indecent words or . . . and so on.

That account of event causation is the main reason that events cannot be identified with facts. If events were facts, $C(e_1,e_2)$ would mean the same as $C(F(e_1),F(e_2))$, but I equate the former rather with the statement that there is some part of $F(e_1)$, call it f_c, such that $C(f_c,F(e_2))$; and that is a quite different story. If I took the other line, and outright identified e_1 with $F(e_1)$, absurd things would follow. I shall devote a paragraph to explaining this.

Fact causation rests ultimately on the idea of one fact's being an NS condition of another. So, if $C(f_1,f_2)$ is true and if f_3 is a much stronger fact than f_1, then $C(f_3,f_2)$ will not be true, because f_3 will be much too rich, too strong, for it to be true that without *it* some sufficient condition for f_2 would have fallen short of sufficiency. There may have been a sufficient condition for f_2 that had f_3 as a part; but f_3 wasn't itself an indispensable part of the sufficient condition, though it *contained* an indispensable part, namely f_1. Now let us apply this. If events were facts, then "$C(e_1,e_2)$" would mean that the companion fact of e_1 was a cause of the obtaining of the companion fact of e_2; in the vast majority of cases, however, the former fact is much too rich to be an NS condition of the obtaining of the other fact. Just yesterday, the job I did in my garden caused a backache. If "the job I did in the garden" named a fact, it would be something like

> the fact that without any preliminary warming up I spent 40 minutes vigorously raking and carrying leaves from a large maple tree, getting them off the lawn and onto the other side of the driveway, using a new plastic rake, alternating between left-sided and right-sided sweeps with the rake, . . .

plus some more. But *that* fact was not an NS condition of my getting a backache, for there was no sufficient condition for the backache that needed *that* fact in order to be sufficient; a small part of the fact was all that was needed, namely that I worked vigorously for 40 minutes without a preliminary warm-up.

According to my account, event-causation statements are fairly uninformative—more so than Kim says they are, though less than would be the case if the Quinean semantics were right. That fact-causation statements are more basic and more informative than event-causation statements—and perhaps also that they are more determinate—has been confirmed in my experience of giving talks about these matters. When I invite an audience to consider how the concept of event causation applies to a given episode, I always use the language of fact causation to give the episode in the first place, and the audience always grasps what they are being asked to think about—they are satisfied that they have been given the situation *an sich*, the God's truth about it. For example:

> A nurse massages a patient's chest, in consequence of which his heart starts pumping again, with the result that he lives for another five years, whereas otherwise he would have died within minutes. After five years, he dies in a traffic accident. Problem: Does the massage cause his death?

Here the language of fact causation allows the case to be presented for consideration, while event causation enters the picture only as a lumpish, inexact, and perhaps misleading way of telling a small part of the story.[1]

53. *Why do we have event causation?*

The relative uninformativeness of event-causation statements is their *raison d'être*. We need such statements because we often know so little of the causal story.

That is what Mackie thought. After belatedly grasping how facts differ from events, he came down on the side of facts, and he asked: "Facts as causes seem to have every advantage over events. Why, then, do we bother to recognize producing [= event] causes as well as explanatory [=fact] causes?"[2] Mackie's answer: "The reason lies, as so

1. John Watling has nicely expounded the point that there is a progressive gain of information as we move from citing objects as causes to citing events, and from that to citing facts. "Are Causes Events or Facts?", pp. 168f.

2. J.L. Mackie, *The Cement of the Universe*, p. 262. Although in this work Mackie does not conflate facts with events, he handles events poorly. He writes (pp. 30f): " 'Event' is just a general term that stands in for such items as 'the hammer's striking the chestnut'. Anxieties about the exact ontology of causation may be postponed for later consideration . . .". But Mackie does not ever get down to the finer details of our event concept. Also, he keeps assuming that all an event's monadic features are essential to it, as here: "All that a law could demonstrate as being necessary for the effect is that an event of a certain sort should have occurred, not that this one in all its concrete detail should do so." (p. 267n)

often, in the extent of our ignorance." He went on to say that a complete explanation in terms of facts—in which causally sufficient antecedent conditions for the explained fact are adduced—"is an ideal which we can hardly ever reach". That is true, but it does not explain why we have a role for event-causation statements; and it is significant that Mackie doesn't go on to argue that, when we fall short of that ideal and can give only partial causal information, event-causation is just what we need. Actually, there are many ways of giving incomplete causal explanations in the language of $C(f_1,f_2)$—"Q because P", and "P's being the case made it the case that Q", and so on—without having recourse to the language of $C(e_1,e_2)$. Oddly, two of the best ways of doing this were pointed out by Mackie himself.

One is the notion of an NS condition, which is a simplified cousin of Mackie's INUS concept. We can say that $C(f_P,f_Q)$ meaning that P's being the case was a needed ingredient in some sufficient condition for Q's being the case. This expresses a state of imperfect information, yet it does so in the language of facts, not events.

The other, which I have touched upon in Section 16, is the explanatory use of Russellian facts. Consider this exchange: "Why is she sick?" "Because she ate some of this stuff." Although an explanation's power may depend upon *how* some individual is referred to in it, often that is not the case. In the present example, the explanation "Because she ate some of this stuff" may be as far as the speaker can go: perhaps he has no opinion about what the stuff is or about how it made her sick, but he knows that those who eat stuff like it usually fall ill, from which he guesses that it is stuff of a kind that sickens, i.e. that causes the eater to be sick by virtue of its inner nature. So the thin, underinformed explanation that he is offering will not suffer if the stuff is referred to in some other way: all he needs is to pick it out transparently, i.e. to point somehow to the bit of the world whose inner nature is, he thinks, a needed ingredient in a full explanation of her sickness. Really, the explanation has the form: "Concerning this stuff: her eating it caused her to fall ill." This is Mackie's idea, and it seems to me just right: it explains why the concept of a Russellian fact is useful, without denying that there are also Fregean facts, and—to come to the present point—it shows how fact-causation statements can express poor states of explanatory information.

Some instances of partial information have the right size and shape to fit "Concerning e_1: it caused e_2" and are not right for capture in the form: "Concerning x: the fact that it was F explains the fact that Q". Oddly, Mackie offers no convincing examples of this and thus no real evidence that event causation is useful to us in expressing low-grade states of explanatory information. Of a particular event-causation statement that nicely fits the statement "The explosion here was caused by Tom's midnight movement", he says that it earns its keep in our scheme of things because "it is easy to tell a story in which someone's actual knowledge of the incident would be accurately expressed by this sentence" (p. 264), but he doesn't tell any such story.

Still, it *is* easy to tell one. If I know that the explosion was a consequence of the fact that Tom moved adverbly at midnight, but I don't know which adverb is right, then my state of knowledge is pretty exactly expressed by saying that the explosion was caused by the movement that he made at midnight. Quite generally, event causation is apt for expressing knowledge to the effect that *some* amplification of a certain fact had such and such as a consequence.

54. *Why event causation is inferior*

I have been assuming that event-causation statements are an inferior breed that need to be justified, but I have not said why. So far, I have made only two points about them: they are not very informative, because they existentially quantify over a class of fact-causation statements, and they are fairly indeterminate, because the membership of the relevant class of fact-causation statements is not determinate. It is not obviously or necessarily true that either of those is a defect at all, and they are not defects that I want to trumpet.

What I do stress is that the language of fact causation is more sensitive and flexible than the other. This fits it for use in reporting causal connections in fine-grained and unmisleading ways of which the language of event causation is quite incapable.

One kind of fine-graining is temporal. In the nurse's massage example that I used recently, the assigning of a truth-value to the lumpish "The massage was a cause of his death" stands in contrast to questions about the truth-values of "The massage was a cause of his dying", ". . . of his dying when he did", ". . . of his dying as late as he did". Of these, the first is false, the second is true but omits something important, the third is true and makes good the omission. The language of facts opens up the whole range of time discriminations which are handled either not at all or else clumsily by the apparatus of events.

Our event concept is poorly adapted to cope with other kinds of fine-graining also. Consider for example an electric motor that is hooked up symmetrically to two sources of power, each circuit having a switch. Current from either source would suffice to make the motor go, though its speed depends on how much current it gets. Now, both switches are closed at the same instant, whereupon the motor starts. How can we explain the start of the motor in the language of event causation? We cannot pick on either one of the relevant events: the stipulated symmetry makes that impossible. One might suggest that the motor's start was caused by each switch-flip, but that is implausible. Against the candidacy of flip 1, we can say that *it* wasn't a cause of the motor's start because it made no difference at all to whether the motor started, and similarly with the candidacy of flip 2. Or we might say that the motor's start was caused by a spatially discontinuous event, namely the fusion of the two switch-flips. But not everyone is happy with such fusions, and in any case this account of the matter is misleading at best, because it seems to imply that the two flips collaborated in getting the motor to start, and that is not so.

If we move from events to facts, all comes clear. What brought it about that the motor started then was the fact that at least one of the switches was closed; it's as simple as that. Furthermore, the fact that both switches were closed caused it to be the case that the motor started as violently as it did rather than more slowly. In short, fact causation gives us the luxuries of disjunction and conjunction, which are not available with event causation.

Then there are the luxuries of negation. That brings me to an especially noxious kind of damage that has been done in moral philosophy by too close adherence to the concept of an event. We can talk about people's responsibility for upshots in either of two idioms. In one of them, we speak about what his actions caused: "His snub caused her distress", or "His snub caused her to be distressed." In the other, we speak about the consequences of how he behaved: "Because he snubbed her, she was distressed." The former belongs to event causation, the latter to fact causation; in the area of moral philosophy that studies responsibility for preventable outcomes, the fact-causation approach is superior. Consider this short story: "Something bad happened because a gate remained open; John could have closed it, but he didn't." We cannot form moral opinions about John's conduct without knowing more. Did he know that closing the gate would have forestalled a disaster? How much of a disaster was it? How easily could he have closed the gate? Was the disaster of a kind that John had a special duty or responsibilty to prevent? And so on. There is much to be thought about here, concerning the moral evaluation of John's conduct in the light of the negative fact that he did not close the gate.[3] But moral philosophers who are still caught in the fog of events, rather than being liberated into the purer air of facts, tend to think that the crucial question is whether John performed an act of omission (rather than merely not preventing something) or whether he counts as having caused the disaster (rather than merely so conducting himself that the disaster ensued). It is easy to see how it happens. Our inclinations

3. The concept of a negative fact about someone's conduct is explained and justified in Jonathan Bennett, "Killing and Letting Die", pp. 55–69.

to use "act" and "cause" in talking about conduct that is negatively relevant to an upshot—e.g. someone's not closing a gate, when this had significant consequences—does reflect what we think was expected or could reasonably have been expected from the agent: if he promised to keep the gate closed, say, and then didn't, that will incline us to credit him with an "act of omission" in not closing the gate and to say that he "caused" the disaster by not closing the gate. Since these considerations are also morally relevant, we get unabsurd results if we let our moral conclusions depend partly on whether there was an "act" and on what it or the agent "caused". I protest at this way of getting the results. "In this case is there an act of omission? Does he cause anything?" These are trivial questions about the *mot juste*, with no deep roots into our general scheme of things: if you answer Yes and I answer No, we are not differing about any matter of fact or philosophy, but merely parting company on a matter of verbal preference. So it is unsatisfactory—to put it mildly—to get from morally relevant premises to moral conclusions through intermediate theses about acts and causes. It is much better to sweep events (and thus acts) aside and talk about the consequences of behaving in one way rather than another.[4]

That is my principal exhibit in the case against events, but there are others. One is Davidson's attempt to found a philosophy of mind on the thesis that some mental events are physical events. I shall discuss this in my next section. Another is Lewis's treatment of Time's Arrow, in which event causation is put to work—made to carry a burden other than that of its own defense—in a manner that essentially depends on the difference between it and fact causation.[5] Lewis has been offering a general theory of counterfactuals that is supposed, among other things, to explain and justify our belief in Time's Arrow,

---

4. Eric D'Arcy, *Human Acts*, takes "act of omission" seriously (pp. 41–57). Other parts of that work, also, are devoted to picking up pieces that would not have been droppped in the first place if the author had turned to facts rather than events.

5. "Counterfactual Dependence and Time's Arrow". Lewis's paper "Causal Explanation" is also expressed in terms of event causation, but need not be. It argues that causally explaining an occurrence is reporting some part of its causal history, so that genuine explanations may be partial in various ways and degrees. This is opposed to the view that, until all the relevant information is included, we don't have an explanation but only a pointer to one. Lewis thinks of causal histories in terms of chains of eventlike items, but that is accidental to his main line of thought in this paper, which is based on a view not specially about events, or even about explanation, but rather about the place of partial information in our lives. This point about Lewis's paper is developed, and other fine things are done, in Peter Railton's "Probability, Explanation, and Information".

that is, our belief that how the world is at a time depends upon how it is earlier but not upon how it is later. Lewis offers to explain this with help from a theory of his according to which most normal counterfactuals run from times to later times, relatively few of them from times to earlier times; the idea being that our notion of dependence comes from the counterfactuals that we accept. Lewis agrees that some normal counterfactuals do run backwards, as for instance "If Stevenson had been inaugurated as President in January 1953, Eisenhower would not have been elected President in November 1952"; and one might regard that as fatal to Lewis's explanation of Time's Arrow, for nobody thinks that Eisenhower's victory depended upon Stevenson's not being inaugurated. Lewis doesn't agree that it is fatal, however. He says in effect that, although the above counterfactual is true, there is no corresponding truth of the form: "If e_1 had not occurred, e_2 would not have occurred". There would be one if there were such an event as Stevenson's noninauguration as President in 1952, and part of the job of Lewis's "Events" paper is to declare that there is not. This is a real use of the concept of event causation: it doesn't model over into anything concerning fact causation and is not comparable with the unhappy use of events and actions in moral philosophy.

It doesn't shake my opinion that event causation should be banned from philosophy, however; quite the contrary. For I contend that the Time's Arrow belief that we actually have is not confined to dependence between events. It is the belief that what is the case at one time does not depend upon what is the case later, whether or not the obtaining of these states of affairs consists in the occurrence of events; from which I conclude that it is not a belief that can be explained and justified by Lewis's general theory of counterfactuals, with its strong but not complete bias against counterfactuals that run backwards in time.[6] This view about Time's Arrow does not rest on hostility to events: I offer it as right, whatever one thinks about events, and I conclude that Lewis's one solid use of the concept of an event is in the service of an error.

---

6. For more on this, see my "Counterfactuals and Temporal Direction".

X

THE FISSION AND FUSION OF EVENTS

55. *Nonzonal fusion*

I have written as though the referents of our perfect nominals are determined by how the grid of our linguistic intentions is applied to the real world, implying that how fine the grid is and what shape its holes have is entirely up to us. Perhaps that is wrong. For all I have shown to the contrary, our event concept may have features that set limits to what events there are at a given zone—limits that remove some of the indeterminacy I have been discussing. For example, when we have no confident answer to the question "Was the fight illegal?", there may nevertheless be a uniquely right answer—one that follows from the given scenario by virtue of indisputable, necessary truths about events. If so, then some of our indecisiveness in applying event names comes from our incompetently wavering between event and nonevent.

Let us ask, then, what limits there are on *nonzonal fusion and fission* of events. An item is the "fusion" of a lot of items if they compose or constitute it: they are all parts of it, and no parts of it lie outside them. A walnut is the fusion of its shell and its kernel; the kernel is the fusion of many cells; each cell is the fusion of a lot of molecules. The family of FOB and PAB is, in 1987, the fusion of myself and my brothers and sisters. Those fusions, like most of the ones we read about, are *zonal*, by which I mean that the zone occupied by the whole is a fusion of smaller zones occupied by its parts. If my greeting and yours are parts of a single exchange, that is zonal fusion; an army's advance may be a fusion of its left wing's advance and its right wing's advance. My present topic, however, is the fusion of two zonally coinciding events to make a qualitatively "richer" or "thicker" event that occupies exactly the same zone, and the fission of an event into qualitatively "thinner" ones, each coinciding with it in space-time. Those are what I call nonzonal fusion and fission.

There are two questions to be faced: (i) "How abstract can an event be?" and (ii) "How unabstract—that is, how near to being concrete—can an event be?" In the light of these, I want to comment on the picture of Quine and Kim as standing at opposite ends of a continuum, representing the extreme "unifier" and "multiplier" positions respectively. This is all right as a picture about Kim's and the Quinean's views about the semantics of event names, but it is misleading when offered as an account of the state of play in the metaphysics of events. Quine's answer to (i) does indeed stand at one extreme; he says that events cannot be abstract at all. There might be a metaphysical position allowing a little abstractness or a bit more or a whole lot or . . . and so on. Kim lies at some distance from Quine on that continuum of possibilities; but he has never said where, and there is no reason to credit him with the extreme position on how abstract events can be.[1] As for the question (ii) about the lower limit on abstractness, i.e. on how unabstract or near to concrete an event can be: Quine's position on that also stands at an extreme, but Kim's may stand there too!

Before plunging on with this, a diagram of possible positions may help:

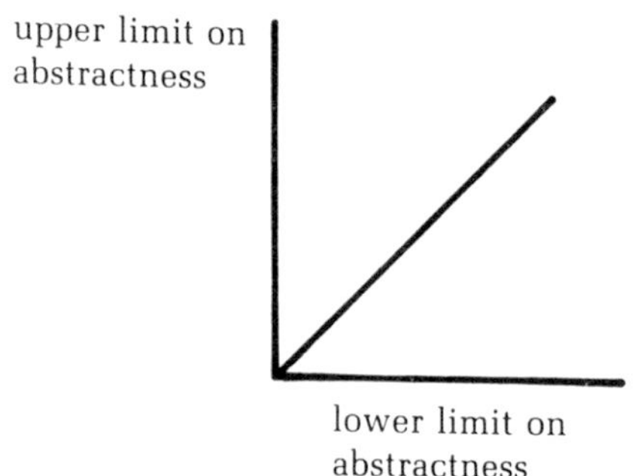

A point on the space represents a theory of events: the higher a theory is on the plane, the greater is the degree of abstractness that it regards as the maximum for any event; the further it is to the right, the greater is the degree of abstractness that it regards as the minimum for any event. That is, the vertical measures the ceiling on abstractness, and the horizontal measures the floor. So all the consistent theories lie on or above the diagonal: a theory below the diagonal would imply, of some degree of abstractness, "No event can be as abstract as this, but every event must be more abstract than this".

Theories on the diagonal are the ones for which floor and ceiling coincide, that is, which don't allow nonzonal fusion or fission of

1. There would be, if he held that there is an event corresponding to every S-P-T triple where S has P at T; but he explicitly denies this.

events. Quine is on the diagonal, down at the point of origin; the only philosopher I know of who was elsewhere on the diagonal is the late N.L. Wilson.[2] I cannot learn from him, however, because I don't know what his real topic was. His theory of "events", so called, was not meant to be answerable to linguistic and other evidence about our ordinary event concept; Wilson brushed all that aside with the grand remark: "We have been hornswoggled by language" (p. 314). Nor was he offering a revised event concept that would be serviceable for scientific purposes. He evidently preferred his event concept as something to think about, but I cannot discover whether or why he regarded it as better to think with.

Kim allows nonzonal fusion and fission: he implies, for example, that a walk might be a nonzonal part of a stroll. So his opinions don't lie on the diagonal. I can find nothing in his writings that definitively rules out concrete events, and certainly his semantic principle does not imply that all events are abstract—merely that a concrete event could not be named briefly unless it occurred at a zone that was qualitatively rather simple. So Kim's position may lie somewhere above Quine on the vertical, implying that events can be considerably abstract and that there is no limit to how unabstract they can be. The same is probably true of Davidson's position before Quine converted him. I don't know of any developed position that lies to the right of the vertical, i.e. that implies that there cannot be concrete events.

It seems indubitable that there is some nonzonal fusion. The spin of the top throughout T is one event, and its synchronous movement across the table is another that coincides with the former, and *the top's whole movement through T* is a third, coinciding with the other two and having them as nonzonal parts. How could anyone doubt it? Well, Lombard doubts it, but he doesn't say why. He writes: "There is, it seems obvious, no event composed of a ball's getting colder and its [simultaneously] rotating."[3] I don't know how to argue against this.

A fortiori, I cannot argue for the thesis of universal nonzonal fusion, which says that any two zonally coinciding events are parts of an event that also coincides with them. Nor can I see any reason to reject it, however. If the universal thesis is right, then any zone at which events occur is the location of a single event that contains all the others as nonzonal parts. That single event is an instance of the

2. N.L. Wilson, "Facts, Events and Their Identity Conditions".

3. Lawrence Brian Lombard, *Events*, p. 238. If this were a rejection of all concrete events, Lombard's position would lie to the right of the vertical. But he tells me that it is not; he thinks there may be events that exhaust what goes on at their zones, and he bases his view about the top on a special worry about rotation.

property that is a conjunction, so to speak, of all the event-properties instantiated at the zone; it will be a concrete event of the sort that Quine acknowledges.

If the thesis of universal nonzonal fusion is right and perhaps even if it is wrong, Davidson's philosophy of mind rests on a virtual triviality. I shall explain.

Davidson asserts the identity not of physical with mental substances, of physical with mental properties, or of physicalistic with mentalistic concepts, but rather of physical with mental events. His argument goes like this: Every cause of a physical event is a physical event, and some mental events are causes of physical events, so some mental events are physical events.[4] As I noted in Section 40, doctrines specifically about events do not inform this argument. I now contend that they undermine it.

We start with the idea, accepted by Davidson too, that there are mental(istic) properties and physical(istic) ones, with no overlap between them. A mental event is a trope containing an instance of a mental property as a part; if it is also a physical event, then it—that same trope—contains a physical property as a part. Now, if (1) mental properties are possessed by physical things and thus are instantiated at the same zones as physical properties, it obviously follows that (2) mental events occupy zones at which physical properties are instantiated. Also, the thesis of universal nonzonal fusion, namely that (3) if there are two events at a zone then there is also an event that is the fusion of them, implies that (2) is strictly equivalent to the thesis (4) that all mental events are physical, which is stronger than the basic doctrine of Davidson's philosophy of mind (stronger because it has "all", not "some"). Thus, Davidson's doctrine turns out to be an understatement of something that follows from thesis (1) which is, these days, a virtual triviality.

Davidson's adherence to Quine's view that there are only concrete events leads to the same conclusion even faster. If we back off from (3), the thesis of universal nonzonal fusion, and say that some coinciding events resist nonzonal fusion into a single event, then—and only then—there may be some significant content in the thesis that (some) mental events are physical. How much content will depend on how far we have moved from (3) and in what direction. This is uncharted territory, but I am not urging anyone to chart it. A proper grasp of how our event concept works should convince us that a worthwhile theory could not be built on double predications on events.

---

4. Donald Davidson, "Mental Events". The conclusion is often stated as "Some mental events are identical with physical events", but I do not follow that pointless formulation.

56. *Nonzonal fission*

Because there is at least some nonzonal fusion of events into thicker events, there is nonzonal fission of events into thinner ones. That much is obvious. It is not obvious whether any events are nonzonally ultimate, that is, have no nonzonal parts that are also events. It might be thought that there are none, i.e. that every event has nonzonal parts that are events; but let us consider the following objection to that thesis of qualitative infinite divisibility:

> If an event is constituted by a single simple property that is instantiated at a zone, then it cannot have nonzonal parts of any kind, and a fortiori cannot have nonzonal parts that are themselves events. Where an event is constituted by a set of properties (a complex property), you can split it by dividing the set of properties into subsets (sorting out the complex property into simpler constituents). But when you are down to one simple property, there is no way of splitting any further.

That is right. Our only understanding of nonzonal fusion and fission is through the idea of dividing a set of properties into subsets or a complex property into constituents. So, if some event was constituted by a property that resisted division into properties that could constitute events, e.g. because it was *simple*, that event would be unsplittable (except zonally).

Locke and Hume thought that color properties such as blueness are simple because the corresponding predicates defy analysis: there are no values of F and G such that "x is blue" is entailed by "Fx and Gx" but not by either conjunct alone, or so they thought. They were wrong, as can be seen by letting F be "is colored" and G be "is either not colored or is blue". This is not to say that being colored and being not-colored-or-blue are simpler properties out of which the more complex property of blueness is composed. It is merely a warning against trying to define simplicity of properties in terms of entailment relations among predicates; the trick with "blue" can be repeated for any predicate.

I don't know whether any events are nonzonally indivisible. It is plausible to think that some are, but this atomistic hunch may have no basis deep and objective enough to deserve a place in a metaphysical scheme. If the hunch is wrong, then the door is wide open to negative events. According to Kant, Ayer, and myself, a negative fact is an extremely general or abstract one—such as the fact that Mario Cuomo is not . . . (and then fill in the gap with a ten-page description that fits Edward Koch) or the fact that at this moment my left foot is not moving with precisely such and such a trajectory.[5] If every such fact attributes to its subject a property and if an instance of such a property can *constitute* an event, then there are negative events.

I cannot produce any convincing examples, because all our actual event sortals pick out events that are not nearly abstract enough to count as negative. I think I know why. A successful event name goes to a zone and picks out, from all the tropes present there, the one to which the property that is named or expressed in the name has a certain relation R. If R were identity, Kim's semantics would be right; but we know that it is not, that R is weaker than identity, and thus that an event name picks out a richer property than the one named or expressed in it. Although R is not weak to the point of tautology (for, if it were, the event name would sweep up every property instance at the zone, making the Quinean semantics right), it is probably weak enough to enable the name to reach into the zone and pick up a trope that is not abstract enough to qualify as negative.

That could be true even if the event name's "property" component were negative. A negative event name, if one could be found, need not name a negative event, because the negative property expressed in the name might have the relation R to a trope that is not negative, in which case the negative name would reach into the zone and grab a nonnegative event. In fact, though, I am not convinced that there are any clear and grammatically decent examples of negative event names.

The line I have been taking leads to the conclusion that either there is a severe limit on how abstract an event can be or there are events that we cannot name. I don't know which disjunct to choose. To adopt the former of them would be, in a way, to let language call the tune. Sometimes philosophers let language call the tune in ways that I would not tolerate. Someone who argues that all events must be changes because it seems odd to speak of something's stasis as "an event" or who sets limits to the zonal fusion of events because the man in the street would not speak of the totality of things I did on my last holiday as "an event" is letting serious metaphysical issues be pushed around by surface features of our language. I can see no reason to do this, rather than carving the world up at the joints by including among "events" not only the items that would ordinarily be so called but also any others that resemble those in fundamental structure and

5. The fact that my left foot is not moving at all is not negative; it is a highly positive fact. Against the contrary opinion, which has been asserted without argument by a line of philosophers from Leibniz through Bentham to Bruce Vermazen (see his "Negative Acts", p. 94), I offer the defense based on an analysis of negativeness in Jonathan Bennett, "Killing and Letting Die", pp. 55–69. The point about immobility as positive is on pp. 65–67.

significance. The kind of "calling the tune" that I have suggested in these paragraphs is different from that and is less clearly objectionable. It involves basing a metaphysical conclusion on a consideration about language, but it is not a trivial point about the *mot juste*. Rather, it concerns how perfect nominals function as event names, which is the most fundamental linguistic phenomenon that the territory of events contains. Indeed, it is almost constitutive of our event concept, as transpired in Section 51, where I showed how far one can go with the idea that events are just facts named by perfect nominals. So even those of us who are not drawn to the surface kind of linguistic point should still be sympathetic to the idea that the semantics of event names set a limit to how abstract events can be. This whole question deserves to be explored further, but I shall not pursue it here.[6]

Lombard has made a proposal for marking off a kind of property that cannot be split so as to give an event nonzonal parts.[7] One of his examples concerns a particle S that moves diagonally downwards through a period of time T. During T it has the property *moving vertically* and the property *moving horizontally*, and the question is "Do these properties constitute two events?" My parachutist who spirals downwards provides a better example, because the difference between rectilinear and circular, being geometrical, is deeper and less conventional than that between vertical and horizontal. However, I shall stay with Lombard's version; the discussion could easily be adapted to the spiralling example.

I assume that if the properties constitute two events they also constitute one, namely the fusion of the two. My question (and Lombard's, I think) is whether they constitute two events or *only* one—a qualitatively atomic event that has no nonzonal parts. Lombard inclines to answer "Only one" because:

> We have a physical theory according to which the forces producing movements of objects are all fundamentally the same and operate in the same way regardless of the direction of the movements they produce. If the horizontal movements of objects were the results of

---

6. Bruce Vermazen, "Negative Acts", and Donald Davidson, "Reply to Bruce Vermazen", have not helped me to a confident view about negative events or event names. For one thing, this material focuses specifically on negative actions, and thus emphasizes issues about intention that are not relevant to my problem. I am also impeded by the remark that "Negative acts do not, strictly speaking, exist" (p. 100), by the remark that "We often seem to count among the things an agent does things that he does *not* do: his refrainings, omissions, avoidances" (p. 217), and by repeated trouble over the difference between perfect and imperfect nominals.

7. Lawrence Brian Lombard, *Events*, Chapter 6. My quotations from Lombard in this section will all be from his pp. 166f; the first has omissions.

> the impartings of momentum by other objects, but downward vertical movements were due to the natural tendency of all things to seek the centre of the universe, then it would be appropriate to say that movements through space were composed of horizontal and vertical movements . . .

. . . so that the total movement of a diagonally moving particle would be composite, having a horizontal and a vertical movement as non-zonal parts. Since that is probably not how things stand, the particle is the subject of just one movement through T.

Lombard says nothing about what forces are at work in the moving of this particle on this occasion, implying that that is irrelevant to how many movements there are. Even if the particle moves vertically because of gravity and horizontally because of magnetic repulsion, still—Lombard seems to think—these are just aspects of a single movement, because they differ in direction and there is no systematic link between that and differences of causal force. But where does direction get its privilege from? Why not say that, in the case I have envisaged, the features differ in that one is gravitationally and the other magnetically caused and that this difference *does* connect systematically—indeed analytically—with different kinds of forces?

Lombard might reply: "My theory doesn't accord any privilege to direction as such. It asks whether any two aspects of an event differ in some respect that is systematically causally tied to different kinds of force, and in my example the only candidate is difference in direction. If the theory attended instead to what forces are actually operative in the example, rather than to differences that are systematically causally tied to different kinds of force, the appeal to what physical theory implies in general would be otiose." So it would, but perhaps that would be a better theory.

Admittedly, it too would have its difficulties. Consider three objects, each moving vertically because something is pushing it down, and each also moving horizontally—one through magnetic attraction, one through mechanical pushing, and the third through a mixture of those two kinds of force. The proposed rival theory would have to say that one particle makes two movements, the second makes only one, and the third . . . ?

With the theory in Lombard's form of it, there are never two motions that fully occupy the same zone. A while back, I took it for granted (except by Quineans) that the spin of a top throughout T is one event and its synchronous movement across the table is another, but Lombard is not entitled to agree, because physical theory tells us that linear and rotary movements can be caused by the same kinds of forces. So the ox's rotation is its loss of rawness after all! We have seen that Lombard doesn't accept this consequence of his theory: with regard to a ball's getting colder and simultaneously rotating he says that there is no such event, although his theory, together with elementary physics, implies that at that zone there is *only* that event.

Lombard also infringes his own theory in treating his other main example. A boy's maturation, he says, is "an event composed of voice lowerings and hair growings" rather than an indivisible event with vocal and hirsute features, because "the growth of facial hair can be traced to factors to which the lowering of the voice cannot (and *vice versa*)". But the growth of facial hair and the lowering of the voice are both biochemical changes that are produced by the forces that govern the interactions of, mainly, carbon, hydrogen, nitrogen, and oxygen. No doubt they "can be traced to different factors" in some sense of those words, but not in any sense that relates to what science tells us about "what the *ultimate* constituents of things are [and] what the changes in ultimate objects consist in".

Even the weaker Lombardian theory that I have suggested—the one that asks what forces are at work in the particular case—still yields a more Quinean result than Lombard wants for the spinning top (or roasting ox) and also for the maturing boy unless zonal differences are brought to the rescue. In some other cases, the strong and weak theories might produce different results. But, if the world makes true a unified theory according to which there is only one basic force, with gravitational and electrical forces being special cases of it, then the two versions collapse into one another and into the Quinean thesis that there are only concrete events.

We can thank Lombard for a provocative if sketchy suggestion, namely: The question of whether P_1^* and P_2^* each constitute an event or whether instead there is only a single event that is constituted by their conjunction may depend on what causal relation there is between the properties of which P_1^* and P_2^* are instances (Lombard's version) or between those two tropes themselves (my weaker version). So far, however, I have not been able to flesh this out into something worth having. It could not yield a very conservative account of our actual event concept, for any version of it will imply the indivisibility of some events that the plain man would cheerfully divide. Still, one might hope that it would capture the heart of our ordinary concept while having other virtues as well, e.g. serviceability for scientific purposes. The hope remains unrealized.

57. *Parts and wholes*

Before turning to zonal fusion and fission of events, let us consider parts and wholes generally.

A thing that has spatial parts is an aggregate: its status as a single thing comes from how its parts relate to one another—as a lot of dust particles may be so related as to constitute a hillock, or planks to make a ship.

Leibniz thought that anything that takes up space is an aggregate, from which he inferred that the rock-bottom constituents of reality have no size at all, this being needed if they are to avoid being aggregates, and thus not ultimate. The bodies of live animals, he thought, hang together in a way that makes them analogous to ultimate simples, but fo the rest he held that differences amongst the aggregates—between a herd of sheep and a diamond, for example, or between one penny and the totality of all coins—are metaphysically negligible.

Quine is like Leibniz in not caring much about how ordinary physical objects differ from extraordinary ones and in having a metaphysical picture in which no kind of spatially extended thing is basic. He does not rely on simple or partless substances, though. Where Leibniz rested his metaphysic on the concept of a particular substance, Quine has space. If he brings "substance" into the story, he must either say with Spinoza that there is only one substance (Space is the substance) or decline to use the count noun "substance" at all and instead use a mass noun that is grammatically like "water" and "porridge" (Space is substance). Thus, whereas for Leibniz the most basic story about a pebble is that it is an aggregate of simple substances, the comparable story for Quine is that a pebble is a part of the one substance or is some substance, like saying that a drop of water is a part of the one ocean or is some water. Still, it is true if unimportant that, in Quine's metaphysic too, a physical object is an aggregate of spatially smaller objects, giving him the question of how a set of objects must be interrelated to compose a larger object. Like Leibniz, Quine is indifferent to what constraints an item must satisfy to count as a physical object *ordinarily so called*. No doubt he would say that whatever items are picked out by physics as fundamental occupants of space are somewhat special, as Leibniz thought animals are.

All of that reapplies to things' temporal parts, if they have them. Quine thinks they do, but Leibniz didn't. A thing with temporal parts would have to be an aggregate of them, and, again, there are differing views about whether there are any sharp, deep criteria by which to aggregate temporally small things into temporally larger ones. Someone might say Yes where the thing in question is an atom, or an organism, or a person, while saying No with regard to artifacts, giving the back of his hand to the "problem" about the ship of Theseus. Someone else might say No across the board.

Where events are in question, both kinds of aggregation are clearly at issue, for events can certainly have temporal as well as spatial parts.

58. *Zonal fusion*

What must be the case about a pair of noncoinciding events for there to be an event that is the (zonal) fusion of them? The strongest possible answer is that nothing is required, i.e. that given *any* set of events occurring at different zones there is an event that is the fusion of them. That may be the position of Judith Jarvis Thomson. What she says seems weaker: given any set of events that share a property, there is the fusion of all of them.[8] But she is generous about what properties there are, counting "is self-identical" and "occurred before today" among them, and apparently allowing brutally disjunctive properties as well—she thinks there is the event that I call Pepper, which is the fusion of my peppering of my breakfast egg this morning and the totality of causes of Caesar's crossing of the Rubicon. So when it comes to event fusion the sky may be her limit.

Anyway, an ontology that includes such an event as Pepper is hospitable, if not in the extreme, then out towards it. Thomson defends this by shifting the onus: "I have no argument for the Principle of Event Fusion. But it seems to me that there is no argument against it either" (p. 82). Let us consider this.

We certainly have the notion of an event with zonal parts that are also events, and we allow that an event may be zonally ragged, as when Amanda's interrupted reproaches and Claude's interrupted apologies add up to a conversation. Are there also events like Pepper, which are ragged and have nothing holding them together?

Thomson equates the question of whether we can "give [these] peculiar event-fusions . . . a place among events" with the question of whether we can "give a plausible account of (i) what their temporal relations are to other events, (ii) what their causal relations are to other events, and (iii) what other events they have as parts and are parts of" (p. 82). Her book gets them over *that* hurdle all right. There is, for example, no problem about locating Pepper: its zone is the fusion of the zones of its parts. That is not a neatly compact way of saying when and where it occurs, but plenty of events whose existence ought to be uncontroversial—for example, Nietzsche's campaign against Wagner—also cannot be located by a simple phrase like "here in this room an hour ago". It's true that we have no way of referring to Pepper except with help from the technical term "fusion". But must a metaphysic of events be confined to events of kinds we name in ordinary thought and speech? I think not. Granted that the man in the street would deny that there is any such event as Pepper, we need to know *why* he would do this—whether there is something deep and hard behind his resistance—before we banish Pepper from our onto-

8. Judith Jarvis Thomson, *Acts and Other Events*, pp. 78f.

logy. These remarks, of course, express a view not about events but about metaphysics.

How freely events can be zonally fused depends, I maintain, on what happens as our metaphysic of events unfolds. Suppose we have a metaphysical theory that does justice to our actual handlings of our event concept and that is cleaner and more economical than any of its unrefuted rivals. Now continue the supposition in each of these three ways (one at a time, of course): (1) the theory owes some of its smoothness to its allowing unrestricted fusion, (2) it can be developed either towards fusion or away from it without this affecting its success in handling the intuitively available data, (3) it comes to grief if fusion is not severely limited.

If either (1) or (2) were the case, that would be evidence that all fusions of events are events. That would make our event concept resemble the concept of a *quantity of matter*, as described by Helen Cartwright.[9] There is a quantity of matter in this cup; right now it occupies a connected portion of space, but it has been widely scattered and will be scattered again. Reflecting on this helps us to see that there are some madly scattered quantities of matter, which we have no practical reason to attend to. There is, for instance, a quantity of matter of which different parts are at this moment parts of the Taj Mahal, my left knee, the planet Mercury, and Philip Larkin's tombstone. There are only philosophical reasons for thinking about it while it is thus dispersed, but there is every reason to suppose that there *is* such a quantity of matter, whether or not we think of it. The question of whether events can be as disconnected as quantities of matter can is an open one and is not to be closed by quick appeals to episodes of naive astonishment or by unlimbering the all-purpose word "surely".[10]

What about the scenario (3), in which our most smoothly efficient way of handling the conceptual facts is in a theory that restricts event fusion? A theory of events might include this: Any two parts of a single event must be causally linked with one another by an ordered set of events each member of which causes or is caused by its successor. (Of course, if a big bang caused all subsequent events, this axiom does not constrain event fusion.) Or a theory might have the stronger axiom: Any two parts of a single event E must be causally linked with one another by an ordered set of events each member of which causes or is caused by its successor and every member of which is a part of E. It might happen that a successful metaphysical theory includes *and*

9. Helen Morris Cartwright, "Quantities".

10. "Events sometimes sum to yield a further and distinct one; yet intuition balks at the notion that such summing is universally permissible (there is surely no one event comprising both Lennon's death and Charles's wedding)." Barry Taylor, *Modes of Occurrence*, p. 25.

needs some such fusion-limiting axiom as that—remove the limit on fusion and the theory falls to pieces or becomes horribly complex, and there is no adequate replacement for it.

Here is a safely undogmatic response to that discovery: retain the theory; describe it as the metaphysics of a certain large species of events, a species including all the kinds of event that we are ever interested in for nonphilosophical reasons; and stay silent about whether any events lie outside it.[11] That could be a reasonable procedure if the line around the species were defined by a strong, clear, deep condition. If the species were untidily gerrymandered to fit snugly around all and only the events that we care about, that would be another story, and not one I am considering.

A riskier response would be to infer that not all fusions of events are events. Objection: "That assumes, absurdly, that the limits on what we can easily theorize about are limits on what is real, as though reality owed us a smooth ride in our theories." I reply that that is a reasonable assumption when, as in metaphysics, what is in question is conceptual reality. When a claim is made of the form "According to theory T, the items picked out by our event concept are . . . ", if what fills the gap is a tolerably simple, economical, manageable set of axioms, and there are no counterinstances, the theory is probably true; but if what fills the gap is a long, tangled story that can't be replaced by something simpler, the odds are that the theory is wrong, because it is not likely that we would have a concept with such an ungainly structure as that.

That is all airy and abstract. If we look for actual theorizing about events that exerts pressure for or against liberality in zonal fusion—not through attitudes to fusion as such but through principles specifically about events—the only candidate I can find is from Lombard. He writes:

> Suppose that a heatwave causes the melting of all the world's snow. If there is such a thing as the world's snow, then its melting surely has a disjointed region of space as its location, since the snow has such a location. However, I am not inclined to think that there is any such thing as the world's snow; and to the extent that there isn't, then its melting does not have a disjointed location, for there is no such event. An event occurs just in case some object changes non-relationally, and is the non-relational change that object thereby undergoes. Each event, then, has some changing thing for its subject. When there is no such thing, there is no event. (pp. 123f.)

Lombard has even more extreme rejections of zonal fusion (see pp. 238–42). He denies, for example, that there is any such event as an

---

11. Thus Jennifer Hornsby, in her review of Thomson's book.

exchange of greetings, because two people don't constitute an object (p. 239).

That is fiercely counterintuitive, and the supposed theoretical basis for it is weak. Granted that an event is a trope[12] and even granted that a trope can exist only at a zone where *something* has the property, it does not follow that what has the property must be *some one object* rather than a scattered aggregate of objects, for example, or a zone. In Lombard's work, these restrictions have no role except to keep "an event" tied to "an object", with the latter understood conservatively, and to deprive the treatment of depth, breadth, and interest that it might have had.

The thesis that events are tropes may seem to limit event fusions. If it does and if the limits are more severe than we want, we had better back off from the position that every event is a trope to the more modest position that every event is a fusion of tropes. This is a minor change; the withdrawal could be orderly and free of casualties. Perhaps it is not even needed, for one might argue as follows: If zone z_1 is the location of trope P_1* and zone z_2 is the location of trope P_2*, then the fusion of the two zones has the property "consisting of two parts one of which instantiates P_1* and the other of which instantiates P_2*"; so the fusion of z_1 and z_2 is the location of a trope that is an instance of that property.

59. *Zonal fission*

If some pairs of events are parts of a larger event, then some events have smaller ones as parts. How far does this go? The strongest answer is that *Every event has spatiotemporally smaller events as parts.* It would be interesting to know whether this ever fails, and, if so, where and why.

The strongest thesis is false so far as temporal parts are concerned. My argument for this has three premises. (1) If time is granular, then there is a lower limit on the temporal fission of events: an event that lasts for only a chronon (a shortest period of time) cannot have briefer parts, because nothing is briefer than a chronon. (2) If there are instantaneous events, these cannot have temporal parts either, for obvious reasons. (3) If time is not granular then there are instantaneous events, including starts and finishes and wins and losses. On the strength of these three premises, I reject the strongest fission thesis so far as temporal parts are concerned.

12. Lombard follows Kim in saying that an event is an exemplifying of a property, and apparently he doesn't think that exemplifyings are tropes. But then I don't know what they are.

Let a "stretched event" be one that lasts for more than a chronon (if time is granular) and for more than an instant (if time is continuous). Then perhaps *Every stretched event has temporally shorter parts that are also events.* This might be disputed by those who think that events must be changes, because they might think that some of the temporal parts of changes are not themselves changes. If all change is continuous, as has often been thought, then every change has temporal parts that are changes. But perhaps some change is discontinuous. That could be so even in a continuous time, but is easier to illustrate in the context of granular time: If a thing changes from being F to being non-F in granular time, there must be at least one pair of adjacent chronons in which it changes; that change is a stretched event, but neither of its temporal parts is an event because neither is a change, and so the change is a stretched event that is incapable of zonal fission along the time line.

Without the premises that all events are changes and that some changes are discontinuous, I cannot mount any case against the thesis that every stretched event has shorter events as parts.

What about an event's having spatially smaller parts that are also events? An event cannot have such parts if it occurs at a spatial point or within an atom of space (if there are any). And it seems undeniable that there are such events. Let P be a plane defined by the centers of gravity of three protons, and L the straight line between the centers of two neutrons. Then consider the event *L's intersection of P at T* where T is an instant; if there is such an event, it occurs at a point. If there are no instants but only temporal atoms, then the event occurs at a spatial atom. If time is granular and space continuous, it may be harder to defend events at spatial points, but I am willing to leave that bridge uncrossed.

60. *Are all events changes?*

Although I have looked at an argument from the premise that all events are changes, I am not convinced of the premise. I take it that all events are property instances; whether they are all changes is the question of what kinds of properties they are instances of. Lombard, who thinks it important that events are changes, says they are "exemplifyings" of *dynamic* properties. A dynamic property is one that an item has by virtue of an alteration in what static properties it has.[13]

13. Lombard defines "dynamic property" in such a way that a thing can have a dynamic property only over an interval, not at an instant, which implies that starts and victories and terminations are not events. My definition allows for instantaneous changes, which seems right: isn't the *ending* of something's being F a perfect paradigm of a change?

This is an intelligible thesis, and on the face of it a plausible one, and I don't deny it. Still, I shall raise a few questions.

Suppose that our event concept does require that all events are changes. Then

an event is an F instance of a dynamic property,

where "F" stands for anything we have to say about zonal limits, upper and lower limits on degree of abstractness, and so on. Now let me invent and define a new word:

a statevent is an F instance of a static property.

Thus, the species *event* and *statevent* are mutually exclusive, and they jointly exhaust the genus *genevent*, defined thus:

a genevent is an F instance of a property.

The chief question in the events-as-changes area is just this: Does *event* differ in interesting structural ways from the *statevent*? Does the dynamic/static difference bring with it other differences that interact so as to give the two species of genevents quite different conceptual gestalts?

Statevents are presumably *states*, so my question is whether the distinction between events and states has much work to do in metaphysics. The distinction does exist and is sometimes insisted upon vigorously,[14] but how much does it really matter?

Three writers on events have thought that it matters considerably, attaching weight to the idea that events are all changes. Let us look at them in turn.

Barry Taylor offers a formidably difficult and technical theory of events, in which great energy goes into developing some ideas of Aristotle's about different kinds of change.[15] This provides what Taylor regards as a classification of events. If not all events are changes, however, we can still retain Aristotle's and Taylor's work as a taxonomy of *changes*, i.e. of one species of events. When Taylor gets around to discussing events as a whole, nothing he says conflicts with that. After a dauntingly formal handling of the preliminaries—the concepts of *fact* and of *change*—what he offers for events as a whole is a brief, casual, inexplicit, underargued treatment of the issues that have commanded the attention of the rest of us. In its main outlines, it reminds one of the Kim-related position criticized in Section 48 above.

Lombard says that his account of events "tries to take seriously

14. For example, by P.M.S. Hacker, "Events and the Exemplifications of Properties". For the opposing view, see C.D. Broad, *Scientific Thought*, p. 54.

15. Barry Taylor, *Modes of Occurrence*, pp. 51–82.

the idea that the concept of change is at the very core of the concept of an event" (p. 79), but the restriction of events to changes really has only mechanical and limiting effects on the work, most of which would go through equally well if he dropped "dynamic" from his account and said merely that events are instances of properties. Right at the end of his book, Lombard purports to use the thesis that events are changes, in arguing against subjectless events:

> The concepts deployed in the construction of my theory have made it impossible that there be subjectless events, events that are not changes in something. I have argued that events are changes, that changes are exemplifyings, and that there can be no exemplifyings unless there are things that exemplify. I do not see how to get a grip on the concept of an event without seeing [it] as bound up with the concept of change [or] how to get a grip on the concept of change without seeing change as what objects undergo. To suppose that there are subjectless events is to suppose that there are events that are not changes; and I don't think I understand such a supposition.[16]

The thesis that events are changes is repeatedly displayed here, but it is doing no work. All the argument needs is that events are exemplifyings and that there cannot be an exemplifying without something that exemplifies.

Frederick Schmitt has sought to make something metaphysically deep of a line between events and states. He distinguishes events, states, and objects by three formulae that differ as follows:

x is an event=necessarily Fx,
x is a state=necessarily not-Fx,
x is an object=possibly but not necessarily Fx.[17]

This is beautiful, and the paper is of the utmost interest, but the value of F upon which it depends, namely an item's "coming into being over its duration", is troublesome enough to leave me finally unconvinced.

61. *Judith Thomson's theory of events*

Judith Jarvis Thomson has presented an elaborately developed metaphysical theory of events, by working out interrelations among the concepts of *event*, *cause*, and *part*. I shall give it two sections, partly

16. Lawrence Brian Lombard, *Events*, p. 242, quoted with omissions.

17. Frederick F. Schmitt, "Events".

for its intrinsic interest but also for the following reason. One might suspect that if our event concept is not sharp edged and does not cut deep into the noumenal dough, it could not support an edifice such as Thomson's. I want to allay that suspicion.

Most of the reason consists in facts about what Thomson does not discuss. Her book does not address the semantics of event names; it says nothing about nonzonal fission and fusion or about whether events must be changes or must have subjects; it does not discuss the rival merits of event and fact causation or consider different analyses of the former. Its principal concerns have little or no overlap with mine.

What it mainly does is take the concepts of event, part, and cause, together with a little temporal terminology and a modicum of logic, and build with these materials. The foundations consist of ten axioms, which I now present. The numbering is Thomson's own; the missing numbers belong to theorems.

Two of the axioms concern the part-whole relation generally:

VIII. If x is part of y, then every part of x is part of y. (p. 76)
XIV. x is y≡x is part of y and y is part of x. (p. 92)

These pose no challenge to any view about the nature of our event concept.

The next two are about causation:

I. Causality is transitive. (p. 6)
VII. No event causes an event that wholly precedes it. (p. 75)

I take it that these are offered as conceptual truths, though the second might be meant rather as a deep contingency. Either way, both are about causation, not events. If either is true for event causation, it is equally so for fact causation. Axiom I does of course constrain one's analysis of event-causation statements, but my own discussion of transitivity shows that the choice for or against transitivity of (event) causation does not interact significantly with my views about how our event concept works.

Then we have three axioms relating *event* to *cause* and *part*:

II. No event causes or is caused by any of its parts. (p. 63)
III. If one event causes another, it causes all its parts. (p. 63)
IV. e_1 causes e_2 ≡ some part of e_1 causes e_2 and no part of e_2 causes or is identical with any part of e_1. (p. 66)

These cannot plausibly be said to be offered just as interrelating the concepts of *cause* and *part*, independently of whether the causes are events or facts. They have all the marks of owing their truth, if indeed they are true, to interrelations among three concepts, one of which is *event*. They are, then, part of the core of Thomson's metaphysic of events, and the purpose of these sections is to reconcile them with my views about indeterminacy and shallowness. It is hard to prove consistency, however. The best I can do is to show these axioms hard at work and invite you to agree that they seem not to mesh with any of the issues that I have been exploring.

Then there is the fusion principle, expressing a certain liberality about what events there are:

IX. For any property F: if some event has F, there is a unique event that is the fusion of all the events that have F. (pp. 78f)

This has some terrific effects on the content of Thomson's theory. It entails, for example, that indefinitely many events have no causes! Specifically, if event Big is the fusion of all the causes of event Small, then Big has no causes. Here is the proof (pp. 75f).

Hypothesis (1): Big is the fusion of all the causes of Small.
Hypothesis (2): Some event c causes Big.

Hypothesis (2) and axiom III jointly entail that c causes every part of Big; that and Hypothesis (1) entail that c causes something that causes Small; that and axiom I entail that c causes Small; that and Hypothesis (1) entail that c is a part of Big; that and axiom II entail that c is not a cause of Big; and that contradicts Hypothesis (2). So, if (1) is true, (2) must be false. Q.E.D.

One's initial attitude to the fusion principle and thus to that argument will be determined by one's views about metaphysics as such—about what the ground rules are, what weight to accord to the various data, and so on—rather than by any views specifically about events. It is not an argument that either confirms or challenges my main thesis about our event concept.

The last two axioms involve Thomson's concept of (in)complete event:

XI. There is at most one complete event that is caused by no event and causes no event.

XV. Every incomplete event is a fusion of complete events. (p. 93)

Having only a poor grasp of what differences these make to the development of Thomson's system, I shall set them aside. But the concept of (in)complete event, which they involve, should be commented on.

62. *Parts and causes in Thomson's work*

If someone runs first north and then south, Thomson says, his northward run is a part of his whole run, to which she adds that she cannot prove this (p. 110). That suggests that she is not working with any explicit theory about how to apply the concept of event-part, such as the theory that the parts of an event map onto the parts of the zone it fully occupies. So far as I can discover, all the event parts that she identifies as such are zonal parts, and I don't see why she shouldn't say, conversely, that (at least down to some small size) any part of a zone that is fully occupied by e is itself fully occupied by a part of e. If that is the working assumption of the book, then its concept of event-part comes directly from that of zone-part.

Thomson's way of interrelating "part" and "cause" is dominated by a formula of which the following is a simplified version (the simplification won't invalidate any of my points):

> D_{5a} e_1 is a part of e_2 ≡ whatever causes e_2 causes e_1, and e_2 does not cause e_1.

This can be found on pp. 74, 83, 90 of Thomson's book.

Although D_{5a} entails axiom III, the latter does have an axiomatic status in the work. It is offered as an "assumption" and treated as a test of an adequate analysis, so that the entailment is meant to count in favor of D_{5a} rather than of axiom III.

D_{5a} is not used to help us apply the concept of event-part in cases where there would otherwise be a diffculty about applying it; and it is hard to see how there could be such cases, if I am right in thinking that in Thomson's theory event-parts are automatically derivable from zone-parts. What D_{5a}—or axiom III—*is* used for is to inhibit some superficially plausible judgments about what causes what. I shall illustrate this with Thomson's argument for the conclusion that two events can have the same causes and effects. This relies on her concept of an incomplete event, which in turn owes a good deal to her liberality about event fusion; it also puts several of her axioms to work, in a way that shows much of the flavor and something of the substance of her work on events. The argument concludes that Davidson's nonduplication principle for events (see Section 38 above) is false.

Thomson writes:

> I shall call an event IE an "incomplete" event just in case there is an event E such that E is caused by part of IE, and E causes part of IE, but E is discrete from IE. A complete event, then, is an event CE such that there is *no* event E such that part of CE causes E and E causes part of CE and E is discrete from CE. ("Complete" because it is in an obvious sense "causally complete".) (p. 70)

By admitting incomplete events into her ontology, Thomson gives herself trouble, as on p. 95, where a certain formula has one disjunct for complete events and two more for two kinds of incomplete event. This might tempt one to exclude incomplete events, and that could be done cleanly, for they are marked off in simple, abstract terms with nothing fussy or ad hoc about them. The temptation is increased by the example through which incomplete events are introduced (pp. 68–71). Given a sequence of events each of which causes the next, Thomson invites us to consider the event we get if we fuse all of those except one that occurs somewhere in the middle. Her liberality with fusion implies that there is such an event, and her definition, given above, implies that it is incomplete. It is a broken causal chain: because it is temporally discontinuous, every causal route from its earlier to its later parts runs outside it. This will not endear it to those whose intuitions of naturalness keep a tight rein on their judgments about what events there are.

However, if we think to save ourselves theoretical trouble by denying such broken causal chains a place among events, we must be prepared to banish some intuitively harmless events. For example, it seems natural to think of the fusion of a certain series of mental and laryngeal events as a single conversation, although they constitute a broken causal chain with the missing links consisting in electrical events in wires or sound waves in the air.

In any case, not all incomplete events (in Thomson's sense) are broken causal chains. Running down a zigzag trail, I kick a small rock that is caused to roll slowly down the hillside and to come out on the next limb of the trail, where it causes me to stumble. In this scenario, Kick causes Roll which causes Stumble. Now, it can hardly be doubted that there is such an event as Run—my whole run down the trail, including Kick and Stumble but not Roll among its parts. Yet Run is an incomplete event in Thomson's sense: there are causal routes *through* it from its earlier to its later parts, but there is also a causal route *outside* it from its earlier to its later parts. Incomplete events, then, have come to stay.

I shall expound Thomson's argument that two events may have exactly the same causes and effects, doing it in terms of my example rather than hers. For purposes of this example, we need a slightly special case of my story about Run and Roll, namely one that satisfies

> Assumption: Every part of Roll causes some part of Run.

This is not asserted to follow from the rest of the story, merely to be consistently addable to it.

The two events we are to consider are Run and an event I'll call Runroll, which is the fusion of Run and Roll. Of these, Run is incomplete, whereas Runroll might be complete. Now let us see why Thomson holds, against Davidson, that they have exactly the same causes and effects.

Here is why they have the same causes. In one direction,

> whatever causes Run
> causes every part of Run (by axiom III), and so
> causes parts of Run that cause Roll (by simple logic), and so
> causes Roll (by axiom I), and so
> causes Runroll (by the trivial converse of axiom III).

In the converse direction, since Run is a part of Runroll whatever causes Runroll causes Run (by axiom III). So the two events have the same causes.

Thomson's account of why they have the same effects (p. 70) is hard to follow and seems to be incomplete or defective. With help from Thomson in personal correspondence, however, I have an argument for this conclusion. It makes use of

> Lemma: Any item that Run causes is discrete not only from Run but from Runroll,

which follows from Assumption by axioms II and III. Now, consider any item x that Run causes. By Lemma, x *is discrete from Runroll.* Furthermore, x *causes no part of Runroll,* because if it did then (by axiom I) Run would cause part of Runroll, which conflicts with axiom II. Also, *some part of Runroll causes* x because Run causes x and Run is part of Runroll. By axiom IV, the three italicized clauses imply that *Runroll causes* x. So we have established that whatever Run causes is caused also by Runroll.

As for the converse thesis that whatever Runroll causes is caused by Run: Suppose that Runroll causes some event x. It is easily demonstrable in Thomson's system (i) that x is discrete from Run and (ii) that it causes no part of Run. All that is needed to build these up into sufficient conditions for Run's causing x is the thesis (iii) that *part of Run causes* x. Working out a proof by reductio of (iii) within the context of Thomson's system is left as an exercise for the reader.

One might resist the first half of Thomson's argument by denying III, or the second half by denying IV, but axioms I and II are hardly controversial, and Thomson has convinced me that it is not easy to hold onto them while denying III or IV. Seeing why is left as a further exercise for the reader, who may find it invigorating.

It is not hard to deal with purported counterexamples. For a while, I liked this one:

> The rock's fall into the water caused the splash; but in the zone occupied by the splash there was a movement of a water molecule that was caused by something quite other than the rock's impact—it just happened to meld in with the molecular movements that were caused by the fall of the rock. In this case, the fall caused the splash but didn't cause every part of the splash.

Presumably Thomson would say that you can please yourself whether you let "the splash" refer to something that includes that molecule's movement, but, if you do, then it is not true that the fall caused the splash, though it did cause most of it.

That seems reasonable, and it is the right line to take for someone wanting—as Thomson pretty clearly does—to construct a fairly stern metaphysic, undeterred by the prospect of coming to conclusions that would sound odd to the untutored person in the street.

XI

ADVERBS AND EVENTS

63. *Explaining entailments*

Davidson uses the concept of an event in a theory about adverbial modification in English.[1] I shall first expound the theory, then explain why it matters, and finally criticize it.

It starts from facts about entailments that hold between some pairs of sentences. Consider the following pair: "During the past year, more oranges were grown in Brazil than kiwi fruit were grown in New Zealand"; "At some time in the past, fruit have been grown in Brazil". These sentences may now be making their first appearance in the whole history of the English language, yet we will all agree that the former entails the latter. This shared knowledge would be mysterious if it didn't proceed from a shared grasp of general principles under which the pair of sentences falls. It seems undeniable that we know and unconsciously apply such principles and that this explains our ability to agree, without collusion, in millions of judgments about which sentences entail which others. In bringing an entailment under such a logical principle, one explains its holding; and in conjecturing that people in general know the principle, one offers to explain their recognizing that it holds.

A pair of sentences may be brought under a logical principle in either of two ways—plain and fancy. We can explain the entailment by "The speed of light is finite and space is curved" of "The speed of light is finite" by bringing them, just as they stand, under this: From (. . . . and - - - -) infer (. . . .). Suppose, however, that we want to explain the entailment by "There are red apples in this box" of "Something is red". A principle that covered these just as they stand would have little scope; but we can bring them under something broader by first rewriting them. For example, if we replace one sentence by "Something is such that: it is red and it is an apple and it is in this box" and the other by "Something is such that: it is red", then the entailment falls under the principle: From (Something is such that: . . . . and - - - -)

1. Donald Davidson, "The Logical Form of Action Sentences".

infer (Something is such that: . . . .). This explains many entailments, so long as we are allowed to regiment the sentences, rewriting them so as to give the principle a grip on them. The more general the principles under which we bring our entailments, the more sentences we must regiment to make them fit.

Davidson wants to do all the explaining through first-order logic, that is, the logic of truth-functions and quantifiers. It would good if that could be done. First-order logic is well understood, simple, and powerful, and so it answers nicely to our desire for a strong, lean, highly general explanatory theory. Insofar as we want merely to get (1) a codification of entailments among English sentences that "explains" them in the sense of deriving them from general logical principles, we are free to settle for first-order logic if it will do the job. But Davidson is hunting bigger game, namely (2) a theory bringing entailments under the logical principles that operate in our minds and give us our knowledge of which entailments are valid. Even if first-order logic could provide (1), it is a further question whether it can provide (2), and it is not clear that Davidson has any independent evidence that it can. He may think that a reason is provided by a theory of his, according to which meaning is essentially linked with truth in a certain way: this could seem to favor first-order logic, since truth looms so large in it. Really, I think there is nothing much in this, but I shall not go into it here.[2] In this chapter, my focus will be on (1) except when I explicitly mention (2).

The project is not to explain all entailments, Davidson says, but only those that hold by virtue of the "logical forms" of the sentences concerned: " '$x > y$' entails '$y < x$', but not as a matter of form. 'x is a grandfather' entails 'x is a father', but not as a matter of form" (p. 125). How are we to draw the line between entailments that hold by virtue of form and ones that do not?

Those features of a sentence that bring it under our logical principles constitute its logical form. So if we know what logic we are using, then if S_1 entails S_2 we can easily tell whether or not these two sentences, *just as they stand*, are related by virtue of their logical form. And, when we are regimenting a pair of sentences so as to get an entailment that falls under logical principles, we can say that we are revealing the logical forms of the original sentences. So far, so good.

What if we are faced with an entailment that does not, just as it stands, instantiate anything general enough to count as a logical principle? How can we decide whether the sentences in it should be regimented so that the entailment becomes—or is revealed to be—formally valid? Here is Davidson's only guidance on this:

---

2. It is discussed in my review of Davidson's *Inquiries into Truth and Interpretation*, pp. 614f.

> There is something arbitrary in how much of logic to pin on logical form. But limits are set if our interest is in giving a coherent and constructive account of meaning: we must uncover enough structure to make it possible to state, for an arbitrary sentence, how its meaning depends on that structure, and we must not attribute more structure than such a theory of meaning can accommodate. (p. 106)

In fact, this sets no limits at all. There is no reason why a coherent and constructive theory should not—if it wanted to get into such details—say that the meaning of "John is a grandfather" depends upon its having the structure "There is something x and something y such that: John is a father of x and x is a parent of y". That implies that the entailment by "John is a grandfather" of "John is a father" holds as a matter of logical form, in first order logic, though Davdison says that it does not. I am not disagreeing him about this entailment—merely remarking that he does not guide us on how to settle such questions.

Earlier on the same page Davidson says that the entailment of P by "Joe knows that P" and not by "Joe believes that P" is a logical truth "that emerges only when we consider the meaning analysis of 'believes' and 'knows' ", and that therefore "we need not view the difference between [the two sentences] as a difference in logical form". He also says: "The request for logical form . . . is answered when we have identified the logical or grammatical roles of the words (or other significant stretches) in the sentences under scrutiny. It goes beyond this to define, analyze, or set down axioms governing, particular words or expressions."[3] These remarks suggest that formal considerations are ones that do not depend on the meanings of individual words, but that cannot be what Davidson means to say, because many of the differences that he regards as formal stem from the meanings of individual words—words such as "if" and "and" and "all". Davidson might say that the meanings of *those* words comes into logical form because the words themselves are formal, but that remark would be part of the problem, not part of the solution.

In his most recent assault on this topic, Davidson still does not say how to mark off formally valid entailments from others. He says, at one point, "There are more inferences that surely ought to be justified as matters of logical form", using "surely", as we all do, to indicate confidence unaccompanied by reasons. A little later, he says something that starts off sounding like a recipe: "To determine the logical form of a verbal expression, reduce the number of places of the underlying verbal predicate to the smallest number that will yield, with appropriate singular terms, a complete sentence." That this is no recipe at all becomes clear in the next sentence: "But do not think you have a complete sentence until you have uncovered enough structure

---

3. Donald Davidson, "Causal Relations", p. 149.

to validate all inferences you consider due to logical form."[4]

However, the entailments that fall squarely within Davidson's project can be intuitively marked off from ones that are marginal or external to it, and those intuitions must rest upon something. I suspect that it is some difference of degree, but I shall not pursue the question. All the entailments I shall discuss are ones that Davidson would call formal, and we need not worry about why.

64. *Adverbs and first-order logic*

We start with adverb-dropping entailments, as when someone believes an informant who says "She is furiously angry" and therefore, when asked "Is she angry?", answers "Yes". There are countless such entailments—"The table collapsed (noisily)", "The rain will fall (soon)", "You make me (extremely) angry", "She went for a walk (through Volterra)". Davidson holds, reasonably enough, that some one logical principle underlies all of these.[5]

It is not obvious that it is a principle of first-order logic. To represent adverb-dropping entailments as mere cases of conjunct dropping, we should have to say that the logical form of "The table collapsed noisily" is exhibited by "The table collapsed and (if the table collapsed it collapsed noisily)". That makes the whole entailment fall under the first-order principle that (P & Q) entails P, but nobody could accept that way of doing it.

Davidson's device for bringing first-order logic to bear on adverb dropping inferences is vastly more promising than that. He proposes that "The table collapsed noisily" means something of the form:

> There was a event such that: it was a collapse, and the table was its subject, and it was noisy,

and that "The table collapsed" means something of the form:

> There was an event such that: it was a collapse, and the table was its subject.

Then the entailment is explained as a routine case of the dropping of one conjunct from an open sentence within the scope of a quantifier. In brief, these adverbs are turned into adjectives that apply to events.

---

4. Donald Davidson, "Adverbs of Action", pp. 232f.

5. David Wiggins, "Verbs and Adverbs", contends that Davidson's program for handling adverbs is worthwhile even if one is not interested in capturing all logical form in the machinery of first-order logic. His difficult paper is adduced as evidence for this, but I do not understand it well enough to form an opinion.

That sketch slightly misrepresents Davidson: where I say "it was a collapse and the table was its subject", Davidson says "it was a collapse of the table". That is, where I use the form "C(x) & Subj(t,x)", he uses the form "C(x,t)", treating collapsing as a dyadic relation between things and collapses that they undergo. My treatment is better for two reasons.[6]

(1) Davidson's compacted treatment suppresses the single "Subj" relation that holds between a collapsing table and its collapse, a running girl and her run, a stabber and his stab. Consider the entailment by "The king insulted the queen" of "The king did something to the queen". It's a perfectly good entailment, and we ought to be able to explain it. You can't do so if you start with

For some x: Ins_3(x,K,Q),

but you can if you start with

For some x: Ins_1(x) & Subj(K,x) & Obj(Q,x);

for then you have only to drop the first conjunct to get a regimented version of "The King did something to the Queen". We need a Subj relation that applies all over our territory because you and I agree that "the King did something to the Queen last night" while disagreeing about what he did; you think he insulted her, I think he hit her. We have inferred our agreed, univocal conclusion from those different premises, so we need Subj and Obj in both premises.

(My topic here is the relation between an event and the substances it involves: the King and the Queen both have this relation to his insult to her and to the blow he gives her. That it is natural to call it Subj in his case and Obj in hers comes from our intuitive sense that the striker acts and the victim undergoes; there is no theoretical significance in this, and often when an event involves two substances they cannot be divided into subject and object—a chess game, for example.)

(2) There is other profit in the finer-grained treatment that breaks up "x is a collapse of the table" into "x is a collapse, and x is of the table". Davidson remained "unconvinced of the advantages in splitting transitive verbs up in this way",[7] but that was in response to a splitting-up proposal that was indeed defective. Here is an example

6. Others have parted company from Davidson in the same way. For example, Hector-Neri Castañeda, Comments on Davidson's "The Logical Form of Action Sentences"; Terence Parsons, "Modifiers and Quantifiers in Natural Language" and "Underlying Events in the Logical Analysis of English".

7. Donald Davidson, Reply to Criticisms of "The Logical Form of Action Sentences", p. 126.

that might carry conviction. When Davidson implies (on p. 157) that "Brutus stabbed Caesar" has the form

For some x: $Stab_3$(B,C,x),

taking it to involve a triadic relation that holds amongst three items just in case the third is a stabbing of the second by the first, he loses his chance of connecting the dyadic ". . . stabs . . ." with the monadic ". . . stabs". The latter is used in "He picked up the dagger and stabbed with it", meaning that he made a stabbing motion with it, perhaps not stabbing anything. Now, a Davidsonian informal logic should cover the entailment from "Brutus stabbed Caesar" to "Brutus stabbed". It can do so if the former is rewritten in the form:

For some x: $Stab_1$(x) & Subj(B,x) & Obj(C,x),

but not if it is left in Davidson's compacted form. Davidson's triadic predicate would let him cope with that entailment only if "Brutus stabbed" meant "Brutus stabbed something", which it doesn't.[8]

From now on I shall pretend that Davidson uses the fine-grained regimentations and the universal "Subj".

Davidson's treatment of adverbs has been subjected to an abundance of negligible criticism, but there is something to be learned from considering the attack on it by Fodor.[9] I mean Fodor's specific attack, not his general complaint that the whole first-order logic project is misguided because it cannot do justice to differences of highlighting, as between "It was Quine who went to Syracuse" and "Where Quine went was to Syracuse" (pp. 310–12). Indeed it cannot, nor can any of its rivals. So far as I can see, *any* viable theory of meaning must keep highlighting out of its foundations, bringing it in higher up, as a decorative extra.

Fodor strangely misidentifies the subject matter of Davidson's theory. As between "John spoke clearly" and "Clearly, John spoke" Fodor says that Davidson's theory is addressed to the *latter*. He tries to explain why (p. 308), but the explanation is wrong, and the explanandum is incredible. Nothing comes of this, however, and I shall not pursue it. Fodor's main offerings are two arguments that do not refute Davidson but do show the need for care in moving from English sentences to their Davidsonian paraphrases.

One concerns such differences as that between two possible readings of "They shot at the house". On one reading, it means that they were at the house when they shot, as distinct from "They shot in the rose garden"; on the other, more natural reading, it means that

8. Davidson comes close to saying all this himself, in his "Adverbs of Action", p. 233.

9. Jerry Fodor, "Troubles about Actions".

they shot towards—or aiming at, or trying to hit—the house. Fodor thinks that this is a problem for Davidson, but really it is no such thing.

According to Fodor, the phrase "at the house", when it serves to say where they were when they shot, operates on the sentence "they shot", so that the whole thing has the form: "At the house: they shot", whereas in the other reading the phrase operates just on the verb "shot", so that the sentence has the form: "They shot-at-the-house". If that is right (which I doubt), then Davidson needs only to say that his is a theory of true ad*verbs*, not of disguised adsentences, so that the original sentence falls within his province only on its second, more natural reading.

If Fodor is wrong about the form of the sentence on its first reading, there is another reply that Davidson can comfortably make. He can say that the sentence has only the form

For some x: x was a shooting, and x was by them, and R(x,the house),

the different readings coming from different values of R or senses of "at".[10] I think that "at" is indeed ambiguous, sometimes meaning "in the place of" and sometimes meaning "towards".

Fodor's remaining argument has been influential: variants on it keep turning up in the literature. Against Davidson's supposed regimentation of "He flew the spaceship to Hesperus" into something of the sort "There was a flying of the spaceship by him, and it was to Hesperus", Fodor objects that "is to Hesperus" is not a predicate of events, in the way that "occurs on June 5th" and "is dreaded by Jessica" are (p. 308), and he offers this as counting against Davidson's treatment of adverbs.

This is based on a misunderstanding. If Davidson offers to lay bare the logical form of "The *Enterprise* flew to Hesperus" by equating it with

There was a flight by the *Enterprise*, and it was to Hesperus,

he does not thereby commit himself to holding that "is to" is an acceptable dyadic predicate relating events to places. That way of stating his position is a stopgap, an intuitive help, a temporary relief from formalism. The official position is that the logical form of "The *Enterprise* flew to Hesperus" is best revealed by

For some x: F(x) & Subj(E,x) & T(x,H).

That last clause might be written "To(H,x)" as a reminder that it corresponds to "to Hesperus" in the original, but it shouldn't be

---

10. Thus Terence Parsons, "Underlying Events in the Logical Analysis of English", p. 256.

thought of as the English phrase "is to". Rather, it stands for something like ". . . occupies a zone whose temporally latest part has a spatial component occupied by . . .".

(Incidentally, Fodor is wrong anyway in saying that "is to Hesperus" is not a grammatically possible predicate of events. Fodor speaks of "the literal ungrammaticality of 'my flying my spaceship was to Hesperus' ". That sentence is indeed ungrammatical, but it uses an imperfect nominal and has nothing to do with events. "My flying of my spaceship was to Hesperus" is grammatically better, though it is hard to feel this because the sentence is stylistically so terrible. Switch now to a derived nominal—"The flight that I made my spaceship take was to Hesperus" or "The flight that I took in my spaceship was to Hesperus"—and the result is impeccable.)

If you see Davidson as using the most naive algorithms to get back and forth between English sentences and their logical-form regimentations, you can easily make him look foolish. That is what Aune does. Davidson holds that, if John amused Mary by walking into the door, then his collision with the door was his giving of amusement to Mary—these are two descriptions of a single event. Aune connects that doctrine (which I shall discuss in Chapter XII) with Davidson's theory of adverbs and contends that Davidson must equate "John amused Mary by walking into the door" with something like this:

For some x: W(x) & Subj(John,x) & Into(door,x) & Amuse(Mary,x).[11]

In fact, that cannot be right, because of subtleties in the "by"-locution that Aune does not mention. But it does not fall to Aune's criticism, as I shall now show.

I have used "Into" and "Amuse" as reminders of which bits of the original sentence correspond to those clauses, and I can say roughly what I mean by them. "Into" stands for the predicate "a collision with . . . was a temporal part of . . .", and "Amuse" stands for "a state of amusement in . . . was caused by . . .". Suppose, then, that we drop the conjunct that tells us that the event was a walking; what are we left with? We have

For some x: Subj(John,x) & Into(door,x) & Amuse(Mary,x),

which means that something that John did included a collision with a door and caused amusement in Mary. That, though not quite right, is free of the absurdity that Aune crams into Davidson's mouth. He says that Davidson must read the above regimentation as "John amused Mary into the door". That is monstrous indeed, but it owes nothing to Davidson's program and everything to Aune's execution of it.

---

11. Bruce Aune, *Reason and Action*; see pp. 29ff.

A more substantial line of criticism of Davidson's program comes from considerations about its scope. There is a rival way of explaining adverb-dropping entailments that covers everything that Davidson's does, and more. Davidson might respond that the rival theory, since it does not stay within the bounds of first-order logic, achieves its wider scope through too great a sacrifice of economy in logical principles. To evaluate this conflict, we shall need to look at the rival theory and compare it with Davidson's in some detail. That will be my task throughout most of this chapter.

There is also sometimes said to be an ontological issue between the two. It is sometimes held against Davidson's theory that "it quantifies over events". If it did, that would be all right, because of course there are events: I heard a crash five minutes ago. In fact, though, Davidson's theory of adverbial modification doesn't quantify over events. What it does do, when understood as a psychological and not merely a logical theory, is to imply that ordinary speakers and thinkers are quantifying over events much of the time—it treats an enormous amount of what we say as covertly asserting that there are events of various kinds—and that is a point in its disfavor. Barry Taylor says that the rival theory treats too many things we say as disguised assertions about worlds,[12] but I cannot see that it does any such thing. Proponents of the rival theory are apt to *explain their theory* in terms of worlds, but that is another thing and a quite innocent one.

65. *Predicate modifiers*

The rival theory was first advanced, more or less independently, by Montague, Parsons, and Clark.[13] I have not mastered the impressive literature that has since been devoted to it, but my present purposes do not require me to.

The theory regiments English sentences to exhibit their logical forms with help not only from names, variables, and predicates, but also from predicate modifiers—expressions that combine with predi-

---

12. Barry Taylor, *Modes of Occurrence*, pp. 6f, 14f.

13. Richard Montague, "English as a Formal Language", pp. 210–13; Terence Parsons, "Some Problems Concerning the Logic of Grammatical Modifiers"; Romane Clark, "Concerning the Logic of Predicate Modifiers". Clark expands and clarifies his views in "Adverbial Modifiers". For an extended, subtle development of this approach, accompanied by sympathetic understanding of Davidson's kind of theory, see M.J. Cresswell, *Adverbial Modification*.

cates to form new ones. They can be thought of as functions from predicates to predicates: "quietly" is a function that takes us from "walks" to "walks quietly", from "bathes" to "bathes quietly", and so on.

Those are adverbs that can validly be dropped from a sentence, that is, the omitting of which cannot turn a truth into a falsehood—unless the sentence is negative or the antecedent of a conditional, etc. Call such (uses of) adverbs *standard.* They contrast with *nonstandard* uses, where the dropping of the adverb is not guaranteed to secure truth. We cannot be sure of preserving truth if we drop the adverb from "They apparently shook hands" or "She allegedly joined the party", but these too can be neatly represented as predicate modifiers. Where standard modifiers take us from a predicate to another with the same or a smaller extension, the nonstandard ones take us to a predicate that may (or must) have a larger extension than the unmodified predicate does, which is why they cannot validly be dropped.

Gilbert Harman has implied that, although predicate-modifier theory has something to say about all adverbs (and, I would add, adjectives), it needs lavish helpings of logic—a separate logical axiom for each adverb—to cover all the entailments. He instances the axiom that would be needed for "slowly": For all x and y, if x has Sl(y) then x has y; and so on through each adverb in our language.[14] Really things are much better than that. All we need is for each predicate modifier to have its place in the following simple taxonomy, adapted from Romane Clark.[15] It is based on the logical relations that one sentence can have to another, namely (1) entailment forwards only, (2) entailment backwards only, (3) equivalence, (4) mutual inconsistency, (5) independence. If f(P) is formed by applying the modifier f( ) to the predicate P, then the possibilities are these:

1. f(P)x entails Px but not conversely. Example of such contracting modifiers are "wave *energetically*" and "fall *heavily*".
2. Px entails f(P)x but not conversely. These are the enlarging modifiers, such as "*arguably* succeed".
3. f(P)x is equivalent to Px. I call these the stand-pat functions, illustrated by "*genuinely* repent".
4. f(P)x entails not-Px. The only good examples I can find of such negating modifiers are adjectives (of which more anon), such as "*fake* Vermeer" and "*pseudo*-intellectual".
5. f(P)x is independent of Px. These are the neutralizing modifiers, as in "*allegedly* embezzle".

---

14. Gilbert Harman, "Logical Form", Section 3.

15. Romane Clark, "Concerning the Logic of Predicate Modifiers". For a helpful overview, see Terence Horgan, "The Case Against Events", pp. 44f.

With this modest apparatus, we can handle the adverb-dropping entailments without having a separate principle for each adverb. All that is needed is to have, for each adverb, the information about whether or not it is standard, i.e. belongs to class 1 or 3. And, by knowing which of the five classes each adverb (and indeed adjective) belongs to, we can handle other entailments as well. In short, if we know where each predicate modifier belongs in a five-part scheme, we can do a vast amount of work with a mere quintet of logical principles.

The predicate-modifier idea has been claimed to have other successes that first-order logic cannot match. Parsons makes one such claim about phrases containing more than one modifier when there is a question about what modifies what. He offers the pair

(1) John painstakingly wrote illegibly.
(2) John wrote painstakingly and illegibly.

(2) does not say whether it was one episode of writing or two, but that is no problem for Davidson and first-order logic.[16] The advantage that Parsons claims for predicate-modifier theory is that it can contrast (1) and (2) by a simple difference of form, whereas first-order logic must tell a tangled story to distinguish them at all. According to Parsons, (1) means something of the form:

(1′) P(I(W(John)))

and (2) means something of the form:

(2′) P(W(John)) & I(W(John)).

At first glance that looks right, but it isn't, because no univocal reading of the "P" operator makes both of those correct. To make (1′) right for (1), we must take P(Pred(x)) to mean, in part, that x took pains to make it the case that Pred(x). But, on that reading of P, the clause P(W(John)) in (2′) entails that John took pains to make it the case that he was writing, which (2) does not entail. It is easy to show also that the reading of P that makes (2′) right for (2) makes (1′) wrong for (1). Still, predicate-modifier theory has plenty of successes, even if that is not one of them.[17]

---

16. Indeed, it may be one for Parsons, though he could probably solve it. A more elaborate version of the same difficulty is urged against the predicate modifier theory by Barry Taylor, *Modes of Occurrence*, pp. 17ff.

17. Examples like these of Parsons' are adduced for different purposes in Romane Clark, "Predication and Paronymous Modifiers". Among the many subtleties in that paper is a convincing distinction between sentence modifiers and copula modifiers.

66. *Stretching Davidson's ontology*

Consider the sentence "Throughout the giving of the evidence, she stonily sat there in silence". It would be implausible to assign to this a different logical form from the sentences that Davidson handles by quantifying over events, but if he treats this in the same way as those, he must allow an episode of motionless sitting as an event. That is fine by me and probably also by Davidson, who has never said that events must be changes and who did once express tolerance for the idea of "such 'movements' as standing fast".[18]

By quantifying over unchanges, Davidson will be smoothing the way for applying his theory to many uses of adverbs to modify not verbs but adjectives. "Marvin was icily silent" entails "Marvin was silent", and it would be uncomfortable for a Davidsonian to have to exclude such entailments from the scope of his theory. It would be better for him to say that the former sentence has the form:

> For some x: x was an episode of silence, and Marvin was the subject of x, and x was icy.

Davidson had better be willing to quantify over some items that run for much longer than hour-long episodes of silence. Otherwise he will have to leave "For 20,000 years the Dover cliffs have been dazzlingly white" out of reach of his theory.

A further stretch in the range of Davidson's quantifiers seems to be demanded by the use of adverbs in timeless contexts. (I owe this point to David Lewis.) The sentence "This mathematical series converges steadily" entails "This mathematical series converges", and it is hardly credible that this entailment should differ in *logical form* from the entailment by "This balloon is shrinking steadily" of "This balloon is shrinking". Davidson apparently has to suppose that the former sentence means:

> For some x: x is a convergence, and x is of this mathematical series, and x is steady.

That is all right in itself, but a mathematical convergence is an intolerable candidate for the label "event". This is not superficial or optional. Even those of us who think that there was a millennia-long event consisting of the staying-white of the cliffs of Dover won't admit into the realm of events an item that is not in time and has no causal properties.

It is presumably obvious that predicate-modifier theory has not

---

18. Donald Davidson, "Agency", p. 49.

the least trouble in dealing with adverbial modification of verbs that do not report change, of negated verbs, and of adjectives. To enable Davidson's theory to handle them, I have had to admit into its ontology many items that some people would not call "events" and some that nobody would call "events". In my view, that enlargement is sheer gain.[19]

It has been suggested, however, that it condemns Davidson's program to being caught in an infinite regress. Given a normal English sentence on the left and a Davidsonian regimentation of it on the right, why should the conjuncts in the latter not be regimented in their turn? If "John sings" is regimented into the form "There is an x such that x *is a singing* and John is its subject" then why should not "x is a singing" be credited with having the form "There is a y such that y is a being-a-singing and x is its subject"? If that is allowed, however, there seems to be no obstacle to an infinite regress—or progress—which is none the better for being inexpressible in civilized English.[20]

The regress doesn't exist if Davidson quantifies only over events, properly so-called; but we are now crediting him with an enlarged theory that quantifies over tropes generally. One might try to fend off the regress, even then, by saying that the theory is to apply only to monadic predications that could be adverbially modified; but are there any that couldn't?

The threatened regress is highly objectionable if the theory that generates it is offered as describing a psychological reality. If the thesis is that, when we move from "This block is perfectly cubic" to "This block is cubic", we do this *by* assigning the former the form "There is an x such that x is an instance of cubicness and this block is the subject of x and x is perfect", and, when we move from "x is adverbly perfect" to "x is perfect", we do this *by* assigning the former the form "There is a y such that y is an instance of being-perfect and . . ." etc., and if this is said to go on to infinity, then we are being credited with assigning to ordinary English sentences an infinitely intricate structure. It may be arguable that sentences *have* that much structure but not that in our ordinary daily handling of our language we have unconscious thoughts in which that much structure is represented.

On the other hand, if the quantifying theory is offered only as "logic of language" and not as psychology, it need not shy away from the infinity. If the latter is present in the theory, that is because proper-

---

19. R. Bartsch, *The Grammar of Adverbials*, tries to make Davidson's ideas work through quantification over items other than events but does not say that the items in question are all tropes.

20. I was made aware of this problem by Eddy M. Zemach, "Events", p. 87.

ties can have properties, which can in their turn have properties, and so on ad infinitum, so that a trope can be the subject of a trope, which can in its turn be the subject of another trope, and so on. For example, this block of wood is cubic, so it is the subject of a trope, an instance of cubicness; since the latter is a geometrical property, the trope is the subject of an instance of geometricalness, which is a higher-order trope; and this may be continuable ad infinitum. If so, the infinity is innocent, considered as logic or metaphysics; if not, there is no infinity.

67. *Two other quantifying theories*

By a series of shifts that are needed to avoid unwanted failures of scope, I have made Davidson's theory virtually identical with one invented by the first theorist of adverb-dropping inferences, Hans Reichenbach.[21] Let us look into this on its own account.

Reichenbach quantifies over specific properties, such as the property of walking in some absolutely specific manner. There are countless different specific walking-properties, that is, properties P such that necessarily something that has P at T walks at T. Thus, "Patrick walks" means that

> For some x: x is a walking-property, and Patrick has x.

Of all the walking-properties, some are quietness-involving. For example, there are properties that include

> walking quietly and with a slight limp at 2 m.p.h. . . .

and all of those are quietness-involving. Again, some walking-properties are gracefulness-involving, and that class overlaps the quietness-involving ones. And so on.

Now we have what we need for a treatment of adverbial modification. To say that Patrick walks gracefully is to say

> For some x: x is a walking-property, and Patrick has x, and x is gracefulness-involving.

---

21. Hans Reichenbach, *Elements of Symbolic Logic*, Section 53; my page references are to the reprint in *The Logic of Grammar*. This Reichenbach material is discussed in Terence Parsons's "Some Problems Concerning the Logic of Grammatical Modifiers", pp. 320–24. Certain other ideas of Reichenbach's are discussed in Davidson's "The Logical Form of Action Sentences".

From that we can infer "Patrick walks" by dropping the final conjunct from the open sentence.

Actually, Reichenbach uses second-order logic. The difference between the two is illustrated by two ways of saying that Roland and Oliver have something in common. In first-order logic we can say

For some property P: Roland has P, and Oliver has P;

while in second-order logic we say

For some f: f(Roland) and f(Oliver).

The former quantifies over properties and asserts a relation of *having* between things and their properties. The latter quantifies in respect of the predicate position in the open sentence. The difference between the two has little significance in logic, I understand, and none in metaphysics or semantics. So we can safely pretend that Reichenbach made his proposal in first-order logic.

Stripped to its formal bones, my Reichenbachian rewrite of "Patrick walks gracefully" is this:

For some x: W(x) & H(Patrick,x) & G(x).

That looks familiar because it is also a bare-bones statement of Davidson's version of "Patrick walks gracefully". The two assign the very same logical form to the statement and differ only in the glosses they put on it. Reichenbach says he is giving two bits of information about a property and saying that Patrick has it; Davidson says that he is giving two bits of information about an event and saying that Patrick is the subject of it. The upshot of my preceding section is that Davidson will do much better if he too says that he is quantifying over property instances, not merely over the ones that would ordinarily be counted as events. If he does so, then he differs from Reichenbach only in quantifying over tropes (property instances) whereas Reichenbach quantifies over properties. That is a real difference, but nothing much hangs on it: any Davidsonian statement of the form "There is a trope which . . . and x is its subject" is interdeducible with a Reichenbachian one of the form "There is a property which . . . and x has it".

Oddly, there is a third approach to adverbial modification that when pressed also turns into a version of Davidson/Reichenbach. I shall expound it as briefly as I can.

If we regiment "The table collapsed" into "For some x, the table collapsed in manner x", and "The table collapsed noisily" into "The table collapsed in manner Noisy", we could bring the entailment between them under the principle

From (. . . [name] . . .) infer (For some x: . . . x . . .).

This idea was canvassed by Anthony Kenny, in the work that first drew Davidson's attention to the whole problem.[22] Kenny rejects it because it associates the verb "collapse" with predicates of different valencies—sometimes monadic, sometimes dyadic, and so on—because the table can also be said to collapse suddenly, in the room next door, with a lurch westwards, onto the floor, and so on, and any combination of these can appear in a single sentence. So we would have to treat "collapse" as "variably polyadic", Kenny says, which would make it radically ambiguous—and similarly with other verbs.[23]

Davidson likes this argument of Kenny's but remarks that he cannot make it a knockdown one by showing how to generate indefinitely many adverbial expansions of the troublesome sort; later on he became more confident of that, though not on impressive grounds.[24] The point about having indefinitely many is presumably this: If there could never be more than seven, say, then the verb "to collapse" could be taken to connote an octadic relation, always, with "The table collapsed noisily" being taken to mean something of the form

$Col_8(t,N,x_1, \ldots, x_6)$

with six existential quantifiers out in front.

Rescher has suggested that it might suffice to have an upper limit not on adverbial modifications but on categories of them.[25] His suggested list of categories—Manner, Means, etc.—tends to confine him to action sentences rather than to event sentences more generally, but never mind that. His idea is that "Patrick walked", for example, means something of the form

For some $x_1, \ldots, x_7$: Patrick walked in manner x_1 by means x_2 at time x_3 . . . and so on.

One might hope that "Patrick walked gracefully" would need one fewer quantifiers:

---

22. Anthony Kenny, *Action, Emotion and Will*, Chapter 7.

23. The assumption that no univocal predicate can have different numbers of subjects is probably false: ". . . constitute a discussion group" seems like a counterexample, and there are others. See Adam Morton, "Complex Individuals and Multigrade Relations"; or Richard Grandy, "Anadic Logic and English". But Kenny is basically right, for the rejected proposal threatens us with variably polyadic predicates that lack the symmetry that all the legitimate ones possess. If John and James and Susan live together (fight, form a gang, outnumber their enemies), then so do James and Susan and John; but it is not true that if the table undergoes a collapse in the manner Noisy, the collapse undergoes the table in the manner Noisy.

24. Donald Davidson, "The Logical Form of Action Sentences", pp. 108, 136.

25. Nicholas Rescher, "Aspects of Action".

For some $x_2, \ldots, x_7$: Patrick walked in manner Graceful by means x_2 at time x_3 . . . and so on,

the limit being a septuply modified use of the verb "to walk" *with no quantifiers*. That is wrong, however, because a verb can be modified in several ways under a single category—most notably the category Manner—so what we need is not "Graceful" as a *name* of the manner in which Patrick walks but rather "graceful" as a *partial description* of the manner in which Patrick walks. Only then can we cope in a tolerable way with the entailment by "Patrick walked gracefully and quietly" of "Patrick walked gracefully". So we have to represent "Patrick walks gracefully" in the form

For some x: Patrick walks in Manner x, and x is graceful,

with the second conjunct understood not as identifying the manner by naming it but as partly describing it by predicating something of it. Then "Patrick walks gracefully and quietly" becomes

For some x: Patrick walks in Manner x, and x is graceful, and x is quiet,

and now all is well.

I have set the other quantifiers aside so as to simplify the discussion, but nothing is gained by readmitting them; since nothing that is said about one could possibly be said about any of the others, we can safely lump them all together. Let us do that, using "Manner" as a fattened-up technical term that covers not only the manner (ordinarily so-called) in which something is done but also where and when and with what help, etc. it is done. Thus, to say that someone walked through Bologna is to say that his Manner of walking was a through-Bologna one, to say that he walked quietly is to say that his Manner of walking was a quiet one, and so on. So we can understand "Patrick walked quietly through Bologna, aided by a walking stick" as saying that

there is a Manner such that: it is the Manner in which Patrick walked, and it is quiet, and it is through Bologna, and it is stick-aided.

It is not hard to see that the abstract form of this is about the same as Davidson's and Reichenbach's regimentation of the same sentence. It is not clear that there is any difference between Reichenbach's theory and my variant on Rescher's proposal: the Manner in which Patrick walked seems to be just the specific walking-property that Patrick had, and I have already pointed out that this differs only algorithmically from the instance of that walking-property that Patrick instantiated.

68. *Nonstandard adverbs*

So, when we work hard on Davidson's and Rescher's ideas about adverbial modification, each turns into Reichenbach's. That is evidence that, if adverbial modification is to be handled in terms of first-order logic, this is how to do it. Let us now consider whether first-order logic is indeed the best tool for the purpose.

Predicate-modifier theory, which stands as a rival to all of these approximately equivalent quantifying theories, uses more resources than they do; recall that the whole point of the quantifying theories was to get certain entailments within the framework of first-order logic. People disagree about how much of a drawback that is in predicate-modifier theory, partly because they do not agree about whether there is a real chance that first-order logic can explain *all* the main outlines of our ways of thinking and talking. Davidson, who thinks there is a chance, might charge that predicate-modifier theory pusillanimously throws in the towel too soon. Others, thinking that the first-order logic project is an *ignis fatuus*, will say that the sooner we stop pursuing it the better. I have no opinion on this matter that I want to express here.

The other differences concern scope. I shall deal with one now, and the other in my next section.

The quantifying theories say nothing about *nonstandard* adverbs, i.e. ones that cannot validly be dropped: "He apparently defaulted", "He almost won", "They scaled the cliff to the first ledge", or about adjectival analogues of these, such as "The museum has a fake Vermeer", "He is a possible candidate", "That is a decoy duck". This silence is of their essence; it cannot be remedied by revising, broadening, or any kind of tinkering. If this is not to discomfit the friends of the quantifying theories, they need independent evidence that these nonstandard adverbs and adjectives ought to be treated differently from standard ones.

Sometimes there is evidence, namely when an adverb clearly operates not as an ad*verb* but as an adsentence, its role being to express an operator on the rest of the sentence. How are we to decide when this is so? Thomason and Stalnaker offer the following criterion:

> Only if *Q-ly* occurs as a sentence modifier can one paraphrase the sentence by deleting the adverb and prefacing the resulting sentence by *It is Q-ly true that.*[26]

This states only a sufficient condition for something to be an adsentence, but its authors think that "it comes close to being a necessary and sufficient condition", and suggest that we might use it to settle

---

26. Richmond Thomason and Robert Stalnaker, "A Semantic Theory of Adverbs", p. 205.

cases that are indeterminate on intuitive grounds. For my purposes, it will suffice to rely on clear intuitions. It cannot be doubted, for example, that "He apparently walked" means something of the form "It is (was) apparently the case that: he walked" or that "He allegedly defaulted" means something of the form "It is (was) alleged that: he defaulted", and it is equally clear that some nonstandard adverbs are not like this. Thomason and Stalnaker cite, against the thesis that all nonstandard adverbs are adsentences, quantitative and proportional ones such as occur in "He almost won", "They scaled the cliff to the first ledge", and "He filled the tank halfway". These adverbs are nonstandard, because any one of the sentences could go from true to false by the dropping of the adverb, and they are not adsentences.

No doubt "almost" could be used as an adsentence, for we could use "He almost ran home" to mean merely "It is almost the case that: he ran home". Some uses of it are more informative than that, however. "He almost ran home" might mean that he almost-ran home, walking so urgently that it was almost a run, or that he ran almost-home, sprinting most of the way and walking the last block. In each of those, "almost" is nonstandard, but in neither of them is it an adsentence. In one it is an ad*verb*, in the other an ad*adverb*.

It is not surprising that there should be nonstandard adverbs that are not adsentences, for hosts of nonstandard adjectives are like that. Nobody would suggest that "This is a counterfeit dollar" means something of the form "Operator: this is a dollar".

Davidson and Reichenbach might hold their ground, saying that nonstandard adverbs are intuitively so different from standard ones that it's not to be expected that a single theory should cover both. Are they so different? I cannot get my untutored mind around this question. When I have a sense that "He gracefully ran home" is radically unlike "He almost ran home", that is because I have been seeing the former sentence as quantified; when I am impressed by how alike they are, that is because I am viewing them through the lens of predicate-modifier theory. A properly grounded answer to the question will have to wait, it seems, for a full development of the two theories.

However, there is a difficulty that may tell decisively against the quantifying theories, in favor of their rival. I shall now expound it.

69. *Dependency*

The difficulty concerns uses of adjectives that I call "noun-dependent" (I prefer that label to "syncategorematic", which is ugly, and to "nonpredicative", which means something else). An adjective is used in a noun-*in*dependent way when "x is an [Adjective] [Noun]" means the same as "x is [Adjective] and x is a [Noun]": to be a cubic box is to be cubic and a box, to be a Bulgarian stockbroker is to be Bulgarian and a stockbroker. When an adjective is used in a noun-dependent way, on the other hand, "x is an [Adjective] [Noun]" does not mean "x is [Adjective] and x is a [Noun]". For example, (1) "He is an incompetent pianist" does not mean "He is incompetent and he is a pianist". If it did, then (2) "He is an incompetent plumber" would mean "He is incompetent and he is a plumber"; and then (1) and "He is a plumber" would jointly entail (2), which they obviously don't.

There is an analogous phenomenon of "verb-dependent" uses of adverbs, which can be illustrated by "Henry walked quickly from Belgium to Turkey". The status of this as verb-dependent cannot be exhibited, as noun-dependency can, right on the surface of the language; it involves the touch of theory that introduces the notion of a walk of which Henry was the subject, saying that if in walking Henry journeyed somewhere, then his walk was his journey. Given that identity statement, we cannot equate "Henry walked quickly. . ." with "Henry was the subject of a walk that was quick . . .", for that would imply that he was the subject of a journey that was quick, which would then have to be equated with "Henry journeyed quickly". But what Henry did was to walk as fast as a man could, from Belgium to Turkey; not for decades has anyone journeyed across Europe as slowly as Henry did!

On the face of it, this is no special problem for Davidson. His theory reduces verb-dependency among adverbs to noun-dependency among adjectives: to say that Henry walked quickly is to say that Henry was the subject of a walk that was quick-for-a-walk, and we can handle *that* in whatever way seems best for ". . . is useful as a muckraker", ". . . is clean for a pig", ". . . is incompetent as a pianist", and for noun-dependency generally.

That approach seems less soothing, from a Davidsonian standpoint, when we consider what is the best treatment of noun-dependent uses of adjectives. Gilbert Harman has suggested that Davidson could handle some of them as "relative modifiers" (*op. cit.*, pp. 294f). So he could; but others would not succumb easily to that treatment, and in any case it would be better if possible to have a more unified treatment of noun-dependent and other adjectives.

Such a unified treatment is splendidly supplied by predicate-modifier theory, according to which "incompetent" is a modifier that turns "is a pianist" into "is an incompetent pianist", turns "was a sonnet writer" into "was an incompetent sonnet writer", turns "will be a plumber" into "will be an incompetent plumber", and so on. Similarly with most uses of "tall", "slow", and countless others. Furthermore, there is something initially reasonable in bringing noun-dependent uses of adjectives under the same theoretic umbrella as all uses of adverbs. In "She is a brilliant organizer" as well as in "He danced awkwardly", something of a descriptive kind ("brilliant", "awkwardly") is connected with the subject *through* the rest of the predicate. The notion of a predicate modifier neatly captures this intuitive sameness of the two phenomena. As for the *in*dependent use of adjectives, as in "leaden casket" and "radioactive liquid": this is merely the special case where the predicate modifier corresponds to something that can be separately predicated of the subject.

If predicate-modifier theory is the best way—and perhaps the only tolerable way—of handling some uses of adverbs, that strengthens the case for letting it handle all of them. Objection: "Theoretical unity is desirable, but not at any price. You are suggesting that we might prefer one theory of adverbs to another just because one leaves out, while the other doesn't, one tiny fraction of the whole territory. Isn't this letting the tail wag the elephant?" I haven't much sympathy with this, even on its own premise. Also, the premise is doubtful: if Davidson stands by his acceptance of Quine's view that only one event can fully occupy a zone, he must classify almost all adverbs as verb-dependent, so that the elephant is almost all tail! I shall explain.

Suppose that John walks and learns at the same time, and let us—in order to come to the crux as quickly as possible—allow that the walk coincides in space-time with the lesson. Then, if there are only concrete events, the walk is the lesson. It follows that no inference of the form "John walks adverbly at T, so he walks at T" can be handled in the simple Davidsonian manner, namely by taking the premise to have the form

For some x: W(x) & Subj(John,x) & At(T,x) & F(x),

where F is an adjective corresponding to the original adverb. Or, rather, that treatment is all right only if it is equally true that John learns adverbly at T, and even more generally that John *verbs* adverbly at T for every verb such that John verbs at T. In short, the simple Davidsonian treatment will work only for adverbs that truly modify every verb that fits the subject at the time; only such an adverb will correspond to an adjective that is directly applicable to the concrete event—i.e. predicable of it *de re*, under any of its names or descriptions.

There are such adverbs or adverbial phrases. For example, if while John walked in Bologna he also verbed, then (whatever "verb" may stand for) he did at that time verb *in Bologna* (adverb), and so we could say that his walk, understood as a concrete event, was *in Bologna* (adjective)—this being true of it under each of its many descriptions.

For adverbs of this kind, though, quantification over events has no work to do. Rather than saying that the walk was in Bologna, we can just as well say that at the time John was in Bologna. Any adverb corresponding to an adjective that directly fits a concrete event will also correspond to one that directly fits the subject of the event. In my example, the adverb "in Bologna" goes over into the adjective "in Bologna", said of John; in other cases, things are trickier than that. But it remains true that when an adverb goes with all the applicable verbs it will correspond to *some* adjective that is true of the subject. I leave it as an exercise to the reader to tackle some of the trickier cases ("John walked through Bologna"). The only exceptions to the above general claim are temporal adverbs ("John walked on Wednesday"); they are best handled as adsentences, but again I leave it to the reader to work out why and how. They still don't offer useful work for Davidsonian quantifications.[27]

In short: if we start with Quine's view about what events there are, adverb-dropping inferences fall into two classes: those where tropes or events have no work to do and those where they do their work only with help from predicate-modifier theory. I offer that as a conclusive reason for thinking that Davidson cannot stand by Quine while also recommending the event concept on the grounds that it is helpful in regimenting adverb-dropping inferences.[28]

He could get out of this bind by parting company with Quine. Indeed, he ought never to have joined forces with him: Davidson wants to do descriptive metaphysics, and Quine's metaphysic of events is defensible only considered as revisionary or excisionary—a decision to *ignore* abstract events rather than an announcement that there aren't any. If Davidson takes that way out, however, dependency is still a problem for him, because he can't come to terms with it until he settles how far back from Quine he is going to go.

Reichenbach had the same problem and knew it. He saw that his treatment of adverbs would be in trouble unless it set limits to the richness of the specific properties over which he was quantifying. Where Davidson has to fend off the Quinean view that there are only concrete events, Reichenbach must keep at bay the view that each of his specific properties incorporates the whole intrinsic truth about the thing that has the property. I don't understand Reichenbach's account of the line that has John's absolutely specific walking property on one

---

27. The ideas in this paragraph are developed, with some differences, in Jonathan Bennett, "Adverb-Dropping Inferences and the Lemmon Criterion".

28. Quine himself wants both at once. In one place, he introduces concrete events and goes on to say: "A reason for being particularly glad to have accommodated events is [that] Davidson has shown to my satisfaction that quantification over events is far and away the best way of construing adverbial constructions." (*Theories and Things*, p. 12.)

side of it and the rest of the story on the other.[29] He explains it, using the phrase "a connective implication of the synthetic kind", referring us to a later chapter for an explanation of this, but after following out the reference I remain in the dark.

So I don't know *where* Reichenbach draws the line, any more than I know where Davidson used to draw it or would draw it now if he split from Quine. This matters greatly, as I now explain. The threat from Quine is that Davidson must say that "John walked noisily" has a different logical form from "John walked in Bologna", because the former but not the latter goes over into a noun-dependent predication on an event. We step back from Quine's metaphysic and are rescued from that conclusion, but—we suppose—the logical form of those two *is* indeed different from that of "John walked quickly", because that goes over into what indisputably *is* a noun-dependent predication on an event. You don't have to be Quine to think that a quick walk is only quick-for-a-walk, because the walk might be a journey and be slow-for-a-journey.

The idea that a walk could be a journey is itself a bit of theory about events. It is pretty well supported by ordinary speech, but we don't yet have any decent theory to back it up, and I contend that the answers to some such questions are considerably indeterminate. Consider again the bailed-out aviator who spirals to earth. It is indeterminate whether "his circular movement" corefers with "his descent to the earth": we can make them sound as though they pick out different events, but we can also make it seem plausible to say that his descent to the earth was a spiralling one, in which case one of its properties was involving-a-circular-component, which seems to imply that "his circular movement" is a name for it. Now, suppose we want to explain the entailment by "Billy Bishop descended at a regular rate" of "Billy Bishop descended". To do this in Davidson's way, we must say that the former sentence means something of the form: "For some x: x was a descent, and BB was its subject, and it was uniform". If the descent is the circular movement, however, that is just wrong; for BB could descend at a regular rate while circling irregularly; on the other hand, if the descent is the circular movement, the Davidsonian treatment is all right. Thus, Davidson's theory of adverbial modification puts differences of logical form at the mercy of issues on which there is no agreement and on which, according to my indeterminacy thesis, there is nothing to agree on. That is a terrific drawback in the theory considered just as logical regimentation; when the theory is taken to offer a description of how our minds work when we draw conclusions, the drawback becomes a fatality.

---

29. Hans Reichenbach, *Elements of Logic*, p. 228.

XII

THE ANSCOMBE THESIS

70. *The Anscombe thesis*

The literature about events and actions says a lot about the word "by" as used in the likes of these: "Borg signified his joy by falling to his knees", "Mellon saved the orchestra by giving it a million dollars", "The state orphaned the boys by electrocuting their parents". These concern intentional human behavior, but some uses of the "by" locution do not: "The explosion dammed the river by sending tons of mud into it", "The arctic air mass damned my holiday by coming south". I shall stick with examples like my first three, because the "by" locution is *more* at home with them. The difference between cases that do and ones that do not involve intentional conduct is unimportant for my purposes.

That is fortunate, because I have no clear grasp of what the difference is. It corresponds to the difference between events that are actions and ones that aren't: actions are a species of events, and our interest in the latter covers not only falls and blizzards and glimpses, but also gestures and hugs and insults. In this chapter and the next two, the question of how our event concept figures in the matter in hand will often be expressed as the question of what role if any the concept of an action plays.

In her book *Intention*, G.E.M. Anscombe considers the case of someone who is killing the inhabitants of a village by putting poison in their well, and she asks how many things he is then doing. She answers "One"—he is performing a single action that is both a poisoning of a well and a killing of some villagers. That answer reflects a general thesis relating the counting of actions to the "by" locution. I call it "the Anscombe thesis"; Anscombe has never explicitly announced it, but she has defended some of its applications and is generally thought to believe it. It says that every instance of the following schema:

> If someone (end)s by (means)ing, then his (end)ing is his (means)ing

is true when the two gerunds are understood as perfect nominals. (When they are understood as imperfect, of course, most instances of the schema are false.) Or, expressed more directly:

> If someone (end)s by (means)ing, then the perfect nominal formed from the statement that he (end)s has the same referent as the perfect nominal formed from the statement that he (means)s.

Some writers have expressed the Anscombe thesis in terms like these: "If a person does something by doing something else, then the two actions are identical". Apart from the solecism with "two" and "identical", this is defective because the Anscombe thesis entails that you cannot do something by doing something *else.*

My second version underlines the fact that the Anscombe thesis belongs strictly to semantics. The metaphysical issues we have encountered—What are events? How concrete/abstract can they be? Are they all changes? Are there limits to how zonally arbitrary they can be?—have no bearing on it. The *semantic* issue between Kim and (say) Davidson is indeed relevant. Kim cannot possibly allow that "Henri's swinging of his axe" refers to the same event as "Henri's felling of the tree"; Davidson, on the other hand, can allow this and does indeed assert it in the case where Henri fells the tree by swinging his axe.

We can be more precise about *what* semantic question is at issue here. Suppose that Henri moved his axe in certain ways, causing breaks in the fibres of a tree trunk, which in turn caused the tree to fall. There is the event Small, consisting of the fusion of all the movements Henri made with his axe, and there is the event Large, which is the fusion of Small and the fall of the tree and the intervening causal chain. Since Henri felled the tree by moving his axe, the Anscombian holds that "the movements Henri made with his axe" and "Henri's felling of the tree" name the same event; since it is indisputable that the former phrase names Small, the Anscombe thesis must be that the latter phrase names Small also. Those who disagree with that seem to hold that "Henri's felling of the tree" names Large rather than Small. That is what the debate is about. It involves no coherent issue about what events there are—only one about what events are named by a certain kind of perfect nominal.

Davidson's Anscombism is independent of the rest of his work on events, except that it entails his rejection of Kim's semantics. It is sometimes seen as an integral part of his treatment of adverbs, but that is wrong. Indeed, when Davidson regiments uses of adverbs by quantifying over events, the Anscombe thesis is a nuisance: adverbial phrases of the form "with the aid of an F" and "by means of an F" might seem to go over into adjectives applicable to events, but if the Anscombe thesis is correct they do not.[1] For example, one might think that Davidson could regiment "Hercules dislodged the rock with a lever" into "There was a dislodging, Hercules was its subject, the rock was its object, and it was done with the aid of a lever". But Hercules dislodged the rock by moving his hand downwards on one end of the lever, from which the Anscombe thesis infers that his dislodgement of the rock was his handmovement; so now we are threatened with having to say that Hercules moved his hand with the aid of a lever. One could, but Hercules didn't. So the Anscombe thesis won't let the adverbial "with the aid of a lever" fall within the scope of Davidson's kind of regimentation. There are more where that came from.

Even without Davidson's theory of adverbs, the Anscombe thesis is a source of some discomfort. Here is an example suggested to me by Michael Kremer. If the gospels are to be believed, Judas betrayed Jesus in the garden of Gethsemane by kissing him. The Anscombian is committed by this to saying that *the kiss that Judas gave Jesus in Gethsemane was his betrayal of him.* Consider the effect of this on the equally biblical statement that *Judas betrayed Jesus with a kiss.* On one natural understanding of this, it combines with the Anscombian identity to yield the conclusion that Judas betrayed Jesus with a betrayal. It might be replied that this conclusion is true and sounds weird only because it is trivial or that the conclusion does not follow because "Judas betrayed Jesus with a kiss" does not really use "kiss" as an action-sortal. The discomfort is not immediately fatal, then, but it is real and should be noted.

In other ways, too, the Anscombe thesis confers truth on things that sound false or peculiar. If the tug on the trigger was the murder, and the tug caused a wound in the victim's body (by causing the firing pin to go forward, which caused . . . etc.), then by the Anscombe thesis it follows that *The murder caused a wound in the victim's body.* Here again, however, the Anscombian has room to move. He can say that the implied statement is unpalatable not because it is false but because it is disorderly: it relates an action to one of its effects yet identifies it in terms of a significantly more remote effect on the same causal chain. In short, the statement is unswallowable because it is tangled. We would have less objection (the Anscombian can say) to "The murder caused a lot of noise", yet it is plainly true that what caused the noise is what caused the wound.

Whether these defensive moves are acceptable depends on what grounds there are for the Anscombe thesis. Let us look into this.

1. This point is developed by Julia Annas, "Davidson and Anscombe on 'The Same Action' ".

71. *What are the reasons for it?*

Barry Taylor, who has shown more interest in Davidson's adverbial work than anyone else, says that Davidson has been seduced into treating too many adverbs as verb-dependent, in the manner of my "with the aid of a stick". He writes:

> It is reasonable, perhaps, that if adverbs are to be assimilated to adjectives, a class of [verb-dependent] adverbs should emerge. What is more problematic is whether *Davidson's* [verb-dependent] adverbs form a preanalytically natural class, or whether they are an artefact rather of welding a mismatched identity-criterion onto his adverbial proposal.[2]

Taylor's view about what gets Davidson into this difficulty is interesting. His examples indicate that the Anscombe thesis is the source of the trouble: he offers a variant on my "with a stick" example and another in which "a walking uphill is by Davidson's criterion also a warning"—presumably because the person gives a warning by walking uphill. What Taylor *says*, though, is that Davidson is forced to make too many adverbs verb-dependent by his "identity-criterion", meaning the thesis "that e_1 is e_2 just in case e_1 and e_2 share all causes and effects".[3] This whole performance makes sense only if Taylor thinks that the causal nonduplication principle entails the Anscombe thesis, so that if Davidson dropped the former he would no longer be under pressure to say Anscombian things about cases where the "by"-locution applies. Never mind the adverbs; let us consider this brand new suggestion about where the Anscombe thesis comes from.

If Davidson had inferred the Anscombe thesis from his causal nonduplication principle, he would have said so, and he hasn't. Still, the logical question stands: Does the causal principle entail the other? It cannot possibly do so. The Anscombe thesis is pure semantics, with no metaphysical implications whatsoever, whereas the causal principle belongs to metaphysics, and, unlike some nonduplication principles, it does not even weakly imply or tend towards any substantive semantic position (see Section 40 above). Stand back at look at it: How *could* the thesis that no two events can share all their causes and effects favor some one answer to the question of what is named by the phrase "Henri's felling of the tree"?

The causal principle might seem relevant to the Anscombe issue if one thinks of the latter as belonging to metaphysics rather than semantics. For then the question cannot be "Does 'Henri's felling of

---

2. Barry Taylor, *Modes of Occurrence*, p. 26.

3. Ibid., p. 25.

the tree' name Small or Large?", and the only thing it can be is "Is Henri's felling of the tree identical with his swinging of the axe?". What on earth can this mean—what nonsemantic problem can it present? Perhaps its devotees think that it is the question "Is Small identical with Large?", and someone who answers Yes to *that* might be thought to have inferred his answer from (i) the causal nonduplication principle together with (ii) the claim that Small and Large have the same causes and effects. In fact, (ii) is false, because Small caused the tree's fall, whereas Large did not. But anyway it is absurd to take the Anscombe thesis to be saying (preposterously) that Small is Large, rather than saying (plausibly) that an expression that some people think names Large really names Small. I don't accuse Taylor of this muddle. I don't know why he sees the causal principle as the source of the Anscombe thesis.

Alvin Goldman has conjectured that the friends of the Anscombe thesis rely on the following argument:

> (i) If two sentences are equivalent, the nominals derived from them cannot refer to different events. (ii) The sentences "Henri felled the tree" is equivalent (near enough) to "Henri acted in such a way that the tree fell in consequence". Therefore (iii) "Henri's felling of the tree" has the same referent as "Henri's action in consequence of which the tree fell", and it seems safe to say that the latter could have the same referent as "Henri's swinging of his axe". So we get the result that the swinging of the axe is the felling of the tree. Similarly with all the other cases.[4]

Goldman objects that (i) is plausible only as applied to gerundial nominals, whereas (iii) needs one that is not gerundial. Maybe, but an idea that I got from Alison McIntyre yields a much more decisive objection. The crux of the proposed argument is the sentence "Henri acted in such a way that the tree fell in consequence", which it nominalizes into a phrase that picks out *what Henri did*, adding a relational description of it—"Henri's action (which, incidentally, made the tree fall)". On the other hand, we can just as well nominalize it into a phrase that picks out *what happened to the tree*, adding a relational description of that—"the fall of the tree (which, incidentally, was caused by Henri's swinging his axe)". The former of those could refer to his swinging of the axe, but the latter couldn't, so the suggested argument is no good. I don't know of anyone who has actually used it.

One of Davidson's two arguments for the Anscombe thesis is that without it we cannot make sense of excuses such as "I didn't know the gun was loaded". He understands this to mean: "Because I didn't know the gun was loaded, I didn't know that my excusable pulling of the

4. Adapted from Alvin A. Goldman, "The Individuation of Action", p. 766.

trigger would be a deplorable shooting of my husband".[5] The excuse doesn't have to be read that way, however. Even if the tug and the homicide were two actions, the excuse could make sense, for it could mean ". . . I didn't know that if I did one of those things I would inevitably do the other".[6]

Apart from one other argument, discussed in my next section, Davidson works not at defending the Anscombe thesis but at explaining why some people disbelieve it. Of those who don't agree that the villain's inundation of the fields was his destruction of the crops, Davidson conjectures that they think that anything properly called "his destruction of the crops" must *include* the crops' failure, i.e. that "when the description is made to include reference to a consequence, then the consequence itself is included in the described event".[7] Later on he develops the point, suggesting that opponents of the Anscombe thesis have "a tendency to confuse events described . . . in terms of terminal states and events described . . . in terms of what they cause".[8] Some of them do, as in this bit of the literature: "If an act description entails that I brought some event about, the act it describes includes that event, any act by which I brought that event about, and any events causally linking such acts with that event." That implies that the phrase "my opening of the flood-gates in circumstances that made it inevitable that the crops would fail" picks out an act of which the crops' failure is a part. This is mistaken, as Davidson says, and someone who accepts it will have a wrong reason for rejecting the Anscombe thesis. We are still looking for reasons in its favor.

Anscombe is apparently trying to defend it in a passage that starts thus:

> Goldman begins his book *A Theory of Human Action* by saying "Suppose John (1) moves his hand, (2) frightens away a fly, (3) moves his Queen . . . [etc. up to (6)]. Has John here performed six acts?" He then ascribes to Davidson and me the answer that John performed only one act in this case.[9]

Anscombe declines to answer the question because the case is underdescribed: Goldman's description would fit if John had moved his right hand, frightened a fly by sneezing, moved his Queen with his foot . . . and so on, up to six. She is willing to guess that Goldman had in mind "a case where he did do all that just by what it is rather natural to call

5. Donald Davidson, "The Logical Form of Action Sentences", p. 109.

6. Thus Lawrence Davis, "The Individuation of Actions", p. 522.

7. Donald Davidson, "Agency", p. 58.

8. Donald Davidson, "The Individuation of Events", p. 177.

9. G.E.M. Anscombe, "Under a Description", pp. 223f.

one act", from which she infers: "When it is taken as Goldman intends, the identity of the act is assumed in giving a lot of different descriptions." The implication is that Goldman and his allies cannot cleanly pick out the cases they think Anscombe is wrong about except in terms suggesting that she is right about them! In a characteristically derisive manner, Anscombe continues: "It reminds me of the would-be sceptical question: can we know that other people see? If one asks which other people, it turns out to be the sighted ones that are meant."

Goldman could agree that John did all that *by* one act, while denying that "all that" constitutes just one act. The force that Anscombe tries to give her "by . . . one act" characterization presupposes the point that is at issue, namely that if John moved his Queen by moving his hand then his hand motion and his chess move were one act. Not that the case has to be described in terms of any counting of acts: Goldman could have employed the kind of language in which Anscombe originally launched her thesis: John moves his hand, which results in a fly's being frightened, and in his Queen's getting a new position, and so on.

It is true—and this seems to be what impresses Anscombe—that in the disputed cases it is implausible to say, "He was doing six things at once". It will take more than that to make the Anscombe thesis philosophically interesting. If it is not a mere piece of fluff picked off the surface of our speech habits, it must show up in more ways than that.

72. *The times of actions*

"By"-statements fall into two large species. There are the time-spanning ones, such as "They ruined the economy by printing too much money", "She doused the fire by throwing sand on it", "He kept the floodwaters back by building a wall". In these, what makes it true that x (end)ed by (means)ing is that fact that because x (means)ed he caused something to occur later.[10] The examples are all causal, but my

10. My shorthand "end" and "means" is not meant to imply that every "by"-statement reports someone's chosen means to a willed end. That would be false. One can, for example, quite unknowingly feed the plants by dumping tea leaves on them. Searle says that Princip pulled the trigger, fired the gun, . . . , avenged Serbia, but adds that he is "inclined" to say that spoiling Lord Grey's summer is not an action of Princip's at all, merely an unintended consequence of one. The reason is not that the limits on intentions set limits on actions: they don't, "because of the possibility of unintentional actions". But Searle does not hint at what his reason is. He may have misled himself by speaking of what Princip did not *by* but *by means of* pulling the trigger. (John Searle, *Intentionality*, pp. 99f.)

focus is on the different though related fact that they are in a sense time-spanning. Other "by"-statements are synchronous, as are "By saying 'I do' she became his wife", "By losing his temper, he fulfilled her prediction", "By raising an arm, he made it the case that ten arms were raised". The truth of these does not come from what x's (means)ing led to later on. In each of them, what makes it true that by (means)ing he (end)ed is a state of affairs that obtains when x (means)s. His loss of temper didn't lead to a subsequent fulfilment of her prediction; it made it the case, there and then, that her prediction was fulfilled. I usually find it more natural to express the time-spanning examples in the form "x (end)ed by (means)ing" and to reverse the order with synchronic cases and say "By (means)ing x (end)ed"; but I can find no significance in this.

Now, nobody who accepts the semantics of Kim and Goldman will accept the Anscombe thesis in any of its applications except for the likes of "He clapped by repeatedly bringing the palms of his hands together hard enough to make a sound" and the degenerate "He raises his arm by raising his arm". Some writers, however, reject Kim's semantics and accept the Anscombe thesis as applied to synchronous "by"-statements, while still rejecting it for the time-spanning ones.

Suppose that Dirk repelled the May floodwaters by building a wall the previous September. By the Anscombe thesis, his repelling of the waters is his construction of the wall; and the temporal objection to this is that the repelling of the waters cannot be, as the construction of the wall is, complete before the waters have risen. Call that the *actio praecox* argument against the Anscombe thesis.

It has some force, but there is also force the other way, from the "no further effort" argument. This says that, if Dirk's repelling of the waters is not completed until the waters have risen and stopped, then there is a time when there is nothing more for him to do and yet his action is not yet completed. It is hard to believe that an action is completed minutes or months after the agent has stopped doing anything that is relevant to it, and it is impossible to believe that "Dirk's repelling of the floodwaters" is not the name of an action.

Beardsley rejected the Anscombe thesis as applied to time-spanning "by"-statements, because he thought the *actio praecox* argument to be fatal. He was willing to argue this even for short time intervals: "The turning on of the light . . . will always take a little more time . . . than the flipping of the switch".[11] He took the "no further effort" counterargument in his stride, asserting that an action can indeed continue when the agent is immobile and even dead:

> Of course activities cease with death, but not necessarily actions: for the event identical to the action has to run its course, and some

11. Monroe C. Beardsley, "Actions and Events", p. 270.

> events, once started, carry through of their own impulse, so that initiating the event is all that is required to act.

When we peel off the redundant "the event identical to", we find Beardsley saying that the action has to run its course after the agent's death. When put thus plainly, it is incredible.

Irving Thalberg thought otherwise, and sought help from a technical concept of the "components" of an action.[12] If that did the other work that Thalberg demanded of it, and incidentally implied that actions can continue after the agent is dead, the latter thesis might come to seem less arbitrary and thus more believable. But the "component" notion doesn't do much good and does some harm: Thalberg's defense of actions that run on after the agent is dead implies that an action may start centuries before the agent is born (p. 30). That is too much.

Judith Thomson, who discovered the time-of-an-action problem, has used a pair of examples to draw the sting of the "no further effort" argument.[13] In one, Adam cleans his floor by pouring Stuff on it, waiting for that to dry, and vacuuming up the residue; Stuff digs out the dirt, making scrubbing unnecessary. While placidly waiting for Stuff to dry, Thomson says, *he is cleaning the floor*, and so his cleaning of the floor is not yet completed. The plausibility of this is supposed to rub off onto her other example, in which Adam cleans his floor by covering it with Superstuff—which makes all the dirt evaporate so that there is nothing more for him to do. Superstuff's work is not completed until it is dry, and Thomson contends that while it is drying Adam is cleaning the floor. If we accept that, we must drop the "no further effort" argument and are free to hold that the felling ends only when the tree falls.

I am not convinced by this. Thomson says that the only significant difference is that Superstuff "plays a larger part" than Stuff does in getting the floor clean (pp. 56f), but that is not so. As well as that metrical difference there is a topological one: when Adam is waiting for Stuff to dry, some of his floor-cleaning activity lies in the future; his total floor-cleaning activity is *divided* by the quiet time when he is still "cleaning his floor", and there is an obvious reason why that might make us willing—if indeed we are willing—to say that he is cleaning his floor at a time when he is drinking coffee.

I find it intolerable to say that Dirk's repelling of the waters—that *action* of his—wasn't over at a time when he had nothing more to do to repel the waters. In my opinion, the "no further effort" argument is

---

12. Irving Thalberg, *Perception, Emotion and Action*, pp. 14f and Chapter 5.

13. Judith Jarvis Thomson, *Acts and Other Events*, pp. 56f.

decisive and is not dented by the efforts of Beardsley or Thalberg or Thomson. As Wordsworth said:

> Action is transitory—a step, a blow,
> The motion of a muscle—this way or that—
> 'Tis done, and in the after-vacancy
> We wonder at ourselves. . . .

So I have to draw the sting of the *actio praecox* argument, which I now proceed to do, by explaining away the intuitions that lie behind it.[14]

At 11 a.m. Henri started chopping at the tree with his axe, continuing up to the stroke of noon, when he stopped and rested all afternoon. The tree was nearly cut through, was bound to fall, and at 12:05 p.m. it did fall. When did Henri's felling of it occur? I say that it stretched from 11 to noon and no further; so I have to explain away the temptation to say that it stretched from 11 to 12:05.

(We can't avoid the problem by confining ourselves to answers of the form: The felling occurred last week, last Wednesday, around the middle of last Wednesday, . . . any answer naming a continuous period that contained the first swing of the axe and the tree's fall. If those are the only permissible answers, then the question "At 12:01 was Henri's felling of the tree completed?" must be defective, and it isn't.)

I introduce the notion of a "consummated felling". An action is a consummated felling at time T just in case it is a felling of something that falls before T. Then at noon the situation was this: Henri's felling of the tree was all over, but it was not yet a consummated felling; it acquired that property a few minutes later. I submit that those who say "The felling can't be over while the tree stands" are really having the thought that a felling cannot be *consummated* while the tree is still standing, which is true but irrelevant to the question of when the felling occurs.

This implies that an event can change its status after it has occurred; and so it can. Although events cannot move or otherwise alter, because they stretch through time rather than lasting through it, they can change relationally, as when a particular event becomes famous or becomes forgotten or comes to satisfy the description "cause of a now-past fall of a tree". Not just events—*anything* can acquire a relational property after it has ceased to exist: Johanna Rosine Wagner

---

14. This treatment was first presented in my "Shooting, Killing, Dying", and later by John F. Vollrath, "When Actions Are Causes", and Robert Grimm, "Eventual Change and Action Identity". Critical remarks have been aimed in its approximate direction by Irving Thalberg in "When do Causes Take Effect?", C.A. MacDonald in "On the Unifier-Multiplier Controversy", Alan R. White in "Shooting, Killing and Fatally Wounding", and Philip Peterson in "The Grimm Events of Causation".

had been dead for thirty-five years when she first became describable as "mother of someone who has composed *Parsifal*".

One writer in a distinguished journal has assumed that an action must exist at a time when it acquires a relational property. Does it then (he asks) stay in existence throughout, or does it take "an ontological holiday" and then "resurface"? Disliking each alternative, he contends that the action has an early part and a late part, with an intervening period during which no part of it is occurring. This argument rests on a simple mistake—as though Johanna had to "resurface" in order to become the mother of someone who had composed *Parsifal*.

My line of thought might go through with the invented "consummated felling" replaced by the ordinary "felling". Then it would say:

> The friends of the *actio praecox* argument are, reasonably enough, taking it that an action doesn't count as a felling until the tree has fallen. From this they validly infer that at 12:01 no completed action yet counts as Henri's felling of the tree, which they wrongly take to mean that Henri's felling of the tree—the action that *will* have that property—has not yet been completed.

There is no logical oddity about this. Logically, it is like "In 1949 the ex-actor who occupies the White House was living in California but wasn't yet an ex-actor."

Here is an interesting passage in which Lawrence Davis, trying to oppose the Anscombe thesis on temporal grounds, is drawn towards it:

> My pulling the trigger and my shooting the prisoner [are] two different acts, since they occupied different though overlapping stretches of time. There is a tendency to object that I was doing only one thing when I pulled the trigger, not two or three or indefinitely many. But we can [say that] I pulled the trigger, and this act amounted to—quickly became a case of—my shooting the prisoner. My pulling the trigger was one event, one act; but this is compatible with its being part of another, longer event that was the second act I performed at the same time.[15]

This would sound peculiar if it were cleansed of its imperfect nominals: the tug that I gave the trigger grew to be a case of my murder of the prisoner. The main point, however, is this: Davis says that we have two acts here, but when he says that one of them "grew to be a case of" the other, he cannot mean that one particular grew to be a case of another particular. He must mean that one act came to fall under some act-sortal— specifically, that the trigger-pulling *came to be a shooting*.

15. Lawrence Davis, "The Individuation of Actions", pp. 525f.

That does not express the temporal objection to the Anscombe thesis; it expresses the Anscombe thesis, with its temporal aspect defended in my way.

73. *Still looking for reasons*

I have offered a line of thought which, if it succeeds, defangs the *actio praecox* argument and thereby allows "no further effort" to have the force that it seems prima facie to have. But the "no further effort" argument (and thus my help for it) offers direct support not to the Anscombe thesis but only to its dating of actions. The Anscombe thesis is wrong if it gets the date wrong, but its getting the date right—as I am sure it does—is no guarantee that it is wholly correct.[16]

Yet the friends of the "no further effort" argument, my earlier self included, have usually credited it with more power than that. Jennifer Hornsby strongly urges it as an argument for the Anscombe thesis;[17] and when Davidson announces "insuperable difficulties that stand in the way of" denying the Anscombe thesis, which he describes as "the conclusion on which our considerations all converge", the only consideration he has offered is the "no further effort" argument.[18]

Someone who accepts the "no further effort" argument as decisively settling *when* x's (end)ing occurs might still refuse to identify it with x's (means)ing. Why would he do that? Well, perhaps because he accepts Kim's semantics or perhaps for other reasons, such as I am inclined to have. I believe that a name such as "Dirk's construction of the wall" refers to an instance of a complex property, which occurs at a zone determined in one dimension by the time it took Dirk to build the wall and in the other three by the spatial locations, throughout that time, of Dirk and his tools and the materials of the wall. The property in question contains the property of building-a-wall as a part or conjunct, but that is not the whole of it. What else is there to the constitutive property? I don't know, and I have contended that there is no determinate answer to that. I don't feel impelled to say that the extra reaches as far as *building-a-wall-that-later-holds-back-floodwaters*. If it doesn't, then the construction of the wall is not the repelling of the floodwaters, and this result is reached without help either from the *actio praecox* argument or from Kim's semantics.

Because I hold that the repelling of the waters is over as soon the

16. This is pointed out by Lawrence Brian Lombard, "Actions, Results, and the Time of a Killing", fn. 26.

17. Jennifer Hornsby, *Action*, pp. 29–32.

18. Donald Davidson, "Agency", pp. 57, 59.

construction of the wall is over, I think that "Dirk's repelling of the waters" names an event occupying the same zone as the one named by "Dirk's construction of the wall": if there is no temporal difference in where the two events are located in space-time, there is no difference at all. This is consistent with denying the Anscombe thesis, because it may be that the two event names pick out different tropes from that zone.

So, granted that the Anscombe thesis is right about dates, the question still stands as to whether it is wrong about anything. When I rejected Kim's semantics, I appealed to firm intuitive data having to do with predications and counting. Contrary to Kim, I argued, it can be true that the kick was an assault, because it can be plainly true that he gave her only one kick and made only one assault on her, and *the kick was an assault*. Data of the same kind can be found for some instances of the Anscombe thesis: she made only one gesture and offered only one insult, and *the gesture was an insult*, so it follows that the gesture that she made was the insult that she offered; and this fits the "by"-locution—she insulted him *by* gesturing in a certain way. I don't believe for a moment, however, that such intuitive data can be marshalled in support of every instance of the Anscombe thesis. Indeed, I haven't been able to work up a single decent example for time-spanning instances of the thesis. But I can't find good intuitive evidence against it in those cases: when I try out sentences of the relevant kind—"That swish of his hand was the jolt he gave to the vase", "That lockout was the destruction of the union", "His work at the pump was his massacre of the villagers"—my reaction is not that they are clearly true or clearly false, but rather that they are damned peculiar things to say or to deny. Beardsley's reliance on the bad *actio praecox* argument led him to a possibly true result, namely that the Anscombe thesis is true for the synchronous but not for the time-spanning cases, but the evidence is neither clear nor conclusive. By now, suspicion should be growing that the Anscombe thesis simply doesn't matter; if it did, there would be more evidence regarding the extent of its truth and the extent, if any, of its falsity.

74. *Logical form and the Anscombe thesis*

I long thought that the best case *for or against* the thesis would come from a good analysis of the "by"-locution. If a clear, fundamental account of how the latter works implies the Anscombe thesis, that secures it (I thought); if it conflicts with the thesis, that refutes it; and if it does neither then that is further evidence that the thesis is negligible, mattering only because of how it has cluttered up the literature.

That was a blind alley, for we know *a priori* that no analysis of the "by"-locution could possibly support the Anscombe thesis. In brief, no Anscombian can allow that the "by"-locution relates an action to an action, for that would imply that the locution is symmetrical, which it plainly isn't. If Peter (end)s by (means)ing, then there is an action a_e that occurs because he (end)s, and there is an action a_m that occurs because he (means)s; but consider what is involved in saying that the statement that Peter (end)s by (means)ing means something of the form

> For some a_1 and a_2: Subj(Peter,a_1) and Subj(Peter,a_2) and E(a_1) and M(a_2) and R(a_1,a_2),

the idea being that the statement is true because a_e satisfies the conditions on the first variable and a_m satisfies the conditions on the second, and that "R" expresses the *by-relation* between actions. Now, if the "by"-locution means anything of that form, i.e. if it relates an action to an action, then an Anscombian must say that it relates an action to itself—for instance, relates a pull to a murder, where the pull is the murder—and *that makes the "by"-locution symmetrical*, which really it is not. No amount of Gricean pragmatics will convince us that it is odd but true that Henri swung his axe by felling the tree, or that Princip pulled the trigger by assassinating the Archduke.

Beardsley accepted the Anscombe thesis as applied to synchronous "by"-statements and also thought that the "by"-locution relates an event to an event. This committted him to holding that the synchronous "by"-locution relates an event to itself, which makes it symmetrical. Beardsley's defense of this aspect of his position is unconvincing.[19] In the course of it, he says that many of these cases are "not all that asymmetrical" and he offers to explain why they seem so. His explanation doesn't fit *any* cases of the synchronous "by"-locution—not even his own chosen example.

Castañeda has suggested that the Anscombe thesis might be turned into something that will let the "by"-locution relate an action to an action.[20] He proposes that thesis be replaced by a qualified identity statement that is not symmetrical, and he offers a choice of three:

---

19. Jay Alan Smith, in "Goldman on Act Individuation", also accepts the Anscombe thesis for the synchronous but not for the time-spanning "by"-locution, on temporal grounds; but he says nothing about (a)symmetry, presumably not intending to analyze the "by"-locution as relating an event to an event.

20. Hector-Neri Castañeda, "Intentionality and Identity in Human Action". This is a review article on Goldman's *A Theory of Human Action*.

(His A-ing qua A-ing) was a B-ing.
His A-ing was (qua A-ing a B-ing).
Qua A-ing: his A-ing was a B-ing.

Castañeda says that the first enlarges our stock of events, while the second enlarges our stock of predicates; I am not sure what the third is supposed to do. He says little about what these qua-events or qua-properties might be. His aim, I think, is merely to sketch opening moves that an Anscombian might make, without saying where we might go from there. I cannot find anywhere to go from there.

So the Anscombian's best hope is that the "by"-locution will turn out on analysis not to be a device for relating an action to an action. Only that gives the Anscombe thesis any chance of being true, admittedly at the price of shrinking its importance still further.

My own account of the "by"-locution will turn its back on the the concept of a particular event and, therefore, on the Anscombe thesis. What motivates me in developing it is an interest in the "by"-locution as something with a rich, varied, hard-working role in our handling of the human scene. It would not be worth the trouble just to answer the boring question of whether "Pétain's speech" can refer to the same event as "Pétain's betrayal of France".

XIII

GOLDMAN ON THE "BY"-LOCUTION

75. *Goldman's program*

Some work by Alvin Goldman will serve as my doorway into the analysis of the "by"-locution. It starts from his rejection of many of the event identities that are implied by the Anscombe thesis, and of some others: for reasons like Kim's, he holds that the signing of a document could not be the bankrupting of a business, that the twitch of an ear could not be a signal to the auctioneer, and that a walk could not be a stroll. He very properly also holds that when a pair of actions is thought by some intelligent people to be a singleton, there is something to be explained:

> According to [my] criterion, pairs of acts such as John's moving his hand and John's moving his queen to QN7 are not identical. But, if not identical, such acts are surely connected in some intimate way. [I want to] explicate the nature of such connections.[1]

Goldman's name for the "intimate connection" he is pursuing is "level generation", but I shall drop the adjective. His initial examples are all expressible in the "by"-locution, and he remarks: "In general, level generation will obtain when the 'by'-locution is appropriate; but [it] will not be completely tied to this locution" (p. 21). That is because the latter does not exhaust the cases where a pair of events might be thought to be a singleton: Goldman holds that a flogging may generate a severe flogging, that a rehearsal can generate a dress rehearsal, that a disaster can generate a blizzard, and so on. These examples don't naturally engage the "by"-locution, but they fall within the province that Goldman sets himself to conquer. He writes defensively: "How *should* one deal with pairs of acts like S's running and S's running at 8 m.p.h., or S's extending his arm and his extending his arm out the car window?" (p. 29)

1. Alvin A. Goldman, *A Theory of Human Action*, p. 20.

Goldman would have done better to let the question "How are we to understand the relation between a_e and a_m when someone (end)s by (means)ing?" stand on its own feet, rather than embedding it in the broader question "How are we to understand the relation between e_1 and e_2 when it is false but plausible to say that e_1 is e_2?" If Kim-Goldman semantics is false, all that is left of the larger question is its overlap with the smaller one, whereas no semantic view can deprive the smaller question of its interest insofar as it forces us to get clear about the "by"-locution. A more specific reason for tackling the small question independently of the large one will emerge in Section 79.

Goldman distinguishes four kinds of generation, three of which constitute his theory of the "by"-locution. I start with them.

(1) In *causal generation*, one action generates another because it causes something to be the case. For example, the push I give the door generates my cooling of the room because it causes the room to cool down. What the push causes is not *my cooling of the room*, but *the room's becoming cool*. When in a causal case someone (end)s by (means)ing, a_m causes a certain event or state of affairs that is systematically connected with the concept of (end). If a_e is a felling, then a_m causes a fall; if a_e is a killing, then a_m causes a death; if a_e is the prevention of a collision, then a_m causes it to be the case that some objects do not collide.

(2) In *conventional* generation, someone who (means)s "counts as" (end)ing because there is a rule or convention according to which (means)ing in those circumstances counts as (end)ing. For example, someone bids at an auction by making a gesture that at that place and time "counts as" bidding. Goldman also brings moral rules in here, saying tendentiously that breaking a promise conventionally generates doing something wrong.

(3) In *simple generation*, a person (means)s in circumstances guaranteeing that someone who (means)s also (end)s; what makes it *simple* generation is that the relevant circumstances do not include causal laws or conventions or rules (p. 26). Thus, if you jump seven feet when George has jumped no higher than six feet, you outjump George; your jump generates your outjumping of him, and it does so "simply" because the relevant circumstance is the simple noncausal nonconventional fact that he has not jumped as high as you have.

Goldman prevents simple generation from overlapping with conventional by including "not conventional" in its definition. That is a hint that something *ad hoc* is going on. Consider the category of *geographical* generation, containing every case where someone's (means)ing counts as his (end)ing because of some geographical circumstance. My present sneeze would geographically generate my addition to today's tally of sneezes in Syracuse. We could segregate this from simple generation by including "not geographical" in the definition of the latter. This proposal is coherent but pointless; no insight is lost by lumping the geographical in with the rest of the "simple" category. I shall now argue that the same holds for conventional generation.

76. *Conventions*

The argument starts a few steps away from the concept of convention.

Goldman says that if *John fished by dangling a baited hook in the water* then what John does with the hook simply generates his fishing. He is uneasy about this and about the likes of "He lied by denying that he had been drinking", because they involve intentions, beliefs, etc. What is wrong with that? In fact, the lying example is perfectly straightforward; the fishing one is not, for a reason that Goldman does not mention.

It is clearly not a case of causal generation. It would be so if "He fished" entailed "He caught fish", for then "He fished by dangling bait" might mean that he dangled bait and this caused fish to get hooked. But it is not so.

In classifying the "fishing by dangling" case as "simple", Goldman implies that there are circumstances C such that if you dangle a baited hook in the water in C it necessarily follows that you are fishing, but he doesn't say what C is. No kind of external circumstance will do the job. We could take a "strict liability" view of fishing: if you dangle a baited hook while standing above water that has fish in it, etc., then *ipso facto* you are fishing. We *could*, but in fact our meaning of "to fish" is not like that: we don't allow that John is fishing unless he is trying to catch fish.

So C has to be an inner circumstance, something to do with the desires or intentions of the person dangling the hook. Here is a try: To say that John fished by dangling a baited hook in the water is to say that he dangled a baited hook in the water while wanting it to be the case that he catches fish. That is clearly wrong. If we strengthen the analysans to ". . . wanting it to be the case that he catches fish on that hook", the error is harder to see, but it is still there. John might want fish to get caught on the hook without thinking that he is improving the chances that they will by dangling his hook in the water; for all he knows, the local fish take only the food that they jump for; John is dangling his hook in the water as part of a corrosion experiment, but he does think it would be nice if, surprisingly, some fish took the bait and got caught. In such a case, John is not fishing, or, anyway, he is not fishing by dangling a baited hook in the water. So that analysans is too weak. I can find no version of C that makes the fishing example fit comfortably into Goldman's category of "simple generation".

In fact, the example belongs to an important species of "by"-statement that has not previously been noticed, namely the *compressed* ones. I submit that "He fished by dangling a baited hook in the water" means something like "He dangled a baited hook in the water because he wanted it to be the case that: he caught fish by dangling a baited hook in the water". The "by"-statement embedded in this is causal: what the fisher intended is that his dangling of the baited hook should cause fish to get hooked. The intention-drenched verb "to fish" lets us express this statement about the causal chain that he wanted or intended to create by simply saying "He fished by dangling a baited hook in the water". Although this could be forced into the "simple generation" box, that would be a distorting, worse than pointless thing to do. I leave it as an exercise for the reader to work out why.

There are hosts of these compressed causal "by"-statements. In general, if to A is to try to bring it about that P_a, then we can use the form "He As by (means)ing" to mean a corresponding thing of the form: "He (means)s intending [or: because he wants] to make it the case that: by (means)ing he brings it about that P_a." Many verbs of hunting, pursuing, etc., are like this: try it with "They hunted for the prisoner by conducting a house-to-house search". The pattern also fits verbs of attack and defense. Consider "She attacked his credibility by pointing out several occasions when he had lied." If she really was *attacking* his credibility, she must have been aiming to produce some result—probably to get the audience to disbelieve him—and have been planning to bring this about by reporting his lies. Here again we have a compressed causal "by". Other examples are the verbs "to signal" and "to warn" and in general all the verbs standing for kinds of illocutionary act. For example, the statement "She invited him in by saying that she was lonely" means, roughly, that she said she was lonely, intending thereby to cause him to come in or to think that she wanted him to come in or the like. The fine-tuning depends on what theory of meaning one accepts; it does not affect the conceptual pattern that I am exhibiting here.

Noncausal "by"-statements can also be compressed. We might say: "He tried for the record by standing on his head for 72 hours", meaning: "He stood on his head for 72 hours because he wanted it to be the case that: by standing on his head for 72 hours he broke a record"; and the "by"-statement in this analysans is noncausal.

Now let us look at Goldman's category of conventional generation. Suppose that this is true: "He raised the bid on the painting by nodding his head." The rules in this auction might be strict liability ones: If you nod your head, you thereby bid, so that if a sneeze makes you nod, a sneeze makes you bid. Or the rules might involve intentions: You bid only if you nod your head *meaning to bid*, that is, intending to have a certain effect on the auctioneer.

The strict liability case does not differ interestingly from typical cases of "simple generation", for in it "By nodding he made a bid" is true because he nodded in circumstances where there was an operative rule saying that he who nods bids, and this does not differ importantly from cases where by nodding he fulfilled a prediction, broke a promise, or counterinstantiated Jones's theory—all of which belong in the "simple generation" category. Three of Goldman's four main examples of "conventional generation" are like this. He stresses that each involves a "rule, convention, or social practice", but that fact just sits there idly. Nothing is done with it to make it look like more important than, for example, the thought that the relevant circumstance might be a geographical fact.

What is noteworthy in Goldman's "conventional" territory does not involve strict liability, has nothing to do with rules, and has everything to do with intention. Consider his favorite example: "He signaled a turn by extending his arm out the window." To signal it is not enough to move your arm in the right way; it doesn't count as signaling unless you have a relevant intention. That applies to everything properly described as "conventional",[2] but the compressed "by"-locution is present in many cases that do not involve conventions or rules. To say that he signaled a turn by extending his arm is to say something like this: *He extended his arm because he wanted it to be the case that: by extending his arm he caused others to know that he was going to turn.* No rule need be involved. Even if he thought up the signal on the spur of the moment, hoping the others would catch on, it is still a perfectly good case of signaling. And it still involves compression, with a hidden causal "by". That concealed structure will trip us up if we don't recognize it, so it *does* need attention, as rules or norms or general practices don't. Now that it has been recognized, however, I shall set it aside and confine myself to uncompressed "by"-statements.

Having no need for "conventional generation" or any descendant thereof, we can reduce Goldman's first three categories to two—the causal and the noncausal. The materials he calls "conventional" are distributed between these, usually after decompression.

77. *Augmentation*

There remains Goldman's fourth category, of what he calls "augmentation generation". Someone's B-ing augmentation-generates his A-ing if he As and this logically entails that he Bs. My walking augmentation-

2. For a crash course on convention, see my *Linguistic Behaviour*, Section 54. For a proper education in it, see David K. Lewis's *Convention*.

generates my walking quickly; my speaking augmentation-generates my speaking in a high-pitched voice. How does my strolling during the storm relate to my walking homewards at that time? Goldman would probably interrelate them by saying that my walking during the storm augmentation-generates them both.

Notice that I have had to express all this with imperfect nominals. That is a reminder that, for Goldman as for Kim, so-called "actions" are really facts about actions. That explains an aspect of Goldman's symbolism, which I should comment on. What is entailed by someone's performing a certain action depends upon how the action is described. Much less is entailed by *Cressida greeted Agamemnon* than by *Cressida gave Agamemnon a greeting kiss*, yet these may be made true by the very same action. Or so one might think. Goldman's Kim-like semantics, however, leads him to think otherwise: he comes close to holding that two names refer to the same action only if their parent sentences are logically equivalent, which frees him to use one symbol to stand either for an action or for the proposition that the action is performed. In the statement "If B is my walking and A is my walking quickly, then B augmentation-generates A because *A entails B*", each schematic letter is used twice for a so-called action and once for a proposition. This double duty is sanctioned by Goldman's system, which comes close to having a perfect mapping of "actions" onto propositions.

That reminds us of what forced augmentation-generation into Goldman's story in the first place, namely his Kim-Goldman semantics of event names. Since I think that that is quite wrong, I want to push this material out again and attend only to Goldman's treatment of the "by"-locution. Even internally to Goldman's account and quite apart from the rejection of the Kim-Goldman semantics, there is a decisive reason for banishing augmentation-generation from the account; I shall explain it in Section 79. Goldman himself has acknowledged that his augmentation category may have been a mistake.[3] I conclude that I shall be doing him no injustice if I now consider him as a theorist of the "by"-locution and attend only to his first three categories, reduced now to two.

78. *Goldman's first three conditions*

Goldman says that two actions A and B are related by generation if and only if they (1) have the same subject, (2) involve different properties, and (3)

3. Alvin A. Goldman, "Action, Causation, and Unity", replying to Castañeda.

(i) Neither is a temporal part of the other,
(ii) It is not correct to say that the agent did one "and then" (or "and later") did the other,
(iii) It is not correct to say that the agent did one of the acts "while also" doing the other,

and (4) satisfy a further condition that I shall treat in my next section. The conditions (3) (ii) and (iii) could be coalesced into the requirement that A and B not be *conversationally additional* to one another. I say "conversationally", because the conditions do not speak of how A is related to B but only of whether it is "correct" to relate them using certain phrases.[4]

The inappropriateness of "and then" and "while also" is presumably the sort of thing Anscombe is steering by when she speaks of "what it is rather natural to call one act". Goldman is here facing up to something that counts against him: if A and B are not related by part/whole or in any way expressible by "and then" or "while also", that is prima facie evidence that A is B, and Goldman is refusing to sweep it under the rug.

But he ought not to have included it in his analysis. Castañeda has attacked this aspect of the analysis, in my opinion rightly.[5] Reporting a wide divergence of view about what it would be "correct to say" regarding Goldman's examples, Castañeda asks what such considerations are doing in a philosophical analysis anyway. They could be part of the output of a good philosophical analysis, i.e. something that an analysis might help to explain, but they should not enter into the analysis as part of the analysans.

Goldman's analysis may not need these two conditions about what it would be correct to say. So far as I can see, if his conditions (1), (2), and (4) did the kind of work he expects of them, they would bear the whole load of the analysis. I have not been able to devise a case of something that Goldman would want to exclude from the range of his level-generation relation and that satisfies the other conditions but fails to satisfy 3(ii) or (iii). His best hope seems to be that these two conditions can be regarded not as parts of his analysis but rather as remarks to aid us pretheoretically to locate the analysans. Before long, however, we shall see that that hope is dashed.

There is no special difficulty with (3)(i). The other conditions are satisfied by the pair: my reading of Shakespeare's *The Winter's Tale* and my reading of the words "Here's flowers for you; Hot lavender, mints, savory, marjoram"; but Goldman doesn't want that pair to fall

---

4. Alvin A. Goldman, *A Theory of Human Action*, pp. 21 and 22 respectively.

5. Hector-Neri Castañeda, "Intentionality and Identity in Human Action", Section 4, up to and including 4.7.

within the scope of his theory, because they don't involve the "by"-locution, and nobody thinks they are one action doubly described. So he excludes them on the ground that one is a temporal part of the other. Incidentally, Goldman's (3)(i) implies that he should not, as in fact he sometimes does, use the *actio praecox* argument against the Anscombe thesis. Anyone who uses that argument must hold that the swinging of the axe is a temporal part of the felling of the tree.[6]

79. *The fourth condition*

Now things start to heat up. In what follows, I shall use the form "P ⥽ Q" to mean that P logically entails or absolutely necessitates Q, and the form "P > Q" to mean that if P had been the case Q would have been the case. Now, Goldman says that A generates B only if

(4) There is a condition C that obtains and is such that
   (i) (B & C) ⥽ A.
   (ii) (not-B & C) > not-A.
   (iii) (B & not-C) > not-A.

In English: something C was the case such that: (i) B's occurring while C obtained would absolutely necessitate (expressed by "⥽") that A occurred; and (ii) if B had not occurred though C had still obtained, A would not have occurred; and (iii) if C had not obtained though B had still occurred, A would not have occurred. (Goldman puts (ii) merely as not-B > not-A, but that is evidently a slip.)

Suppose that Heinz (A) breaks a promise by (B) losing his temper. Let condition C be the fact that he promised not to lose his temper and that nothing has happened to release him from that promise. Then (i) Heinz's losing his temper while C obtains absolutely necessitates that he breaks a promise; (ii) if he hadn't lost his temper but had made the promise, he would not have broken a promise; and (iii) if he hadn't made the promise but did lose his temper, he wouldn't have broken a promise.

Conditions (ii) and (iii) are meant to exclude idle or vacuous values of B or C, requiring that both B and C were *operative* in the performance of A. However, they are far from being adequate as they stand: it is not hard to construct cases of the "by"-locution to which they do not apply. Goldman might have done better to leave counterfactuals out of it, and to say instead:

(ii′) not-(C ⥽ A)
(iii′) not-(B ⥽ A)

6. This point is made by Lawrence Brian Lombard, "A Note on Level-Generation and the Time of a Killing".

Those would ensure nonidleness, while keeping the lid on the Pandora's Box of troubles springing from the counterfactual formulations. Whether it would run into other troubles instead I do not know.

Goldman's condition (4), thus amended, neatly covers hosts of noncausal "by"-statements: the Athenians widowed Xanthippe by killing Socrates (C = they were spouses at the time); the driver broke the law by going at 60 m.p.h. (C = the law forbade driving faster than 55 m.p.h.); Bannister set a world record by running a mile in under four minutes (C = up to that time nobody had been clocked as running a mile that fast).

Causal cases don't fit so smoothly. Goldman requires that (B & C) entail A, that is, absolutely necessitate its performance. So his idea must be that in a causal "by"-statement C includes not only facts about the circumstances in which the person Bs but also the relevant causal laws. That may still not be strong enough to do the job. If the causal laws of the actual world are not deterministic, then in a situation where a village was threatened by fire, but *Kate saved the village by opening the floodgates of the dam*, there is no truth C about causal laws and the environment at the time of the opening of the gates which, when conjoined with "Kate opened the floodgates of the dam", strictly entails that the village was saved.

Perhaps Goldman could weaken 4(i) to something probabilistic, making it weak enough to capture the causal "by"-statements while still strong enough to do justice to the noncausal ones. I haven't explored this possibility carefully, because the problem has no analogue in my own analysis of the "by"-locution, which I shall present in my next chapter.

A problem that Castañeda has raised for Goldman's analysis will also confront mine (*op. cit.*, p. 249). Recall that Goldman's whole story is this: B generates A if and only if: (1) they have the same subject, (2) they involve different properties, (3) neither is part of or conversationally additional to the other, and (4) there is a condition C such that . . . etc. Castañeda has offered a simple proof that, given two logically independent truths A and B, there is *always* a C that satisfies Goldman's (4). It follows that (4) adds nothing to the content of the analysis, whose whole weight therefore falls upon the suspect conditions (1) through (3), with the latter's emphasis on what it is "correct to say".

Castañeda's proof is simple. It consists in letting C be (A ≡ B). That value of C satisfies Goldman's three clauses in (4) and my suggested replacements for two of them. C's being truth-functional doesn't prevent it from occurring *in* counterfactuals such as (ii) and (iii) or entailment statements such as my (ii′) and (iii′).[7]

If Goldman is to rescue his theory from this disaster, he must

7. Hugh J. McCann, "The Trouble with Level-Generation", p. 484, thinks otherwise but gives no reason.

tighten the constraints on C. I once wasted my own and students' time trying to keep Castañeda's trivialization at bay by strengthening the clauses in (4). While we were trying to choose from an array of five or six possible strengthenings, David Lewis devised a trivialization that got past all of them at once.

We should never have tried to do the job through logical tinkering. On encountering Castañeda's value of C, one's immediate reaction is that it is "not what we had in mind" when we first met Goldman's (4) and found it plausible, because it is conceptually parasitic on A and B. That initial reaction ought to be trusted and the analysis strengthened by reference to the difference between honestly free-standing conditions and ones that are constructed out of A and B. In my own analysis, that is the line I shall take (see Section 84).

Now I can show why, quite apart from the wrongness of the Kim-Goldman semantics, Goldman ought not to have lumped "augmentation generation" in with the rest. In fact, he seems to have forgotten it when he required (i) that ((B & C) ⥽ A). What value of C satisfies this when B is Sebastian's walking and A is his strolling? If from my breach of promise you subtract my loss of temper, you are left with my promise not to lose my temper; if from Goering's widowing of Emma you subtract his suicide, you are left with the fact that they were married at the time; but if from Sebastian's strolling you subtract his walking, you are left with . . . what? The only possible answer is the fact that (Sebastian walks ⊃ Sebastian strolls). That satisfies Goldman's (4)(i) and (iii), but, for (ii) to be satisfied, we must strengthen it into the biconditional (Sebastian walks ≡ Sebastian strolls).[8] There is really is no better candidate for the job. But that is Castañeda's value of C! In short, the only way to make the analysis cover "augmentation-generation" is to allow C to take just such Castañedan values as make a mockery of the analysis across the rest of its territory. That proves that "augmentation" is a cuckoo in the nest.

Strictly, what are excluded are the augmentation cases that cannot be treated as ordinary noncausal generation. Goldman says that Bill's shooting generates his jump-shooting because his jump-shooting entails that he shoots; but he could instead say that the shooting "simply" or noncausally generates the jump-shooting because it occurs in circumstances C—namely at a time when Bill is in the middle of a jump—and so considered the case can be brought within the scope of his analysis. Significantly, it is a case where the "by"-locution is appropriate. How did Bill jump-shoot? By shooting (when he was in the middle of a jump).

With gratitude for good leads and salutary warnings, I now leave Goldman's account of "generation" and start afresh in an attempt to analyze the "by"-locution.

---

8. The story runs a little differently if Goldman's (ii) is replaced by my (ii)′.

XIV

AN ANALYSIS OF THE "BY"-LOCUTION

80. *Contrasting two patterns of analysis*

When Goldman introduces causal generation, he emphasizes that, when the Hunts depressed the price of silver by selling too fast, the causal flow ran from their selling not to their depressing of the price but to the price's fall—not to what they did to the price but to what the price did. Quite generally, what makes a causal "by"-statement true is a causal relation between the agent's (means)ing and something that is *systematically connected* but *not identical* to his (end)ing. Goldman, however, announces his theory as one about a relation between two *actions*—the (means)ing and the (end)ing. I say he announces it in that way; in the upshot, his entire account of "level generation" is stated in terms of facts or propositions. Goldman thinks that those map onto actions, but that belief plays no part in the working out of the theory. Nor does it figure in the informal discussions, where Goldman says things like ". . . he would not have signalled" rather than " . . . his signal would not have occurred".

My account of the "by"-locution partly overlaps Goldman's discussion, but it stands in sharp contrast to his official view of what he is doing. Where he says he is treating the "by"-locution as a way of relating actions, I see it as a way of relating facts. There are *a priori* reasons for wanting to see it my way, if possible.

(1) My kind of analysis is more conservative, less intrusive, with regard to the end clause. That clause is a whole sentence reporting a fact about the agent's conduct, such as *The Hunts depressed the price of silver.* My analysis will have to operate on that, digging out of it the associated fact that *the price of silver fell*. Goldman also alludes to that fact in explaining what makes the case a causal one, but he has to operate on the end clause again, to dig out of it a reference to an event, namely *the Hunts' depressing of the price of silver.* So Goldman needs two digs to my one.

(2) My kind of analysis can be faithful to the means clause, which is always an imperfect nominal—try it out with adverbs and adjectives or with direct and genetive objects. We can say: "He silenced the rattle by tightening the screws", but the genetive-object version, "He silenced the rattle by his tightening of the screws", is poor English. It would be all right if "by" were replaced by "by means of", thus turning it into something analogous to "He silenced the rattle by means of a push and a tug" or ". . . with the help of a cushion" or ". . . with the aid of his wife". None of these belongs to the "by"-locution that I am trying to understand.

I raised the question: How does the Anscombe thesis look in the light of a viable analysis of the "by"-locution? If I succeed with my analysis, the answer will be clear. It is that as we wrestle with the "by"-locution the Anscombe thesis is *invisible*: it is couched in terms that are irrelevant to any clear understanding of how the locution works. "Was his swinging of the axe his felling of the tree?"—this will look serious only to someone whose eye has drifted away from the actual "by"-locution onto a sterile theory about it.

81. *An analysis of the "by"-locution*

In both causal and noncausal "by"-statements, the end clause entails something to the effect that the subject of the clause—the "agent" in the "by"-statement—was instrumental in its coming to be the case that P_e, where P_e is a fact or state of affairs systematically associated with the verb phrase that I formalize as "(end)". Sometimes the associated fact is handed to us on a plate, being explicitly expressed by a sentence nested in the end clause: "He brought it about that *his employees hated one another*", "She let it be the case that *the car ran down the hill*". The latter example is stilted and unnatural, though. In statements about allowing and letting, we are more likely to use a noun-infinitive form than a full nested sentence, as in "She let the car run down the hill" or "She allowed the car to run down the hill". And not only with "let" and "allow". It is just passable English to say "He made it the case that the lid fell off", but it is more idiomatic to say "He made the lid fall off". It is a routine exercise to move back and forth between nested sentences and these noun-infinitive constructions, and I can see no difference in meaning between them. From now on I shall use the phrase "nested sentence", to cover both.

To say that *someone* was instrumental in its becoming the case that P is to say that *some fact about his conduct* has this as a consequence. If, as some philosophers think, an agent can be efficacious other than through facts about his behavior, that is irrelevant to understanding the "by"-locution. Incidentally, I don't use "conduct" and "behavior" to imply agency, in any sense that excludes falling freely through space and inadvertently trembling: if a cup falls as a result of a person's inadvertent trembling, there is nothing wrong with saying "He spilled the wine by trembling while holding the glass". Indeed, it may be safe to understand "x was instrumental . . ." merely as "Some fact about how x *moved* was instrumental . . .".

There is a difficulty, however. The subject of a "by"-statement need not be a movable thing at all; it could be an armistice, a blizzard, a climb, a dance, a fumble, a meal, a purchase, a rodeo, a snarl, or a wake. These do not move and do not conduct themselves in any way, so the above account does not apply to them.

Then what are we to say about the instrumentality of events? When the instrumentality is causal, the answer is simple: what makes it the case that event x is causally instrumental in its becoming the case that P_e is that x is a cause of P_e's obtaining. The storm spoiled the picnic—it caused the picnic to be spoiled. But sometimes the instrumentality is not causal: for example, "The storm set a record (by dumping two feet of snow in one night)" does not report a causal relation between the storm and the record. Suggested solution: "The setting of the record was a noncausal consequence of the storm, so the general idea that we need is that of *consequences of events*, sometimes causal and sometimes not." That is no good. A causal consequence of an event is just an effect of it, something that it causes, but "noncausal consequence of an event" is meaningless, as will be clear to everyone who grasps the difference between events and facts. Nor will it do to say that the new record was a consequence of the fact that there was a storm. However, it could be described as a consequence of the fact that there was *that* storm. Using terminology that I introduced in Section 52, the new record was a noncausal consequence of some part of the storm's companion fact, that is, the fact that a certain zone was . . . [and now follows a specification of the trope that constituted that storm]. That gives us a unified account for both causal and noncausal cases where the subject is an event. The causal statement "The storm spoiled the picnic" can be expressed simply as "The storm caused the picnic to be spoiled", but, according to my analysis of event causation in Section 52, that is equivalent to saying that the spoiling of the picnic was a (causal) consequence of some part of the storm's companion fact.

This unified linking of events with the facts that they causally or noncausally bring about, though satisfactory in itself, is troublingly different from how a particular agent connects with the facts that it or he or she brings about. The storm did such-and-such because of some consequence of *a part of its companion fact*; John did such-and-such because of some consequence of *a fact about his conduct*. If there is no unifying formula that nontrivially covers both of these, it seems to follow that there is something close to an ambiguity in (say) the verb "to throw" as used in "I threw him on his back" and "The explosion threw him on his back". This is uncomfortable but not intolerable. Anyway, it seems to be true. From now on, I shall mostly confine myself to agents, occasionally turning aside briefly to bring in events as well.

What about end clauses that don't have full sentences nested in them? Well, to the extent that we understand a sentence "[NP] [VP]", we know which sentences it entails of the form "[NP] is instrumental in its becoming the case that [S]". Of all the values of S that make this true, the one that has a place in my analysis is *the strongest noninstrumental* S for which the entailment holds. The fact expressed by this sentence is what I shall call "the end fact", symbolized by P_e. For example, "Alex boiled the water" entails

Something happened to the water
The water's physical state altered
The water boiled
Someone made the water boil
Alex made the water boil.

The third of these is the end fact P_e. The first two don't qualify because they are weaker, the last two because they are instrumental, that is, they speak of a state of affairs not merely as obtaining but as being brought about. Here are some more examples of sentences and their end facts: He fells the tree / the tree falls; She legitimizes the child / the child becomes legitimate; He reduces the price of silver / silver becomes cheaper; He nets the fish / the fish comes to be in a net. That is the best I can do to explain my concept of the end fact.

I have spoken of what is entailed by each end clause, but I need a mutual entailment, an equivalence. Here it is, with the dummy predicate "K" standing for a long story that has yet to be told: Each end clause whose subject is x is equivalent to "x has a role of kind K in its becoming the case that P_e", which is short for "Some fact about x's conduct has a role of kind K in its becoming the case that P_e."[1] In these formulae, "K" stands for certain constraints that the role must satisfy—conditions on *how* the behavioral fact is instrumental in P_e's becoming the case—their exact nature depending on details of the end clause under analysis. For example, the sentences "John boiled the water" and "John brought it about that the water boiled" have the same end fact, namely *The water boiled*, but they impose different constraints K on the role of John's conduct in the water's coming to boil. In both cases the role is *causal*, but only one of them implies that the relevant causal chain did not run through the will of another

1. Or, if x is an event: Some part of x's companion fact has a role in its becoming the case that P_e.

agent: I can bring it about that the water boils by ordering you to boil the water, but I can't boil the water that way. Reserving a full account of the K constraints until later, I can give my account of the "by"-locution immediately. Here it is: Where "x (end)s . . ." means

> *Some fact about* x's *conduct* has a K role in its becoming the case that P_e . . .

the addition ". . . by (means)ing" means

> . . . namely *the fact that* x *(means)s.*

Putting it together, then, "x (end)s by (means)ing" means

> The fact that x (means)s has a K role in its becoming the case that P_e.

To illustrate this roughly: "He felled the tree" says that *something* about his conduct led to the tree's coming down, and "He felled the tree by swinging his axe" says *what*; "He made it unanimous" says that *something* about his conduct led to the vote's being unanimous, and "By saying Aye, he made it unanimous" says *what*; and so on.

A fact about x's conduct that is referred to in the means clause could in turn be reported in an end clause. He dammed the river by creating a log jam; he created a log jam by rolling logs down the bank; he rolled logs down the bank by . . . , etc. The sequence must stop at the *basic* fact about how he behaved, which will ordinarily be a fact about how he moved. What makes a fact about x's conduct basic is that it could not occur as the end clause in a "by"-statement, except a degenerate one such as "He closed his eyes by closing his eyes".

The foregoing analysis secures the unitariness of the "by"-locution, protecting us from having to suppose it to be ambiguous. We need not say, for example, that "by" has a logical meaning and a causal meaning: according to my analysis, it has just the one meaning, which is essentially that of " . . . namely, the fact that . . ." plus an operator that turns an imperfect nominal into its parent sentence. (Furthermore, this applies equally when the subject is an event. "The wake cheered everyone up . . . by reminding them of how little they had liked the deceased"—"Some part of the wake's companion fact led to everyone's being more cheerful . . . namely the fact that at that zone people were reminded of how little they had liked the deceased".)

Any account of the "by"-locution that did make it ambiguous as between causal and noncausal would be thereby condemned. Suppose I had promised not to make a noise, and then *I broke my promise by making a noise, which I did by turning on a siren.* That conjoins a noncausal "by" with a causal one, and it seems intolerable to suppose that there is any kind of bump, any meaning shift, between the first "by" and the second. That there isn't is confirmed by fact that we can condense part of the story into the nonconjunctive sentence: "I broke my promise by turning on a siren", in which the one occurrence of "by" combines work by the two occurrences in the conjunctive version. If "by" were ambiguous, the condensed sentence would be a zeugma and would strike us as absurd or comic, like "She went home in a taxi and a flood of tears".

For more evidence, remember that "by"-statements are answers to "How?" questions, and consider how one can answer these. (1) "How did he bring it about that there were ten upraised arms?" Causal: "By telling ten people to raise their right arms." Noncausal: "By raising an arm when there were already nine arms raised." (2) "How did he bring it about that she is the fattest person in the village?" Causal: "By encouraging her in her sugar habit." Noncausal: "By getting all the fatter villagers to move to the city."[2] It is wildly implausible to suppose that in such cases the answers interpret the question in different senses; and if "How . . . ?" is univocal, then so is "By. . .". It is good, therefore, to have an account of the "by"-locution that makes it univocal.

82. *Positive and negative*

We have a rich stock of ways of connecting agents to upshots of their behavior, with the upshots being expressed in nested sentences. For example: "make it the case that", "let it be the case that", "bring it about that", "allow it to be the case that", "see to it that", "so behave that in consequence", and there are others. A sentence with any of those as its principal verb phrase will mean something of the form: "Some fact about x's conduct has a K role in its becoming the case that P_e." As I have already said: what K is depends upon what the end clause is, and if it is a nested-sentence end clause, what K is depends on which of the above or other similar expressions is its principal verb phrase. In some cases K is empty—for example, when the principal verb phrase is "so behave that in consequence". If a fact about my conduct has *any* working role, causal or not, in the award's not being given, then "I so behaved that in consequence the award was not given" comes out as true.

Most nested-sentence end clauses, however, say more than merely that some fact about x's conduct was instrumental in making P_e

2. "If all the 3,500 million people in the world who are more despicable than you were taken out and shot for their shortcomings, you would be the most despicable creature on the face of the earth." Michael Frayn, *Constructions*, 70.

obtain. One source of their extra strength is the fact that most of the principal verb phrases are either positive ("make", "bring about", "force") or negative ("let", "allow", "permit"). Where one of the former group is used, what is said is true only if a positive fact about the agent's conduct relates appropriately to its being the case that P_e. For example, if, when ten arms were already raised, Alfred could have raised an arm but didn't, he may have *let* it be the case, but he certainly didn't *make* it the case, that only ten arms were raised.

In causal cases, it may happen that the relevant behavioral fact is positive but negativeness enters the scene further down the causal chain running from the behavioral fact to P_e. In such a case, the verb "to let" is appropriate, and "to make" etc. are inappropriate. Consider two scenarios in each of which a gate is swinging towards the closed position: (i) I could but don't stop it with my foot, and it closes; (ii) I kick away a rock which would have stopped it from closing, and it closes. These have an equal claim to being accounted cases of *letting* the gate close. Where a causal chain is involved, it seems, "let" and "allow" are apt to be appropriate if there is negativeness anywhere along the chain even if not at its behavioral first member. In the noncausal cases, the negativeness must be in the fact about behavior, because there is no chain.

There may be forms of words that imply positiveness in the behavioral fact but allow negativeness further down the causal chain if there is one. To my ear, "bring about" is like that. The truth of "x lets y move" requires that there be negativeness somewhere along the line; "x makes y move" requires positiveness everywhere along the line; and "x brings it about that y moves" requires positiveness in the fact about how x moves but tolerates negativeness further along the causal chain—or so it seems to me.

I have shown elsewhere how to distinguish negative from positive facts without relying on the trivial line between sentences that do and ones that don't contain an odd number of occurrences of "not", "un-", "non-", and the like.[3] My account does not reflect all the niceties of "let", "allow", etc., but I think it is the best *basis* for a full treatment of those words. The details need not delay us here. All I am laying claim to is the idea of a positive/negative line through a lot of verb phrases that we can use to connect conduct with upshots.

So far as I can discover, every form of words on the negative side of the line—"let", "allow", "permit"—implies something about what the agent knows or should know. Suppose that the gate comes to be closed and that I could have stopped it from closing by interposing my foot. Does it follow that I *let* the gate close, or *allowed* or *permitted* it to close? I can find nobody who says Yes. Apparently we won't use any of

3. Jonathan Bennett, "Killing and Letting Die", pp. 55–65.

these verbs unless the agent knew or ought to have known that he could prevent P_e from obtaining. For example, a woman died of smoke inhalation in Dubrovnik last night; if I had phoned her just before the fire started, she would have survived. A negative fact about my behavior led to her dying at that time, but I didn't *let* her die, because I was not related to her in any way that gave me a responsibility for knowing that—or even wondering whether—a phone call from me would be useful to her.

Similarly with noncausal cases. The organizers of United Way were anxious to reach the same mark as last year, and at the last moment they were a hundred dollars short. I could have given them the money, and I didn't, but we don't say that I allowed the total to stay below last year's unless I knew or should have known what the situation was.

Suppose that the fire that killed the woman was started by some device which, through a horrible fluke, was sensitive to an ordinarily harmless kind of radio signal and that what triggered the device was a signal sent out, all innocently and responsibly, by a distant amateur radio operator. Did he bring it about that she died at that time? Most of my native informants say Yes, indicating that the epistemic constraint is absent from the positive side of the line. This too holds in noncausal cases. It is obvious that by paying a hundred dollars to the United Way I might bring its total up to last year's mark without having the faintest idea that I was doing so.

In practice, nested-sentence end clauses are more often negative than positive. Indeed, if I had not wanted to treat the positive/negative divide, I would have omitted the explicit nested-sentence or noun-infinitive form from my story, as too minor to be worth the trouble: I would have settled for getting straight about "He weeded the lawn" and would have left "He brought it about that the lawn was free of weeds" to take care of itself. But nested sentences and noun-infinitive forms are our chief and almost our only linguistic vehicle for the negative cases, so they need to be attended to.

If we want to say that the relevant behavioral fact is negative, it seems that we have to use nested sentences with "let" or "allow" or the like.[4] Some forms of words, however, do not entail that the behavioral fact is negative but are consistent with its being so. For instance, by not sneezing, I may foil your prediction; by not being at the theater this evening, you might let me down; by not reporting that my address

4. It has been objected that "He neglects her" does not have a nested-sentence form yet entails that some negative fact about his conduct is instrumental in P_e's being the case. But what is P_e in this case? The sentence seems to entail nothing of a noninstrumental kind, and thus to lie outside the scope of my analysis. Significantly, there are no good ways of completing "He neglects her by . . ." with an imperfect nominal in the gap.

has changed, I could break the law. Each of these has in the background something of the form "[attitude] [positive proposition]"—you predicted that I will do A, you said that you would meet me, the law requires that I report my new address—and the statement about foiling or letting down or breaking is made true by a behavioral fact that is contradictory to that positive proposition, i.e. by a negative behavioral fact.

That is one way in which the same form of words could be made true by either positive or negative behavioral facts. A second way is exemplified by this: if x is to blame for the fact that P_e or if it is x's responsibility to ensure that P_e does not obtain, we will sometimes use the normally positive language of "x verbs y" to report x's role in P_e's coming to obtain, even if the relevant behavioral fact is negative. He killed the houseplants by letting them die when it was his job to keep them alive. This idiosyncrasy of "kill"—that one can kill by letting die—is shared by some other dyadic verbs: she saved the Jewish family by not reporting them to the SS; he destroyed the government by not intervening in the debate. The majority of verbs don't have it. Suppose that it is my job to keep the gate open, that I see it swinging shut and know I can stop it by interposing my foot, that I deliberately stand aside and watch the gate close, and that this is a bad way to behave; still nobody will say that I closed the gate. Similarly for "fell the tree", "crumble the cake", "flatten the carton", "disperse the leaves", "pile up the dust", "dirty the carpet", "light the fire", and so on.

The odd positive-negative feature of "kill" and "save" and "destroy" (and "help" and "harm" and some others) seems to be a bubble forced onto the surface of our language by underlying moral pressure. That would help to explain where the line falls between verbs that have the feature and ones that don't: it is a line between verbs that commonly carry a moral or evaluative charge and ones that don't. A similar moral bubble comes to the surface of our uses of the verb "to cause", also, but I would never give that any place in an analysis of the concept of causation.

83. *Instrumental verbs*

We can relate an agent to an upshot without using a nested sentence, by employing what I shall call an instrumental verb, that is, a dyadic verb V such that "x Vs y" entails that some fact Q about x's behavior contributes to y's acquiring a certain property P_v. We know what P_v is by knowing what V means, this being a special case of knowing what P_e is by knowing what the sentence "x (end)s" means.

Many instrumental verbs are causal: V is causal if "x Vs y"

entails that some fact about x's behavior is *causally* instrumental in y's acquiring the property P_v. Causal verbs include "boil", "cook", "beget", "fell", "lift", "fertilize", "reap", and thousands of others.

I shall not give the concept of a causal verb much work to do. I shall have a lot to say about "by"-statements that are made true by causal facts, but not all of those will involve "causal verbs" in my sense of that phrase. Consider the verb "destroy", for instance. "He destroyed the firm" could be true because he set off a causal chain that led to the firm's destruction; but it could instead be true because he signed his name under circumstances C which, conjoined with his signing his name, *entailed* that the firm didn't exist any longer. I cannot find any philosophically important difference between causal verbs and ones that can but need not be made applicable by causal facts. (There are no instrumental verbs that cannot be made applicable by causal facts.)

One special class of causal verbs is worth noticing. Typical members of it are "kick", "punch", "shove", "slap", "kiss", "stroke", "pat", "eat", "bite", "drink", "swallow". These certainly are "causal" in my sense: if I kick someone, a certain fact about my behavior causes him or her to come into contact with my foot. What makes the "kick"-like verbs special is that (i) P_v is a relation to some part of x's body and (ii) x *immediately* causes y to acquire P_v. If I start up a machine that a minute later thrusts my booted foot into your midriff, it need not ever be the case that I have kicked you. Feature (i) is obviously special. So is (ii), for most causal verbs can be applicable on the strength of a causal chain running from x's movement to y's acquiring P_v. Still, some verbs seem to have (ii) and not (i)—for example, "He *painted* the wall".

Because of those two features, we can know whether x Vs y, where V is "kick"-like, merely by knowing what happens up to the instant that x stops moving in relevant ways; we can know whether John kicked Henry if we observe them both up to when John's boot stops moving; similarly with kissing, swallowing, and the rest. This contrasts with causal verbs of the sort that generate the "no further effort" difficulty, where the question of whether x Vs y depends on what results later on from x's movements.

(This feature of "kick"-like verbs limits the kinds of means clause that can occur in "x (end)s y by (means)ing". Roughly speaking, the means clause must be something that gives pretty well all the information that the end clause gives: it is not right to say "She slapped him by raising her hand" or "She slapped him by touching him". If the means clause says all that the end clause does, what gives the whole statement its point? Well, the means clause may elucidate the end clause: "He walked by repeatedly losing his balance and then regaining it by putting one foot in front of him and then putting his weight onto that",[5] or it may add further details: "She kissed him by pursing her lips while holding them firmly together and pressing them briefly against his left cheek." None of this matters much.)

In Judith Thomson's definition of "V is a causal verb" the definiens has two conjuncts—a complex one that I shall not discuss, and another saying that *V accepts events as subjects.*[6] That second conjunct serves, in her hands, to draw the line between "kill" and "kick": you may be killed by a substance such as a person, an animal, or a rock or by an event such as a fall, an explosion, a fit of anger, and so on, but you can be kicked only by a substantial kicker—"It is not possible for an event to kick anything".[7] So "kick" is not a causal verb, although it satisfies her first conjunct and clearly has things in common with "kill".

Why can't an event kick something? Simply because "x kicks y" means "x moves its foot . . ." and events don't have feet. Similarly with all the other "kick"-like verbs: they either mean something about specific parts of x's body ("punch", "kiss", "eat", "bite", "drink", "swallow") or at least mean that x did such and such with *some* part of its body ("shove", "slap", "stroke", "pat").

That points to a routine procedure for defining verbs so that they are not "causal" in Thomson's sense. Let V be a paradigm causal verb—your favorite occupant of that role. If we define a verb V_1 so that "x V_1s y" means that x Vs y by moving some material part of itself, it follows that events cannot be subjects of V_1 because no part of an event is a portion of matter. Thus, for example, although events can be killers, only material things could be kill_1ers. Again, we can define V_2 so that "x V_2s y" means that x intentionally Vs y. That would exclude events and also some physical substances from being subjects of the verb. Events cannot be kill_2ers, and nor can bullets.

Thus, many of the verbs that fail to be "causal" in Thomson's sense, because they cannot take events as subjects, are thoroughly "causal" in my sense. In the same passage where Thomson plausibly remarks that illocutionary act verbs such as "answer" and "insist" and "warn" are not causal, she unapologetically implies that in her taxonomy "murder" is not a causal verb either (pp. 224f). But such matters of terminology are usually not important, and my objection would collapse if "causal" were replaced by "purely causal", say.

The verbs in question are a mixed bunch. They won't take

5. "Around us clothed mammals alternately lose and recover their balance in a regulated error known as 'walking'." Peter De Vries, *Let Me Count the Ways*, p. 118.

6. Judith Jarvis Thomson, *Acts and Other Events*, p. 133.

7. Ibid., p. 220.

events as subjects, because they require their subjects to have feet, to last through time, to think. . . . That too is unimportant. What matters is whether the verbs that *can* take events as subjects comprise a species with enough conceptual unity to be worth marking out in a philosophical theory. I suspect that they don't, but I cannot be sure without having mastered the intricate theoretical network in which Thomson puts to work her idea that events can melt chocolate, dam rivers, bankrupt farmers, and so on.

84. *"Pictured as the sole input"*

In most statements that relate an agent to an upshot without expressing the upshot in a nested sentence, two further constraints are at work. Each applies across a wide range, which makes them worth a section each.

The first is present in many nested sentence forms as well, so some of my examples will be like that.

What do we demand of a situation if we are to be willing to say that *He felled the tree? She legitimized the baby? He made it the case that ten arms were raised?* Well, in each case some fact about the person's behavior must have been instrumental in bringing it about that the tree fell, the baby became legitimate, there were ten arms raised. And—I now add—the behavioral fact must be one that we picture as being, in the circumstances, the *only* input into P_e's obtaining.

Let me first explain "in the circumstances". I take the "circumstances" to consist in some condition C that does not logically involve either the behavioral fact Q or the upshot P_e. That is in the spirit of what I said in Section 79 about Castañeda's trivialization of Goldman's account. Furthermore, I mean a condition C that is settled at the time when the behavior occurs, either because it already obtains or because it is certain to obtain later. The second disjunct is needed. We would regard "By switching his vote, he made assent unanimous" as true if, when he switched his vote, it was settled that everyone else would vote Yes, even if they hadn't yet done so. Another example: "By bogeying the 18th hole, Miller gave the victory to Palmer" could be true even if Palmer was playing behind him, if Palmer's eventual score is thought of as inevitable, as a fixed fact. This notion of an independent fixed fact is doubly vague, but I think this mirrors a respect in which many sentences relating conduct to upshots are vague.

Now I must explain my clause about Q's being pictured by us as in the circumstances the *only* input into P_e's obtaining. I mean by this that our informal intuitive picture of the situation presents (Q & C) as *alone* bringing it about that P. In many cases—the noncausal ones—

our informal intuitive picture is complete: there are no other relevant factors. He sets a record for the mile because (Q) he runs the mile in four minutes at a time when (C) no one has ever before run a mile that fast; those alone bring about, with absolute necessity, a state of affairs P_e in which a record comes into being. In many and perhaps all causal cases, however, (Q & C) is not all that goes into P_e's becoming the case, even if we allow C to include all causal laws; but our willingness to report the situation in the language of what the agent did depends on whether the other causal inputs are conspicuous enough to intrude upon our informal intuitive picture.

If the relevant causal chain has significant temporal length, there will be many other causal inputs along the way, but if they consist mainly in the holding steady of background conditions—as the fuse slowly burns, the earth continues to turn, the wind keeps a steady velocity, no meteorite falls, etc.—they represent normality, all quiet, things as usual. They therefore don't enter our informal picture and aren't intuitively registered by us as causal inputs at all, and so they don't stop us from reporting the situation in terms of what the agent did—he "brought it about that the house burned" or "he set fire to the house". We don't talk like that, however, if the causal chain depended upon many intervening coincidences. Here is how I once put it:

> I kick a rock which starts a landslide which crashes into a lake and sends out a wave of water which drowns you as you stand in the stream fishing. In this case I kill you. . . . Now alter the story a bit: the kicked rock starts a landslide only because it happens to coincide with a crash of thunder; the wave goes your way only because it happens to reach the junction at one of the rare moments when the control gates are set to the left; and the water catches you only because by chance that is the moment when you are hastily wading across the stream. The fact that the causal route from my movement to your death involves several intervening coincidences seems to imply that in this case I do not kill you.[8]

That illustrates the "few intervening coincidences" condition, which Lewis calls the "stability" condition—the requirement, in his phrase, that the causal chain not depend on "an exceptionally large and miscellaneous bundle of circumstances all being just right".[9]

It is not the requirement that the causal chain be *secure*, with each element likely to lead to the next. On the contrary: if I built a randomizer into my fire-starting mechanism, giving it only one

---

8. Jonathan Bennett, "Killing and Letting Die", p. 71.

9. The phrase and the point of this paragraph are from David K. Lewis, Postscript to "Causation". Lewis had already contributed to my own earlier treatment of this matter.

chance in ten of causing a fire to start, that will not deter us from saying that I burned down the house. That is because this causal chain, although not likely to lead to P_e, did not conspicuously depend for its chance of doing so on a suitable conjunction with chancy external circumstances.

I am offering two theses here. (i) When a fact Q about x's conduct contributes causally to P_e's being the case, we do not report this in the language of what x did—saying that x brought it about that P_e or that he started the fire, felled the tree, repaired the bicycle, bankrupted the firm, or the like—if we are conscious of the causal chain as involving a number of intervening coincidences. (ii) The reason for (i) is the fact that our use of the language of "what x did" is tied to the notion of x's behavior as seeming to function, against the background of existing independent conditions C, as the *sole* input into P_e's coming to obtain.

A special case should be mentioned. Suppose that x's behavior starts a causal chain that runs to P_e's being the case, the chain depending on several coincidences, and imagine x, being superhumanly skilful and prescient, to have foreseen these coincidences and to have relied on them to get to P_e, this being what he was after. In that case, x clearly *does* bring it about that P_e, does dam the river or close the door or whatever. I agree with Lewis that we can handle this without tacking on a disjunct, though my way of doing so differs from his. I suggest that if the agent foresees the intervening coincidences then in his picture of the situation the outcomes of the coincidences are fixed, settled, established at the time when he acts. That makes them part of the given circumstances C in which he acts, which restores to truth the statement that Q and C are pictured as together providing the whole input into P_e's becoming the case.

This idea about something's being "pictured as providing the sole input" is not clear and distinct; I let it into my book only because I believe that it does work in our everyday thinking. I could still have an account without it. I could say that what is needed is that (Q & C) lead to P_e in some manner other than through a causal chain containing many intervening coincidences; that would cover the noncausal cases and the causal ones where the chain is stable. But a superficial condition that draws the line in the right place doesn't explain what is going on—*why* we should draw a line there. That is what I offer to do with my "pictured as the sole input" idea.

85. *No wholly intervening agency*

Here is a repeat of the story up to here, with one addition. For any instrumental verb V, there is a property P_v such that "x Vs y" entails that some fact Q about x's conduct is instrumental in y's acquiring P_v, and that this instrumentality does not run through a causal chain that is "unstable" in Lewis's sense or involves anything negative or—this being the addition—runs wholly through the will of an agent. I shall explain.

If I pull a lever that starts a machine that rolls a stone that swings a balance that rotates a wheel that closes a circuit that starts a second machine that closes the gate, and if all this is "stable" in Lewis's sense, then *I close the gate*. If, on the other hand, I bully or bribe or persuade you to close the gate, *I don't close the gate*. The meanings of our instrumental verbs will tolerate long, complicated causal chains, but not ones whose whole effectiveness runs through the will of an agent.[10]

I don't say "the will of *another* agent", for a reason given by David Lewis. Suppose that I cause myself to close the gate: at noon I set up a delayed-action mechanism, knowing that when it kicks into action at dusk it will irresistibly tempt me to close the gate. In that case, what qualifies me as the one who closes the gate is what I do at dusk, not what I do at noon. The applicability of an instrumental verb seems to depend on whether the relevant chain runs through the agency of someone—not necessarily someone else.

The conceptual phenomenon I am pointing to requires that the relevant causal chain runs through the will of an agent, not merely through an agent's voluntary behavior. If I persuade you to put extra vitamins into your food, that doesn't make it true that I enrich your food intake; but the latter is true if I sneak vitamins into your food, which you then unsuspectingly eat. In each case, the causal chain from my behavior to your swallowing better food includes voluntary behavior of yours, but only in the former case do I act on your will; in the other, I merely affect what results from your unswayed exercise of your will.

I have said that the phenomenon requires, further, that the causal chain from behavior to upshot run "wholly" through someone's will. The need for the qualification "wholly", to which I was alerted by Alastair Norcross, comes from cases like the following. I pick up the wrench and start turning a bolt with it; this causes you to apply another wrench to the nut at the back so that it doesn't turn with the bolt; and the final result is that the bolt is tightened. What I did with my wrench caused it to be tight, and the causal chain ran through your will; yet we don't hesitate to say that I tightened the bolt. The reason seems to be that the chain didn't run wholly through your will.

That suggests an explanation of why our instrumental verbs are

---

10. This constraint is discussed by Judith Jarvis Thomson, *Acts and Other Events*, p. 128; Donald Davidson, "The Logical Form of Action Sentences", pp. 110f; Alvin A. Goldman, *A Theory of Human Action*, p. 23; Lawrence Brian Lombard, "Actions, Results, and the Time of a Killing".

sensitive to facts about intervening agency. It looks as though the cases where my behavior leads to y's acquiring P_v but, because of how your will figures in the situation, it is false that I verb y, are also cases where *you* verb y. I tightened the bolt, and you didn't; whereas, if I bully or bribe or persuade you to close the gate, I don't close the gate, and you do. That suggests that it is because you did that I didn't; and when at noon I launch the chain that causes me to close the gate at 5 p.m., what I do at noon doesn't count as closing the gate because what I do at 5 p.m. counts as that.

That explanation is not much good. It seems to require that we think of such roles as that of gate-closer as indivisible, but we don't; we are quite willing to say, sometimes, "together they closed the gate". Perhaps we say that only when the two instrumentalities are hooked up in parallel rather than in series, but why? That is the problem, not the solution.

Here is another possible solution: Instrumental verbs are applicable only on the basis of (almost) unbreakable causal chains, the point being that the will of a free agent is always a weak link. For that is just wrong about instrumental verbs: I can demolish a building through a causal chain containing a one-chance-in-ten randomizing device. The proposed explanation is also wrong on the other side: if I lay seige to the will of a pliable person, subtly (or brutally) making it virtually certain that he will close the gate, it still isn't true that I close the gate.

Lewis holds that the "no intervening agency" condition comes from the requirement of stability or "few intervening coincidences". He suggests that we think of a causal route running through the will of an agent as unstable, highly sensitive to circumstances: there are so many ways a person's behavioral course can be tilted by physically tiny changes in his environment. In the odd cases where that is not so, our usual attitude to intervening agency has a momentum that lets it still influence our speech, Lewis writes:

> We might know very well that this dull thug before us would never think twice about killing for a small fee. Therefore we might be sure that when you hire him, the causal chain from your action to the victim's death is as inexorable and insensitive as if it had passed instead through some strong and sturdy machine. But we might know this, and yet be halfhearted in putting our mouths where our minds are. Some vestige of our habitual respect [for the sensitivity of most people to circumstances] might well influence how we speak.

The employer of the dull thug *is* a killer—Lewis is suggesting—and we are merely squeamish about saying so. Alternatively, Lewis has a fall-back position: our meaning for the verb "to kill" requires a causal chain with no intervening agency, sensitive or not, because (i) insensitivity or stability of causal mechanisms is built into the meanings of our instrumental verbs, (ii) people are usually behaviorally sensitive to circumstances, and (iii) we prefer to keep our meanings simple rather shaping them to fit snugly around special cases. I agree with him that there is little to choose between the two positions.

Probably one of them is right. I have looked hard for nested-sentence constructions that fall under the "stability" or "few intervening coincidences" constraint but not under "no intervening agency", but I have not found any that stand up under pressure.

The fact that "no intervening agency" is strenuously at work in all our instrumental verbs, whatever the reason for it, completes the case for saying—as I now do—that "kill" is not serviceable in fundamental moral thinking about positive and negative. When writers trying to explore the positive/negative difference in moral philosophy contrast "kill" with "let die", they accompany the positive/negative contrast with at least three others: instrumental verb versus nested sentence, silence about what is known versus a strong epistemic constraint, and a strong "no intervening agency" constraint versus silence about intervening agency. Because of the moral bubble in the meaning of "kill", indeed, a clean positive/negative distinction is not even an ingredient in this stew. It is a pity that the kill/let-die formulation of the issue was launched in the first place.[11]

86. *Idiosyncrasies in instrumental verbs*

Many instrumental verbs make special demands on the causal chain from Q to y's acquiring P_v. Indeed, the constraints on the causal chain may vary not only from one verb to another, but even from one community to another in respect to a single verb. Suppose I contribute to a tree's falling by digging the earth away from its roots and burning them through; do I *fell* it? I am inclined to say No, but that seems to be partly because in communities with which I am familiar that is not a standard way of getting trees to fall. I don't know how many instrumental verbs have such special sensitivities, but many do not. When Davidson writes that "we would [not] say the doctor removed the patient's appendix" if he "brought it about that the patient has no appendix . . . by running [him] down with his Lincoln Continental",[12] what he says seems false; I can find no such sensitivity in the verb "to remove".

---

11. Jonathan Bennett, " 'Whatever the Consequences' ". I try to repair the damage in "Killing and Letting Die".

12. Donald Davidson, "The Logical Form of Action Sentences", pp. 110f.

Judith Thomson, who has done more with instrumental verbs than anyone else, makes provision for the various differences amongst them.[13] She introduces a relation of Ownership between an agent x and an event e, defining it as follows: x Owns e ≡ x causes everything e causes. Thus, Booth Owns Lincoln's death, but so also does the person (if there is one) who caused Booth to kill Lincoln, yet that person did not kill him. It follows, then, that there is more to killing someone than Owning his death.

To capture the idea of not merely causing a death but killing, not merely causing the log to split but splitting it, not merely causing the clothes to be packed but packing them, Thomson introduces a whole class of tighter relations between agents and events. You don't kill someone, she says, unless you Own_{kill} some event that causes him to die; you don't fell a tree unless you Own_{fell} an event that causes it to fall; you don't melt some chocolate unless you Own_{melt} some event that causes it to melt; and so on. By not even considering whether there is a single differentia that marks off Owns from each of these tighter relations, Thomson implies that she thinks not, and that is why I see her as providing for those individual nuances that I have been discussing—the ones I think to be unmanageable.

Thomson's handling of them is extremely abstract: she does not say in detail what it is for someone to $\text{Own}_{\text{smash}}$ or $\text{Own}_{\text{fertilize}}$ an event, and she offers no help in deciding what to say—did he melt it? did she injure him?—in hard cases. She is open about this, as of course she must be, given her schema for defining the special $\text{Ownership}_{\text{verb}}$ relations. The schema says that, if e is an event, then x $\text{Owns}_{\text{verb}}$ e ≡ x [verbs] everything that e [verbs]. So I Own_{kill} an event if and only if I kill everything it kills; I $\text{Own}_{\text{freeze}}$ an event if I freeze everything it freezes; and so on. This schema does not and is not meant to help us to draw any lines. If we ask it "Did Thatcher sink the Belgrano?", it tells us that that depends on whether she $\text{Owns}_{\text{sink}}$ some event that caused the sinking of that ship. Well, a certain torpedo attack e caused the sinking, and we may know that Thatcher caused e. But did she, then, Own_{sink} e? To answer that under the guidance of Thomson's schema, we must discover whether Thatcher sank everything that e sank, which involves discovering whether Thatcher sank the Belgrano, which is the question we came in with.

I haven't been able to make Thomson's schema do any other work for me either. I continue to think that the manageable part of the instrumental-verb story is the part I have told—the part that is common to all the verbs.

Dyadic verbs that relate agents to upshots without entailing that the relationship is causal also have their own individual require-

13. Judith Jarvis Thomson, *Acts and Other Events*, Chapter 10.

ments. Suppose that Congress today passes a retroactive law about the validity of marriages, with the result that George's marriage to Martha last year becomes valid; as George has since died, Martha is now a widow. At the time he died, she was not, because under the law as it then existed she had not been validly married to him. So Congress's passing the law has completed the sufficient conditions for Martha to be a widow, but it would be odd and probably just false to say that Congress had *widowed* her. On the other hand, it would be all right to say that it had *legitimized* the child that she had by George.

These idiosyncrasies in individual verbs are of no philosophical interest in themselves. As long as we know of their existence and have some idea of what they are like, we are free to concentrate on the conditions that mark off large blocks of territory—positive/negative, "see as sole input", and "no wholly intervening agency". Not even those are essential to my main thesis in this chapter, namely that the "by"-locution is a way of relating facts, not of actions or events. When the lively issues about how to understand the "by"-locution are banished from the domain of events, what remains is meagre indeed, that being my main thesis in this book.

BIBLIOGRAPHY

Achinstein, Peter, "The Causal Relation", *Midwest Studies in Philosophy* 4 (1979), pp. 369–86.

———, *The Nature of Explanation* (Oxford University Press: New York, 1983).

Annas, Julia, "Davidson and Anscombe on 'The Same Action' ", *Mind* 85 (1976), pp. 251–57.

Anscombe, G.E.M., "Under a Description", *Noûs* 13 (1979), pp. 219–33.

Aristotle, *Physics*.

Armstrong, David M., "Identity through Time", in P. van Inwagen (ed.), *Time and Cause* (Reidel: Dordrecht, Holland, 1980), pp. 67–78.

Aune, Bruce, *Reason and Action* (Reidel: Dordrecht, Holland, 1977).

Bartsch, R., *The Grammar of Adverbials* (North Holland Publishing Co.: Amsterdam, 1976).

Beardsley, Monroe C., "Actions and Events: the Problem of Individuation", *American Philosophical Quarterly* 12 (1975).

Beauchamp, Tom L., and Rosenberg, Alexander, *Hume and the Problem of Causation* (Oxford University Press: New York, 1981).

Bennett, Jonathan, "Adverb-Dropping Inferences and the Lemmon Criterion", in LePore and McLaughlin (ed.), pp. 193–206.

———, "Analytic-Synthetic", *Proceedings of the Aristotelian Society* 59 (1959), pp. 163–88.

———, Comments on Dretske's "The Content of Knowledge", q.v.

———, "Counterfactuals and Temporal Direction", *The Philosophical Review* 93 (1984), pp. 57–91.

———, "Event Causation: the Counterfactual Analysis", *Philosophical Perspectives* 1 (1987).

———, "Killing and Letting Die", in S. McMurrin (ed.), *The Tanner Lectures on Human Value* II (University of Utah Press; Salt Lake City, 1981), pp. 45–116.

———, *Linguistic Behaviour* (Cambridge University Press: Cambridge, 1976).

———, "Shooting, Killing, Dying", *Canadian Journal of Philosophy* 2 (1973), pp. 315–23.

———, Review of Davidson's *Inquiries into Truth and Interpretation*, in *Mind* 94 (1985), pp. 601–26.

———, *A Study of Spinoza's Ethics* (Hackett: Indianapolis, 1984).

———, " 'Whatever the Consequences' ", *Analysis* 26 (1966).

Boer, Steven E., "Meaning and Contrastive Stress", *The Philosophical Review* 88 (1979), pp. 263–98.

Brand, Myles, "Identity Conditions for Events", *American Philosophical Quarterly* 14 (1977), pp. 329–77.

———, *Intending and Acting* (M.I.T. Press: Cambridge, Mass., 1984).

Broad, C. D., *Scientific Thought* (Routledge and Kegan Paul: London, 1923).

Brody, Baruch, *Identity and Essence* (Princeton University Press: Princeton, N.J., 1980).

Campbell, Keith, "The Metaphysics of Abstract Particulars", *Midwest Studies in Philosophy* 4 (1981), pp. 477–88.

Carnap, Rudolf, *Meaning and Necessity* (Chicago University Press: Chicago, 1956).

Cartwright, Helen Morris, "Quantities", *Philosophical Review* 79 (1970), pp. 25–42.

Castañeda, Hector-Neri, Comments on Davidson's "The Logical Form of Action Sentences", in Rescher (ed.), pp. 104–12.

———, "Intensionality and Identity in Human Action and Philosophical Method", *Noûs* 13 (1979), pp. 235–60.

Chisholm, Roderick, "Events and Propositions", *Noûs* 4 (1970), pp. 15–24.

———, "States of Affairs Again", *Noûs* 5 (1971), pp. 179–89.

Chomsky, Noam, "Some Remarks about Nominalization", in D. Davidson and G. Harman (ed.), *The Logic of Grammar* (Dickenson: Encino, Calif., 1975), pp. 262–89.

Clark, Romane, "Adverbial Modifiers", in R. Severens (ed.), *Ontological Commitment* (University of Georgia Press, 1974), pp. 22–36.

———, "Concerning the Logic of Predicate Modifiers", *Noûs* 4 (1970), pp. 311–35.

———, "Predication and Paronymous Modifiers", *Notre Dame Journal of Formal Logic* 27 (1986), pp. 376–92.

Clatterbaugh, Kenneth C., "Leibniz's Doctrine of Individual Accidents", *Studia Leibnitiana*, Sonderheft 4 (1973).

Cresswell, M.J., *Adverbial Modification: Interval Semantics and Its Rivals* (Reidel: Dordrecht, Holland, 1985).

Cummins, Robert, and Gottlieb, Dale, "On an Argument for Truth-Functionality", *American Philosophical Quarterly* 9 (1972), pp. 265–69.

D'Arcy, Eric, *Human Acts* (Oxford University Press: Oxford, 1963).

Davidson, Donald, "Actions, Reasons, and Causes", in his *Essays*, pp. 3–20.

———, "Adverbs of Action", in Vermazen and Hintikka, pp. 230–41.

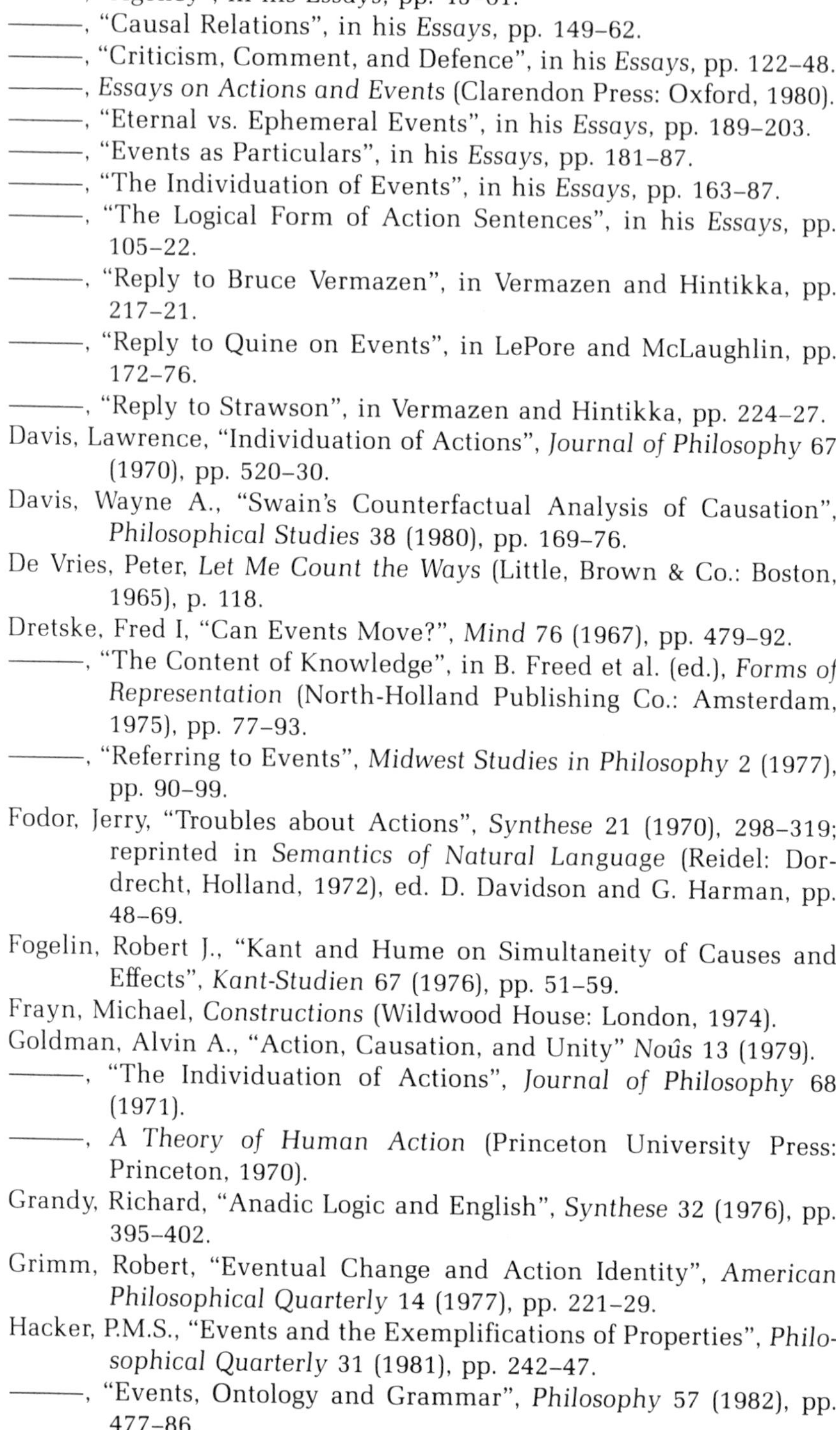

———, "Agency", in his *Essays*, pp. 43–61.

———, "Causal Relations", in his *Essays*, pp. 149–62.

———, "Criticism, Comment, and Defence", in his *Essays*, pp. 122–48.

———, *Essays on Actions and Events* (Clarendon Press: Oxford, 1980).

———, "Eternal vs. Ephemeral Events", in his *Essays*, pp. 189–203.

———, "Events as Particulars", in his *Essays*, pp. 181–87.

———, "The Individuation of Events", in his *Essays*, pp. 163–87.

———, "The Logical Form of Action Sentences", in his *Essays*, pp. 105–22.

———, "Reply to Bruce Vermazen", in Vermazen and Hintikka, pp. 217–21.

———, "Reply to Quine on Events", in LePore and McLaughlin, pp. 172–76.

———, "Reply to Strawson", in Vermazen and Hintikka, pp. 224–27.

Davis, Lawrence, "Individuation of Actions", *Journal of Philosophy* 67 (1970), pp. 520–30.

Davis, Wayne A., "Swain's Counterfactual Analysis of Causation", *Philosophical Studies* 38 (1980), pp. 169–76.

De Vries, Peter, *Let Me Count the Ways* (Little, Brown & Co.: Boston, 1965), p. 118.

Dretske, Fred I, "Can Events Move?", *Mind* 76 (1967), pp. 479–92.

———, "The Content of Knowledge", in B. Freed et al. (ed.), *Forms of Representation* (North-Holland Publishing Co.: Amsterdam, 1975), pp. 77–93.

———, "Referring to Events", *Midwest Studies in Philosophy* 2 (1977), pp. 90–99.

Fodor, Jerry, "Troubles about Actions", *Synthese* 21 (1970), 298–319; reprinted in *Semantics of Natural Language* (Reidel: Dordrecht, Holland, 1972), ed. D. Davidson and G. Harman, pp. 48–69.

Fogelin, Robert J., "Kant and Hume on Simultaneity of Causes and Effects", *Kant-Studien* 67 (1976), pp. 51–59.

Frayn, Michael, *Constructions* (Wildwood House: London, 1974).

Goldman, Alvin A., "Action, Causation, and Unity" *Noûs* 13 (1979).

———, "The Individuation of Actions", *Journal of Philosophy* 68 (1971).

———, *A Theory of Human Action* (Princeton University Press: Princeton, 1970).

Grandy, Richard, "Anadic Logic and English", *Synthese* 32 (1976), pp. 395–402.

Grimm, Robert, "Eventual Change and Action Identity", *American Philosophical Quarterly* 14 (1977), pp. 221–29.

Hacker, P.M.S., "Events and the Exemplifications of Properties", *Philosophical Quarterly* 31 (1981), pp. 242–47.

———, "Events, Ontology and Grammar", *Philosophy* 57 (1982), pp. 477–86.

Harman, Gilbert, "Logical Form", in Davidson and Harman (ed.), *The Logic of Grammar* (Dickenson: Encino, Calif., 1975), pp. 289–307.

Horgan, Terence, "The Case Against Events", *Philosophical Review* 87 (1978), pp. 28–47.

Hornsby, Jennifer, *Actions* (Routledge and Kegan Paul: London, 1980).

———, Review of Judith Thomson's *Acts and other Events*, *Philosophy* (1979), pp. 253–55.

Johnson, Major L., Jr., "Events as Recurrables", in K. Lehrer (ed.), *Analysis and Metaphysics* (Reidel: Dordrecht, Holland, 1975), pp. 209–26.

Jones, J.R., "Are the Characteristics of Things Particular or Universal?", *Philosophical Review* 58 (1949), pp. 152–70.

Kaplan, David, "How to Russell a Frege-Church", *The Journal of Philosophy* 72 (1975), pp. 716–29.

Katz, Bernard D., "Kim on Events", *Philosophical Review* 87 (1978), pp. 427–41.

Kenny, Anthony, *Action, Emotion and Will* (Routledge and Kegan Paul: London, 1963).

Kim, Jaegwon, "Causation, Emphasis, and Events", *Midwest Studies in Philosophy* 2 (1977), pp. 100–103.

———, "Causation, Nomic Subsumption, and the Concept of an Event", *Journal of Philosophy* 70 (1973), pp. 217–36.

———, "Causes and Counterfactuals", *Journal of Philosophy* 70 (1973), pp. 570–72.

———, "Events and their Descriptions: Some Considerations", in N. Rescher et al. (ed.), *Essays in Honor of Carl G. Hempel* (1969), pp. 198–215.

———, "Events as Property Exemplifications", in M. Brand and D. Walton (ed.), *Action Theory* (Reidel: Dordrecht, Holland, 1980), pp. 159–77.

———, "On the Psycho-Physical Identity Theory", *American Philosophical Quarterly* 3 (1966), pp. 277–85.

Kripke, Saul, "Naming and Necessity", in D. Davidson and G. Harman (ed.), *Semantics of Natural Language* (Reidel: Dordrecht, Holland, 1972), pp. 253–55.

Landesman, Charles, "Actions as Universals: an Inquiry into the Metaphysics of Action", *American Philosophical Quarterly* 6 (1969), pp. 247–52.

Lees, Robert B., *The Grammar of English Nominalizations* (Indiana University: Bloomington, 1963).

Leibniz, G.W., *New Essays on Human Understanding*, translated and edited by P. Remnant and J. Bennett (Cambridge University Press: Cambridge, 1981).

Lemmon, E.J., "Comments", in Rescher (ed.), pp. 96–103.

LePore, E., and McLaughlin, B. (ed.), *Actions and Events: Perspectives* on the *Philosophy of Donald Davidson* (Basil Blackwell: Oxford, 1985).

Lewis, David K., "Causal Explanation", in his *Philosophical Papers*, vol. 2, pp. 214–40.

———, "Causation", in his *Philosophical Papers*, vol. 2, pp. 159–72. Postscripts pp. 172–213.

———, *Convention* (Harvard University Press: Cambridge, Mass., 1969).

———, "Counterfactual Dependence and Time's Arrow", in his *Philosophical Papers*, vol. 2, pp. 32–52.

———, *Counterfactuals* (Harvard University Press: Cambridge, Mass., 1973).

———, "Events", in his *Philosophical Papers*, vol. 2, pp. 241–69.

———, *Philosophical Papers*, vol. 2 (Oxford University Press: New York, 1986).

———, Postscripts to "Counterpart Theory and Quantified Modal Logic", *Philosophical Papers*, vol. 1 (Oxford University Press: New York, 1983), pp. 39–46.

Locke, John, *An Essay Concerning Human Understanding*.

Lombard, Lawrence Brian, "Actions, Results, and the Time of a Killing", *Philosophia* 8 (1978), pp. 341–54.

———, *Events: a Metaphysical Study* (Routledge and Kegan Paul: London, 1986).

———, "A Note on Level-Generation and the Time of a Killing", *Philosophical Studies* 26 (1974), pp. 151–52.

MacDonald, C.A., "On the Unifier-Multiplier Controversy", *Canadian Philosophical Quarterly* 8 (1978), pp. 707–14.

Mackie, J.L., "Causes and Conditions", *American Philosophical Quarterly* 2 (1965), pp. 245–64.

———, *The Cement of the Universe* (Oxford University Press: Oxford, 1974).

Martin, R.M., "Events and Actions: Some Comments on Brand and Kim", in M. Brand and D. Walton (ed.), *Action Theory* (Reidel: Dordrecht, Holland, 1980), pp. 179–92.

McCann, Hugh J., "Individuating Actions: the Fine-Grained Approach", *Canadian Journal of Philosophy* 13 (1983), pp. 493–512.

———, "The Trouble with Level-Generation", *Mind* 91 (1982), pp. 481–500.

Montague, Richard, "English as a Formal Language", in his *Formal Philosophy* (Yale University Press: New Haven, 1974), pp. 188–221.

Moore, G.E., "Are the Characteristics of Particular Things Universal or Particular?", *Proceedings of the Aristotelian Society*, suppl. vol. 3 (1923), pp. 95–113.

Moravcsik, J.M.E., "Strawson and Ontological Priority", in R. J. Butler (ed.), *Analytical Philosophy*, second series (Barnes and Noble: New York, 1965), pp. 106–19.

Morton, Adam, "Complex Individuals and Multigrade Relations", *Noûs* 9 (1975), pp. 309–18.

Mourelatos, Alexander P.D., "Events, Processes, and States", *Linguistics and Philosophy* 2 (1978), pp. 415–34.

Parsons, Terence, "Modifiers and Quantifiers in Natural Language", *Canadian Journal of Philosophy*, suppl. vol. 6 (1980), pp. 29–60.

———, "Some Problems Concerning the Logic of Grammatical Modifiers", *Synthese* 21 (1970), pp. 320–33.

———, "Underlying Events in the Logical Analysis of English", in E. LePore and McLaughlin (ed.), pp. 235–67.

Peterson, Philip, "The Grimm Events of Causation" (unpublished).

Quine, W.V., "Events and Reification", in E. LePore and McLaughlin (ed.), pp. 162–71.

———, "The Problem of Meaning in Linguistics", in his *From a Logical Point of View* (Harvard University Press: Cambridge, Mass., 1953), pp. 47–64.

———, *Theories and Things* (Harvard University Press: Cambridge, Mass., 1981).

———, "Two Dogmas of Empiricism", in his *From a Logical Point of View*, pp. 20–46.

———, *Word and Object* (M.I.T. Press: New York, 1960).

Quinton, Anthony M.,"Objects and Events", *Mind* 88 (1979), pp. 197–214.

Railton, Peter, "Probability, Explanation, and Information", *Synthese* 48 (1981), pp. 233–56.

Reichenbach, Hans, *Elements of Symbolic Logic* Section 53; reprinted in D. Davidson and G. Harman (ed.), *The Logic of Grammar.*

Rescher, Nicholas, "Aspects of Action", in Rescher (ed.), pp. 215–20.

———, (ed.), *The Logic of Decision and Action* (University of Pittsburgh Press: Pittsburgh, 1967).

Rosenberg, Alexander, "On Kim's Account of Events and Event-Identity", *Journal of Philosophy* 71 (1974), pp. 327–36.

Russell, Bertrand, *The Analysis of Matter* (Dover: New York, 1954).

Sanford, David H., "Causal Relata", in LePore and McLaughlin (ed.), pp. 282–93.

———, "The Direction of Causation and the Direction of Conditionship", *Journal of Philosophy* 73 (1976), pp. 193–207.

Schlesinger, George N., "Events and Explicative Definitions", *Mind* 93 (1984), pp. 215–29.

Schmitt, Frederick F., "Events", *Erkenntnis* 20 (1983), pp. 281–93.

Searle, John, *Intentionality* (Cambridge University Press: Cambridge, 1983).

Shoemaker, Sydney S., "Identity, Properties, and Causality", *Midwest*

Studies in Philosophy 4 (1979), pp. 321–42.

Smart, J.J.C. "Further Thoughts on the Identity Theory", *The Monist* 56 (1972), pp. 149–62.

Smith, Jay Alan, "Goldman on Act Individuation", *Australasian Journal of Philosophy* 56 (1978), pp. 230–41.

Stalnaker, Robert, "Possible Worlds", *Noûs* 10 (1976), pp. 65–75.

Stout, G.F., "The Nature of Universals and Propositions", *Proceedings of the British Academy* 1912.

Strawson, P.F., "Causation and Explanation", in Vermazen and Hintikka (ed.), pp. 115–35.

———, *Individuals: An Essay in Descriptive Metaphysics* (Methuen: London, 1959).

Swain, Marshall, "A Counterfactual Analysis of Event Causation", *Philosophical Studies* 34 (1978), pp. 1–19.

Taylor, Barry, *Modes of Occurrence: Verbs, Adverbs and Events* (Basil Blackwell: Oxford, 1985).

Thalberg, Irving, *Perception, Emotion and Action* (Oxford University Press: Oxford, 1977).

———, "When Do Causes Take Effect?", *Mind* 84 (1975), pp. 583–89.

Thomason, Richmond, "Some Isues Concerning the Interpretation of Derived and Gerundive Nominals", *Linguistics and Philosophy* 8 (1984), pp. 73–78.

Thomason, Richmond, and Stalnaker, Robert, "A Semantic Theory of Adverbs", *Linguistic Inquiry* 4 (1973), pp. 195–220.

Thomson, Judith Jarvis, *Acts and other Events* (Cornell University Press: Ithaca, 1977).

———, "Individuating Actions", *Journal of Philosophy* 68 (1971), pp. 771–81.

van Inwagen, Peter, "Ability and Responsibility", *Philosophical Review* 87 (1978), pp. 201–24.

———, "Indexicality and Actuality", *The Philosophical Review* 89 (1980), pp. 403–26.

Vendler, Zeno, "Causal Relations", *Journal of Philosophy* 64 (1967), pp. 704–13.

———, "Facts and Events", in his *Linguistics in Philosophy* (Cornell University Press: Ithaca, 1967), pp. 122–46.

Vermazen, Bruce, "Negative Acts", in Vermazen and Hintikka (ed.), pp. 93–104.

Vermazen, Bruce, and Hintikka, Merrill (ed.), *Essays on Davidson: Actions and Events* (Clarendon Press: Oxford, 1985).

Vision, Gerald, "Causal Sufficiency", *Mind* 88 (1979), pp. 105–10.

Vollrath, John F., "When Actions are Causes", *Philosophical Studies* 27 (1975), pp. 329–39.

Wallace, John, "Some Logical Roles of Adverbs", *Journal of Philosophy* 68 (1971), pp. 690–714.

Watling, John, "Are Causes Events or Facts?", *Proceedings of the Aristotelian Society* 74 (1973-74), pp. 161–70.

White, Alan R., "Shooting, Killing and Fatally Wounding", *Proceedings of the Aristotelian Society* 80 (1979-80), pp. 1–15.

Wierenga, Edward and Feldman, Richard, "Identity Conditions and Events", *Canadian Journal of Philosophy* 11 (1981), pp. 77–93.

Wiggins, David, "Verbs and Adverbs, and Some Other Modes of Grammatical Combination", *Proceedings of the Aristotelian Society* 86 (1985–86), pp. 273–304.

Williams, Donald C., "The Elements of Being", *Review of Metaphysics* (1953); reprinted in his *Principles of Empirical Realism* (Thomas: Springfield, Ill., 1966).

Wilson, N.L., "Facts, Events and Their Identity Conditions", *Philosophical Studies* 25 (1974), pp. 303–21.

Yagisawa, T., "Counterfactual Analysis of Event Causation and Kim's Examples", *Analysis* 39 (1979), pp. 100–105.

Zemach, Eddy M., "Events", in Y. Yovel (ed.), *Philosophy of History and Action* (Reidel: Dordrecht, Holland, 1978), pp. 85–95.

INDEX OF PEOPLE

Note: Numbers not identified as chapters are section numbers.

Achinstein, Peter, 14
Annas, Julia, 70
Anscombe, G.E.M., 70f
Aristotle, 36, 60
Armstrong, David M., 47
Aune, Bruce, 64
Ayer, A.J., 56

Bartsch, R., 66
Beardsley, Monroe C., 40, 48, 72–74
Beauchamp, Tom L., 18
Bennett, Jonathan, 14, 18, 20, 28, 36, 38, 54, 56, 63, 69, 76, 82, 84, 85
Bentham, Jeremy, 56
Berkeley, George, 5
Boer, Steven E., 14
Brand, Myles, 38, 45, 46, 48
Broad, C.D., 60
Brody, Baruch, 38

Campbell, Keith, 6
Cargile, James, 47
Carnap, Rudolf, 21
Cartwright, Helen Morris, 58
Castañeda, Hector-Neri, 35, 64, 74, 78f, 84
Chisholm, Roderick, 23, 36
Chomsky, Noam, 2
Clark, Romane, 65
Clatterbaugh, Kenneth C., 36
Cresswell, M.J., 65
Cummins, Robert, 16

D'Arcy, Eric, 54
Davidson, Donald, 4, 6, 13, 16, 21, 23, 30f, 35, 36, 38, 42f, 45f, 54, 55, 56, 62, ch. 11, 70f, 73, 85, 86
Davis, Lawrence, 71, 72
Davis, Wayne A., 22
De Vries, Peter, 83
Dretske, Fred I., 14, 46

Feldman, Richard, 48
Fodor, Jerry, 64
Fogelin, Robert J., 18
Frayn, Michael, 81
Frege, Gottlob, 16

Goldman, Alvin A., 29, 35, 36, 48, 71, ch. 13, 80, 84, 85
Gottlieb, Dale, 16
Grandy, Richard, 67
Grimm, Robert, 72

Hacker, P.M.S., 60
Harman, Gilbert, 65
Hirsch, Eli, 47
Horgan, Terence, 16, 36, 65
Hornsby, Jennifer, 58, 73
Howard, Frances, 28
Hume, David, 21, 56

Johnson, Major L., Jr., 36, 49
Jones, J.R., 6

Kant, Immanuel, 56
Kaplan, David, 15
Katz, Bernard D., 33
Kenny, Anthony, 67
Kim, Jaegwon, 14, 21, 22, ch. 5, 36f, 40, 41, 45, 48–51, 55, 58, 70, 73, 75, 77
Kremer, Michael, 19, 70
Kripke, Saul, 15, 24

Landesman, Charles, 23
Lees, Robert B., 2
Leibniz, G.W., 6, 7, 36, 56, 57
Lemmon, E.J., 41f, 46

Lewis, David K., 13, 18, 19, 20, 22, 24–28, 38, 46, 54, 66, 76, 79, 84f
Locke, John, 7, 36, 41, 56
Lombard, Lawrence Brian, 24, 28, 37, 38, 43, 55, 56, 58, 60, 73, 78, 85

McCann, Hugh J., 36, 48, 79
MacDonald, C.A., 72
McIntyre, Alison, 71
Mackie, J.L., 16, 18, 53
Martin, R.M., 36
Montague, Richard, 65
Moore, G.E., 6, 7
Moravcsik, J.M.E., 6
Morton, Adam, 67
Mourelatos, Alexander P.D., 49

Newton, Isaac, 47
Norcross, Alastair, 28, 85

Parsons, Terence, 64f, 67
Peterson, Philip, 72
Plato, 47

Quine, W.V., 38, 41f, 44–50, 55, 57, 69
Quinton, Anthony M., 6, 46

Railton, Peter, 54
Reichenbach, Hans, 46, 67–69
Rescher, Nicholas, 67f
Rosenberg, Alexander, 18, 33, 35
Russell, Bertrand, 46

Sanford, David H., 14, 18
Schlesinger, George N., 48
Schmitt, Frederick F., 60
Searle, John, 72
Shoemaker, Sydney S., 47
Smart, J.J.C., 41
Smith, Jay Alan, 48, 74
Spinoza, Baruch, 7, 47, 57
Stalnaker, Robert, 46, 68
Stout, G.F., 6
Strawson, P.F., 5, 13, 18
Swain, Marshall, 22

Taylor, Barry, 16, 58, 60, 64, 65, 71
Thalberg, Irving, 72
Thomason, Richmond, 2, 68
Thomson, Judith Jarvis, 36, 38, 46, 48, 58, 61f, 72, 83, 85, 86

van Inwagen, Peter, 24, 46
Vendler, Zeno, 2f, 11f, 16, 51
Vermazen, Bruce, 56
Vision, Gerald, 21
Vollrath, John F., 72

Wallace, John, 49
Watling, John, 52
White, Alan R., 72
Wierenga, Edward, 48
Wiggins, David, 64
Williams, Donald C., 6, 36
Wilson, N.L., 38, 51, 55
Wordsworth, William, 72

Yagisawa, T., 22

Zemach, Eddy M., 66

INDEX OF TOPICS

Note: Numbers not identified as chapters are section numbers. For example, the Anscombe thesis is discussed in Chapter 12 and in Sections 75 and 80.

"a cause" vs. "the cause", 12, 18
abstract/concrete 6, 35, 41, 55f, 69
act of omission, 54
actio praecox argument, 72f, 78
action vs. event, 70, 80
adsentence, 68f
adverb, 6, ch. 11, 70f
adverbial idea, 48
allomorph, 14
allowing, 82, 85
Anscombe thesis, ch. 12, 75, 80
asymmetry "fact", 28
atemporal "event", 66
augmentation generation, 77, 79

bracket notation explained, 1
"by"-locution, ch. 12–14, *especially* 81
"by"-locution, asymmetry of, 74
"by"-locution, causal, 64, 72, 75f, ch. 14
"by"-locution, compressed, 76
"by"-locution, noncausal, 72, 76, ch. 14
"by"-locution, unified, 81
by-relation, 74

Castañeda's trivialization, 79, 84
causal law, 18, 20, 21
causal verb, 83
causation, continuity of, 18, 21
causation, event, 8, ch. 4, 45, 47, ch. 9
causation, fact, 8–10, 13, ch. 3, ch. 9
causation, four approaches, 17
causation, transitivity of, 19, 21, 24, 61
causation, weakness of, 19
cause and effect, 11f
cause vs. forcer, 8
cause, direction of, 18
change, 36, 42, 56, 59f
companion fact, 51f, 81
conceptual analysis, 1, 7, 38, 56, 78, 80
concrete event, ch. 7
concrete/abstract, 6, 35, 41, 55f, 69
continuity of causation, 18, 21
conventional generation, 75f
counterfactual, 20, 22–28, 45, 54
counterpart, 25
counting of events, 4, 32, 34, 49, 71

data on semantics of event names, 49
data on event essences, 23f
data on event identity, 4, 32, 73
dependency, 69, 71
direction, causal, 18
discontinuous event, 58

effect and cause, 11f
essence and time, 24, 28
essence of event, 22–24, 26–28, 48, 53
event and fact, 3, 30f, 33, 51
event and object, 46f
event and state, 60
event as agent, 80, 83, 86
event as change, 36, 42, 56, 59f
event as triple, 36
event as trope, 6, 36, 41, 51, 56, 58, 66f
event causation, 8, ch. 4, 45, 47, ch. 9
event concept, dispensability of, 6
event concept, indeterminacy of, 7, 25, 26, 27, 50f, 54
event concept, supervenience of, 5f
event identity, 4, 32, 38, 40
event name, 1, 3, 27; *see* nominal, perfect
event names, Kim's semantics for, ch. 5, 48f, 51, 55f, 70, 72f, 77
event names, Quinean semantics for, 40, 43–45, 48f, 51, 55f, 69
event sortal, 1
event vs. action, 70, 80
event, constitution of, 33, 37, 40, 56
event, discontinuous, 41, 58
event, essence of, 22–24, 26–28, 48, 53
event, fission of, 56, 59
event, fusion of, 55, 58, 61f
event, incomplete, 62

event, location of, 5, 36, 42, 43, 45, 58
event, size of, 5, 59
event, subjectless, 5
event, uncaused, 61
events, counting of, 4, 34, 49
explanation, 13, 30

fact and event, 3, 30f, 33, 51
fact causation, 8–10, 13, ch. 3, ch. 9
facts and the "by"-locution, 80
facts, fineness of, 4, 15
fission of event, 56, 59
Fregean proposition and fact, 15, 35, 53
Frege-Davidson argument, 16
fusion of events, 55, 58, 61f

highlighting, 14, 35
"how?" and "by", 81

identity of events, 4, 32, 38–40
immanence thesis, 47
incomplete event, 61f
indeterminacy of event concept, 7, 25, 26, 27, 50f, 54
individual accident, 6
instrumental verb, 83
intervening agency, 85
INUS condition, 18

"kick"-like verb, 83

letting, 82, 85
level generation, ch. 13
location of event, 36, 42, 43, 58
logical form, 6, 63, 66, 69, 74
logically proper name, 15

mass term vs. count term, 49, 57, 58
metaphysics and semantics, 37f, 40, 43, 48, 72
modal continuant, 25
monism, Davidson's, 4, 40, 55
moral considerations, 19, 54, 75, 82

name and sortal, 3
necessity of origins, 24
negative/positive, 54, 56, 82, 85
"no further effort" argument, 72f
nominal, derived, 1f, 64
nominal, gerundial, 2f, 71
nominal, perfect vs. imperfect, 2–4, ch. 5, 48, 51, 64, 72, 80
nominal, that [S], 3
nonduplication principle, 38, 40, 41, 48, 62, 71
nonstandard vs. standard adverbs, 65, 68
noun-dependent adjective, 69, 71
noun-infinitive form, 10, 16
NS condition, 18–20, 52f

object and event, 46f
opacity, 9, 44
Ownership, 86

part and whole, 27, 34, 57, 61f
particulars, 35
positive/negative, 54, 56, 82, 85
pragmatics, 12, 16, 19, 28, 44f, 70
predicate modifier, 65, 68f
pronoun, 23
properties, quantified over, 67

Russellian proposition and fact, 15, 35, 53
semantics and metaphysics, 37f, 40, 43, 48, 72
semantics for event names, Kim's, ch. 5, 48f, 51, 55f, 70, 72f, 77
semantics for event names, Quinean, 40, 43–45, 48f, 51, 55f, 69
simple property, 56
size of event, 5, 59
sortal and name, 3
space as substance, 36, 47, 57
standard vs. nonstandard adverbs, 65, 68
state and event, 60
state of affairs, 3
subject and object, 64
subjectless event, 5
supervenience, 5f

temporal atom, 59
temporal part, 24, 46f, 57
"the cause" vs. "a cause", 18
Theseus, ship of, 7, 57
time and event essence, 24
time discriminations, 54
time of action, 72f
time's arrow, 54
transitivity of causation, 19, 21, 28, 61
transparency, 9, 15f
triple, event as, 36
trope, 6, 36, 41, 51, 56, 58, 66f

uncaused event, 61
unchanges, 66
unifier/multiplier, 55

verb-dependent adverb, 69, 71
V-fact, 16, 35

whole and part, 27, 34, 57, 61f

"zone", term explained, 5